פִּרְקֵי אָבוֹת

PIRKEI AVOTH

Ethics of the Fathers

WITH COMMENTARY BY
Rabbi Meir Matzliah Melamed ז"ל

Copyright © 2007 David F. Altabe

Library of Congress Cataloging-in-Publication Data

Mishnah. Avot.

Pirkei Avoth = Ethics of the Fathers: thoughts of the sages of the Talmud / commentary by Matzliah Melamed; translated by David Altabé.

p. cm.

Includes bibliographical references and index.

ISBN: 978-0-88125-970-4 (alk. paper)

1. Mishnah. Avot – Commentaries. 1. Melamed, Meir Masliah. 11. Altabé, David F. 111. Mishnah. Avot. English. 1V. Title. v. Title: Ethics of the Fathers.

BM506.A2E5 2007

296.1'234707–dc22

2007023020

Published by:

KTAV Publishing House, Inc.

930 Newark Avenue

Jersey City, NJ 07306

www.ktav.com

Phone: 201-963-9524

Fax: 201-963-0102

info@ktav.com

פִּרְקֵי אָבוֹת

PIRKEI AVOTH

Ethics of the Fathers

COMMENTARY BY
Rabbi Meir Matzliah Melamed ז"ל

TRANSLATED FROM THE SPANISH BY
David Fintz Altabé

KTAV Publishing House, Inc.
Jersey City, NJ

～ Dedication ～

My aunt, Lina Fintz, gave me her copy of Rabbi Matzliah Melamed's commentary on the *Pirkei Avoth*, and so it is to her that I owe my gratitude for first bringing this valuable work to my attention. As a member of the Cuban Sephardic Congregation of Miami Beach, Florida when Rabbi Melamed was the officiating rabbi, she knew him well and admired him. My uncle Israel Fintz was a member of the Board of Trustees of the congregation in the early sixties when the congregation was founded by Sepharadim who fled from Castro's Cuba.

I also dedicate this translation to the revered memory of Rabbi Matzliah Melamed in appreciation of his work and personal friendship.

David Fintz Altabé

CONTENTS

Rabbi Meir Matzliah Melamed ז״ל viii

Translator's Note ix

Acknowledgments xi

Introduction xii

Ethics of the Fathers 1

Chapter I 3

Chapter II 27

Chapter III 53

Chapter IV 85

Chapter V 117

Chapter VI 169

RABBI MEIR MATZLIAH MELAMED ז"ל

The learned rabbi was born in Izmir, Turkey of a rabbinical family. He studied for the rabbinate at the Rabbinical Academy in Istanbul, and in Israel. Subsequently, he emigrated to São Paulo, Brazil where he published in 1962 *A Lei de Moises*, the translation into Portuguese of the Torah with commentaries. His work is studied in theological seminaries, both Jewish and Christian in Brazil.

He later officiated in Mexico City, and was chosen to represent the Jewish community at the invocation of the Mexico City Olympic games in 1968. He was appointed rabbi of the Cuban Sephardic Congregation in Miami Beach, Florida in 1971. His writings in Spanish include Jumash Hamerkaz, a translation with commentaries of the Torah, the Sidur Hamrkaz, a translation with explanation and commentaries of the book of prayers according to the Sephardic ritual, as well as the prayerbooks used on the major festivals, Rosh Hashanah, and Yom Kippur. While serving as spiritual leader of the Cuban Sephardic Congregation (now Torath Moshe) in Miami, he published the Passover Haggadah with commentaries and the *Pirkei Avoth*. He died in Miami in 1989. All of these works are available through the International Sephardic Educational and Cultural Center, 10808, Santa Monica Blvd., Los Angeles, CA 90025 or by searching under his name on the internet. This translation of his commentaries on the Pirkei Avoth is the first of his works to be published in English.

TRANSLATOR'S NOTE

My reasons for translating Rabbi Matzliah Melamed's commentary on the *Pirkei Avoth* are twofold. To begin, his explanations of the Talmudic passages contained therein are not only illuminating, but also of a profoundly humanistic nature, more so than other commentaries that I have read. *Pirkei Avoth or The Ethics of Our Fathers,* written by rabbis mainly for the moral edification of the Jewish people, are universal in their message to all humanity. They are a guide leading to the path of harmony in human relations. They provide insights into human nature valid for all time. Upon reading them, one gains insight into the true meaning of the Torah.

My second reason is more personal. I had the privilege of meeting personally with Rabbi Matzliah Melamed on three distinct occasions. One would never guess, on speaking with him, his voluminous writings in the field of Jewish exegesis. His sincere humility belied his vast learning and achievements. Or perhaps, it was because he was so learned that he lived the message of the *Pirkei Avoth*. He greeted all with the respect due to the spark of divinity infused in us by the Creator. But it was more than respect or humility; he exuded warmth that enveloped you while in his presence. It is this love of humanity that pervades his commentary, and that is why I deem it so important to bring it to the English speaking public, Jewish or Gentile.

Though the *Pirkei Avoth* are addressed mainly to men, Jewish ethics apply equally to men and women, and indeed, it is often the woman who will remind the man of what is ethical. As it says in Proverbs 1:8, "Fear the instruction of thy father, and do not forsake the Torah of thy mother."

The Biblical passages quoted are taken from the Jerusalem Bible (Koren Publishers, Jerusalem, 1992). Its style may seem archaic to the modern reader for its use of the second person, 'thee' and 'thou'. It is my opinion, nevertheless, that these archaisms lend to the solemnity of the Holy Writ.

For the translation of the passages of the *Pirkei Avoth*, I have relied on those included in *The Book of Prayer* (*Siddur haTefiloth*) edited and translated by Rabbi Dr. David De Sola Pool of blessed memory. This was published by the Union of Sephardic Congregation in New York in 1960, and is still in use in many Sephardic synagogues in the United States and perhaps elsewhere in the English speaking world. On occasion, I have modified the wording where I thought it might be necessary in order to make it more comprehensible to the modern reader. I am indebted to Rabbi Daniel Green of Miami for his recommendation that I do so.

It is my hope that my translation of Rabbi Matzliah Melamed's commentary will serve to clarify the meaning of passages of the *Pirkei Avoth* that may be puzzling because of the concise style of the rabbis of the Talmud. Also, I subscribe to the wish expressed by Rabbi Matzliah Melamed at the end of his work that peace and universal brotherhood reign in all human beings as children of our Father, the Lord. May this work contribute to that end.

David Fintz Altabé

ACKNOWLEDGMENTS

First, I wish to express my acknowledgment and humble gratitude to our Creator for enabling me to complete the translation of Rabbi Matzliah Melamed's commentary on the *Pirkei Avoth*. May it inspire the English reader to a greater understanding of the principles of divinely ordained ethical behavior as elucidated by the Sages of Israel and to live by them for the good of all mankind.

I thank Dr. Jose Nessim of the Sephardic Educational Center of Jerusalem for his encouragement to undertake this project, and for his permission to have it published.

My deepest gratitude goes to Rabbi Dr. M. Mitchell Serels, Secretary of the American Society of Sephardic Studies for his appreciation of the value of the work. I thank him for making available funds bequeathed by the late Dr. Rachel Dalven, an accomplished scholar in her own right, for the publication of the scholarly works of others. By establishing this publication fund, Dr. Dalven continues the noble work she performed in her lifetime advising and encouraging those interested in Sephardic Studies in their research.

I thank Mr. Zachary Levy, Treasurer of the American Association of Jewish Friends of Turkey for advancing funds toward the publication of this book. The organization was founded to recognize the magnanimity of the Ottoman sultans in granting refuge to the Jewish exiles from Spain in 1492, and to the harmony that has since existed between Jews and Turks. The *Pirkei Avoth,* and Rabbi Matzliah Melamed's commentary provide a guide to good relations among all peoples, and coincide with the mission of the AAJFT.

ETHICS OF THE FATHERS

פרקי אבות

All Israel (1) has a share in the world to come, as is written, "Thy people shall all be righteous (2): they shall inherit the land forever; they shall be the branch of my planting, the work of my hands, that I may be glorified." (Isaiah LX:21).

כָּל יִשְׂרָאֵל יֵשׁ לָהֶם חֵלֶק לָעוֹלָם הַבָּא, שֶׁנֶּאֱמַר: וְעַמֵּךְ כֻּלָּם צַדִּיקִים, לְעוֹלָם יִירְשׁוּ אָרֶץ, נֵצֶר מַטָּעַי מַעֲשֵׂה יָדַי לְהִתְפָּאֵר.

---

(1) This paragraph does not form part of the *Pirkei Avoth*, yet it is found in the Talmud (*Sanhedrin* 10, 1). It is customarily recited at the beginning of each chapter of the *Pirkei Avoth* to remind us that one who fulfills what is said in this tract deserves the reward for the righteous in the World to Come.

(2) It is inconceivable that a Jew may be unjust or that he or she may conduct him or herself so irreproachably as to not merit the enjoyment of the fruits of the World to Come reserved for the just.

Compared in numbers with any other nation in the world, we Jews count among us not only the greatest percentage of contributors to all the sciences, but also the lowest percentage of delinquents. It is easy to prove this by visiting the prisons of any country. This is due, in my opinion, to the transmittal of the ethnic character of the Jews. I firmly believe that, with the exception of some examples of close assimilation that bears fruit only in the second or third generation, the Jewish spirit remains always in the mind of one who was born a Jew. It is proven that parents tend to pass on to their children the general spiritual and mental characteristics of their ancestors even when children do not resemble their parents, a concept known as atavism.

Certainly, the Jewish people have undergone changes to a greater or lesser extent in their character in the course of history; nevertheless, we can affirm that in spite of physical and moral variations (as among

Sephardic and Ashkenazic coreligionists in general) that no one can escape, our people have preserved their unique character. In other words, the heritage received from our fathers Abraham, Isaac, and Jacob, and our prophets and sages, is felt among Jews in an undeniable way after a two thousand year trajectory throughout history.

The word *kol* (כל) meaning "all" represents the initials of Kohen and Levy, and tells us that Kohen and Levy, like Israel (the three groups of the Jewish people) all of them, without exception, have a portion in the world to come, even those who are *am ha-aretz* (ignorant in matters of religion). These words *"kol Israel"* can also be interpreted in the following manner: all who possess the noble virtues of our patriarch Jacob, whose honorific title is Israel (see Genesis XXXII:29) will have a share in the world to come. Nevertheless, this does not exclude the righteous of any nation on earth regardless of race, religion, or color, as is said in the Talmud: "The pious of all nations have a share in the world to come." (See *Tos. Sanhedrin* 13)

Chapter 1 פרק א'

VERSE 1:1

1:1. Moses received the Torah (1) from God who appeared to him on Mount Sinai, and transmitted it to Joshua; Joshua to the elders (2), the elders to the prophets (3); and the prophets transmitted it to the men of the Great Assembly (4). They recommended three things: deliberate when passing judgment (5), have many disciples (6), and make a fence (7) around the Law.

א מֹשֶׁה קִבֵּל תּוֹרָה מִסִּינַי, וּמְסָרָהּ לִיהוֹשֻׁעַ, וִיהוֹשֻׁעַ לִזְקֵנִים, וּזְקֵנִים לִנְבִיאִים, וּנְבִיאִים מְסָרוּהָ לְאַנְשֵׁי כְנֶסֶת הַגְּדוֹלָה. הֵם אָמְרוּ שְׁלֹשָׁה דְבָרִים: הֱווּ מְתוּנִים בַּדִּין, וְהַעֲמִידוּ תַלְמִידִים הַרְבֵּה, וַעֲשׂוּ סְיָג לַתּוֹרָה.

---

(1) Everyone knows from what is written in the *Pentateuch*, that Moses received the Torah, the written Law, from God who appeared to him on Mount Sinai. Therefore, the commentators tell us that the Torah mentioned here refers to the Oral Law; that is, the explanations of the laws, passages, symbolisms, allegories, etc. contained in the Torah, which Moses, after having received it (the Oral Law), transmitted to Joshua. It was then passed on down from generation to generation until it was finally compiled in the Talmud (from 300 B.C.E. to 500 C.E.) and its commentaries.

(2) It would be more correct to say *la-zekanim* (to the elders), which would include the elders of the entire period of the Judges, from Joshua to Eli.

(3) Samuel was the first prophet, and Malachi, the last.

(4) The Great Assembly, begun by Ezra the Scribe (approximately 440 B.C.E.) upon his return from Babylonia, was composed of 120 wise men, who formed the corpus of the traditional and religious teaching

of the Jewish people, laying down new rules without deviating from the essence of the Law of Moses. The sages of the Great Assembly established our liturgy and decided upon the books that make up the canon of the Jewish Bible to this day. As for the Sanhedrin, made up of seventy members, this was the legislative body of the Jewish people, and had supreme political authority.

(5) One who is precipitous in making a judgment is likely to make a mistake. He or she should not say, "This case has occurred two or three times before this; I will decide it in accordance with the previous ones." but should examine the case meticulously once and again, for perhaps there may be something new in it that was previously omitted. The men of the Great Assembly used to advise the judges in particular to study any case from all points of view, and take into account all possible contingencies.

(6) There exists, in this regard, a contradiction between the rabbinical academies of Hillel and Shammai. The latter required many qualities of a student before accepting him, while the former admitted all, for he judged that many sinners could be rehabilitated through the study of the Torah, which is considered the Divine Truth that all have the same right to know.

(7) The word "fence" signifies here the rabbinical decrees and regulations designed to keep a persoen far from any transgression of the precepts of the Law. For example, the Torah prohibits working on Shabbat; the rabbis decreed *muktzah*, the touching of tools, money, etc., as well as riding a horse, carrying from one place to another any object that may be used to perform any labor, as being prohibited activities on the Sabbath and Festivals, etc. Such prohibitions are called *seyag* (fence) around the Torah. Said *seyag* serves to warn a person not to commit any error before it is too late. Thanks to these *seyagim*, the Torah is preserved intact as the particular treasure of the Jewish people.

VERSE I:2

1:2. Simeon the Just (1) was one of the last survivors of the Great Assembly. He would say, "The world is held upright on three pillars: the Law (Torah) (2), worship (3), and acts of kindness (4).

ב שִׁמְעוֹן הַצַּדִיק הָיָה מִשְׁיָרֵי כְנֶסֶת הַגְּדוֹלָה. הוּא הָיָה אוֹמֵר: עַל שְׁלשָׁה דְבָרִים הָעוֹלָם עוֹמֵד, עַל הַתּוֹרָה וְעַל הָעֲבוֹדָה וְעַל גְּמִילוּת חֲסָדִים.

---

(1) Both grandfather and grandson were called Simeon, and both served as high priest. The grandfather lived from 310 to 231 B.C.E., and his grandson, from 213 to 133 B.C.E. We do not know for sure if the reference here is to the former or to the latter.

(2) The Torah is considered *Etz Hayim* (The Tree of Life), and is the revelation of God to mankind. Only the Torah can lead to the practice of the truth (of God), justice, and peace. Without the Torah, human life in its true meaning would be impossible.

(3) Here this signifies the services at the Temple of Jerusalem, and the sacrificial offerings that were made there. Now that the Temple is no longer in existence, prayer, substitutes for the ancient service, above all, when it is made with a contrite spirit, and with a humble and broken heart. A person who prays in this way offers as sacrifice his own flesh and blood. This was deduced from the words of King David (Psalm LI:18) "For Thou desirest not sacrifice, or else I would give it, Thou delightest not in burnt offerings. The sacrifices of God are a broken spirit. A contrite and humbled heart, Oh God, Thou wilt not despise."

In my opinion, *Avodah* (worship) signifies, not only the practices of the Temple cult and prayer (*Avodah shebalev* – worship of the heart), but also any kind of constructive work (*avodah* also means work), and the observance and practice of the precepts of the Torah.

(4) *Gemilut Hasadim* means something more than simple charity that

is given to the needy. It signifies good deeds that are performed for the living and for the dead, and for the poor and for the rich. One practices *gemilut hasadim* by giving money or through physical sacrifice. Visiting the sick, lending money without interest to one who needs it, accompanying the dead to their final resting place, etc. are examples of *gemilut hasadim*. In short, *gemilut hasadim* are any good deeds that are performed for the benefit of one's fellow human being.

In my humble opinion, Simeon the Just refers, in particular, to the survival of the Jewish people. The neglect of these three things can bring about the disappearance of our people. Israel without the Torah is no longer Israel, and can be easily absorbed and assimilated by other nations. The same may be said of the famous solidarity of the Jewish people, without which they could no longer exist.

VERSE 1:3

| 1:3. Antigonos of Soho (1) received the tradition from Simeon the Just. He used to say, Do not be like servants who serve their master expecting to receive *peras* (a prize or reward) (2), but like servants who serve their master without expecting a reward; and may the fear of heaven (3) be within you. | ג אַנְטִיגְנוֹס אִישׁ סוֹכוֹ קִבֵּל מִשִּׁמְעוֹן הַצַּדִּיק. הוּא הָיָה אוֹמֵר: אַל תִּהְיוּ כַּעֲבָדִים הַמְשַׁמְּשִׁין אֶת הָרַב עַל מְנָת לְקַבֵּל פְּרָס, אֶלָּא הֱווּ כַּעֲבָדִים הַמְשַׁמְּשִׁין אֶת הָרַב שֶׁלֹּא עַל מְנָת לְקַבֵּל פְּרָס, וִיהִי מוֹרָא שָׁמַיִם עֲלֵיכֶם. |

---

(1) Soho is the name of a city of the tribe of Judah.

(2) The word *peras* (Heb.) comes from the Greek and means reward or gift. It is different from *sahar* (payment) that a person receives from his master or employer for the work he or she has done. Here the word *peras* is used in the sense of *sahar*, for it is a Jewish belief that the just are compensated for their good deeds.

It was not the intention of Antigonos to state that there is no compensation for the good deeds one performs. He wished, rather, to explain that we should serve God without self-interest in mind. The person who adores God out of love and not for the reward he hopes to receive (like a child who behaves well in expectation of a gift) has greater merit than one who does so for self interest or out of fear of punishment. The last recommendation of Antigonos means that we should have *mora* (awe), or *yirat ha-shamayim* (fear of heaven), which should not be taken to mean fear or terror, but rather reverence, respect, submission, and devout adoration of our Creator.

(3) It is customary in Jewish literature to avoid mention of the name of God, and to write instead: *Shamayim* (heaven), *Hakadosh Baruch Hu* (The Holy One, Blessed be He), *Ribono shel Olam* (Master of the Universe), *Meleh Malhei Ha-Melahim* (King of Kings), *Makom* (Place), etc.

VERSE 1:4

1:4. Yose ben Yoezer of Tzeredah (1), and Yose ben Yohanan (2) of Jerusalem, received the Oral Law from those previously mentioned. Yose ben Yoezer used to say, Let your house be a meeting place for sages (3); walk behind the dust of their feet (4) and thirstily absorb their words.

ד יוֹסֵי בֶּן יוֹעֶזֶר אִישׁ צְרֵדָה וְיוֹסֵי בֶּן יוֹחָנָן אִישׁ יְרוּשָׁלַיִם קִבְּלוּ מֵהֶם. יוֹסֵי בֶּן יוֹעֶזֶר אִישׁ צְרֵדָה אוֹמֵר: יְהִי בֵיתְךָ בֵּית וַעַד לַחֲכָמִים, וֶהֱוֵי מִתְאַבֵּק בַּעֲפַר רַגְלֵיהֶם, וֶהֱוֵי שׁוֹתֶה בַצָּמָא אֶת דִּבְרֵיהֶם.

---

(1) Tzereda is the name of a city of the tribe of Manasseh.

(2) These rabbis as well as others until Hillel and Shammai are listed in pairs and known by the term *zugot* – pairs. The first bore the title of *Nasi* (president of the Sanhedrin, that is, the National Council

composed of seventy members). The second held the post of *Av bet din* (president of the Supreme Court of the Law). The *zugoth* preceded the *tannaim*, the authors of the Mishnah in the course of one hundred fifty years.

(3) When wise men wish to meet, have them do so in your house for in this way you can learn more and more from them.

(4) It was the custom for the master to walk ahead of his disciples, who followed him listening to his words. (One who walks behind someone receives the dust of the feet of the one ahead of him); and when seated, the disciples sat at a lower level than the master.

VERSE 1:5

1:5. Yose ben Yonatan of Jerusalem would say, keep your house wide open (1) and let the poor be like members of your family (2). Do not talk too much with a woman, even your own wife (3), and, of course, with another man's wife. For this reason the sages say, one who engages in excessive conversation with women (4) inflicts harm upon himself, neglects the teachings of the Torah, and, finally, will end up in purgatory (5).

ה יוֹסֵי בֶּן יוֹחָנָן אִישׁ יְרוּשָׁלַיִם אוֹמֵר: יְהִי בֵיתְךָ פָּתוּחַ לִרְוָחָה, וְיִהְיוּ עֲנִיִּים בְּנֵי בֵיתֶךָ, וְאַל תַּרְבֶּה שִׂיחָה עִם הָאִשָּׁה. בְּאִשְׁתּוֹ אָמְרוּ, קַל וָחֹמֶר בְּאֵשֶׁת חֲבֵרוֹ. מִכָּאן אָמְרוּ חֲכָמִים, כָּל הַמַּרְבֶּה שִׂיחָה עִם הָאִשָּׁה, גּוֹרֵם רָעָה לְעַצְמוֹ, וּבוֹטֵל מִדִּבְרֵי תוֹרָה, וְסוֹפוֹ יוֹרֵשׁ גֵּיהִנֹּם.

---

(1) The tent of Abraham had openings on all four sides so that the needy would not tire looking for the entrance.

(2) This means that one should treat them with warm friendship.

(3) This statement refers to unnecessary topics of conversation, trivialities, etc., which lead to lustful thoughts. However, a man may speak as much as he wants to with his wife about matters dealing with the household, the family, children, etc.

(4) In my humble opinion, when a woman is uncultured, her husband should speak to her only of necessary matters, but if the wife is cultured and intelligent, a man may ask her advice, as it says in the Talmud: "If your wife is short, bend down and ask her advice." Elsewhere, the Talmud (*Shabbath* 33) states that women have an enlightened spirit. All women have knowledge regarding their tasks. (see Talmud, *Yoma* 66). A good woman is the best companion of her husband and children. God gave greater intuition to women than to men (*Nida* 45). On the other hand, in the Talmud (*Yevamot* 63) it is said: "What is more bitter than death? A bad wife." As we can see, our religion does not belittle in any way the merits of women. Proof of this is Deborah, a prophetess and a woman of great valor, as it says in the Bible (Judges IV:4–5): "…she judged Israel at that time… and the children of Israel came to her for judgment."

(5) *Gehinam* is usually translated as "hell." It is found mentioned in Jeremiah (Ch. XXXII:35): "In the valley of *Ben-Hinom*, which is south east of Jerusalem… the pagans would sacrifice human beings to Moloch." Later, the term *Gehinam* came to signify hell due to the horrible torment that people suffered there, in contrast to *Gan Eden* (the garden of delights), commonly translated as "paradise, " located purportedly in Mesopotamia, where God placed Adam and Eve. *Gan Eden* and *Gehinam*, when mentioned in Jewish literature, pertain solely to the dwelling place of the soul.

VERSE 1:6

1:6. Joshua ben Perahia and Nittai of Arbel (1) received the tradition from the previous pair. Joshua ben Perahia would say, get yourself a teacher for your studies (2) and a companion (3), although it may cost you (4), and judge all men charitably (5).

ו יְהוֹשֻׁעַ בֶּן פְּרַחְיָה וְנִתַּאי הָאַרְבֵּלִי קִבְּלוּ מֵהֶם. יְהוֹשֻׁעַ בֶּן פְּרַחְיָה אוֹמֵר: עֲשֵׂה לְךָ רַב, וּקְנֵה לְךָ חָבֵר, וֶהֱוֵי דָן אֶת כָּל הָאָדָם לְכַף זְכוּת.

---

(1) Arbel is a place north of Tiberias.

(2) Do not remain without a teacher; even if the one you find is not very competent, for it is always better than studying alone.

(3) This refers to a study companion. Good books can also be considered man's friend. Nowadays, it is difficult to find friends in whom you can confide anything, especially secrets. The best examples in the Bible of pure and selfless friendships were those of David and Jonathan among men, and of Naomi and Ruth among women. When Honi (Onias – *See Mahzor Ha-Shanah*, p. 51) awoke from his seventy-year sleep, and found himself without anyone he knew, he exclaimed, "It is better to die than to live without friends."

(4) Although it may cost you money, sacrifices, etc

(5) This means that we have to be charitable in our judgment when we are in doubt as to whether or not our companion is good. Also, we should not allow ourselves to be misled by appearances, and thus, be inclined to mistrust our fellow man in any matter. When we hear someone speak against a person, we should try to defend him or her. This is one of the best norms of conduct a human being should have. It is called in Hebrew *"l'hafech zechut"* which means: to tip the balance in favor of our companion. If we do so, God will do likewise with us.

VERSE 1:7

1:7. Nittai of Arbel was wont to say, keep away from an evil neighbor (1). Have no association with a wicked person, and do not fail to believe in final retribution. (2).

ז נִתַּאי הָאַרְבֵּלִי אוֹמֵר: הַרְחֵק מִשָּׁכֵן רָע, וְאַל תִּתְחַבֵּר לָרָשָׁע, וְאַל תִּתְיָאֵשׁ מִן הַפֻּרְעָנוּת.

---

(1) In the morning service called *"Bircat ha Shahar"*, in the prayer that begins *"Yehi Ratzon"*, we pray that God should deliver us from a wicked neighbor among other evils. In addition to the problems and unpleasantness that bad neighbors can cause, our rabbis said that we, ourselves, can receive punishment for their bad actions. It is written in the Mishnah (*Negaim* 12, 6): "Woe to the wicked one, and woe to his neighbor!" The wickedness of an evil person often brings about the deterioration of a good one's character. It is the opinion of some rabbis that the bad neighbor refers to the "*yetzer ha-ra*," the evil inclination that lurks in the heart of man, and that we should not allow ourselves to be carried away by it.

(2) When we see an evil person prospering, and not being punished immediately for the evil he or she commits, do not despair, for sooner or later, those who are evil will receive their just deserts. On the other hand, if good people suffer, and are not rewarded for their good deeds, they should not refrain from keeping up their good works, for reward always comes in time.

VERSE 1:8

1:8. Judah ben Tabbai, and Simeon, ben Shatah, received the tradition from Joshua and Nittai. Judah ben Tabbai used to say, act not as lawyers do (1). When the litigants stand before you, consider them both guilty, but when they are no longer in your presence, consider them innocent (2) once they have accepted the decision.

ח יְהוּדָה בֶּן טַבַּאי וְשִׁמְעוֹן בֶּן שָׁטַח קִבְּלוּ מֵהֶם. יְהוּדָה בֶּן טַבַּאי אוֹמֵר: אַל תַּעַשׂ עַצְמְךָ כְּעוֹרְכֵי הַדַּיָּנִין, וּכְשֶׁיִּהְיוּ בַּעֲלֵי הַדִּין עוֹמְדִים לְפָנֶיךָ, יִהְיוּ בְעֵינֶיךָ כִּרְשָׁעִים, וּכְשֶׁנִּפְטָרִים מִלְּפָנֶיךָ, יִהְיוּ בְעֵינֶיךָ כְּזַכָּאִין, כְּשֶׁקִּבְּלוּ עֲלֵיהֶם אֶת הַדִּין.

---

(1) *"Keorehei ha-dayanim"* (like lawyers) means literally like those who influence the mind of judges in favor of a person before judgment is passed. It also refers to those who influence the mind of an arbiter or anyone else as lawyers do during the course of a trial.

Likewise, one should not suggest ideas to litigants so that they may defend their case, as for example, by telling them to proceed in such and such a manner in order to win the case. This is what lawyers do, but you should not do the same, even when you know that your friend has reason on his side. On the contrary, you should allow him to tell the whole truth, and let the judge decide the issue. No one should influence a judge in favor or against either party to a dispute before the trial begins.

(2) Although one of the litigants may be acting falsely during the trial, do not deem him a liar, even if in the end he is found guilty. It is preferable to consider him a penitent who will not repeat the same error.

VERSE 1:9

1:9. Simeon ben Shatah (1), would say, examine the witnesses very carefully (2), and be very exacting with your words, so that the witnesses do not find a basis for giving false testimony (with the aim of winning the case). (3)

ט שִׁמְעוֹן בֶּן שָׁטַח אוֹמֵר: הֱוֵי מַרְבֶּה לַחֲקוֹר אֶת הָעֵדִים, וֶהֱוֵי זָהִיר בִּדְבָרֶיךָ, שֶׁמָּא מִתּוֹכָם יִלְמְדוּ לְשַׁקֵּר.

---

(1) This rabbi was the brother of Queen Alexandra Salome, the wife of King Yannai (Ist Century B.C.E.). It was he who founded the first elementary schools of his time.

It is said about him that when he was still poor, he had asked one of his disciples to buy a camel from an Arab. Upon examining the animal, he found a precious stone in its collar. He then told his student, "I bought the camel and not the precious stone, return it to the Arab immediately!" When the Arab received the stone, he exclaimed, "Blessed be the God of Israel." This statement was taken by the rabbi to be an act of *"kiddush HaShem"* (sanctification of the Holy Name of God) and more precious than all the riches in the world.

(2) This recommendation by Simeon hen Shatah stems from the bitter experience that he had with his own son when the latter was executed for a crime he did not commit. It was only after the execution that it was proven that there was no basis for the accusation, and that if the witnesses had been examined thoroughly, the false accusation would have been brought to light.

(3) Inexact words could suggest to the witnesses ideas that may influence them to distort their testimony.

VERSE I:10

1:10. Shemaya and Avtalyon (1) received the tradition from Judah and Simeon. Shemaya said, love work (2), hate mastery (3), and do not try to become too familiar with those in political power (4).

שְׁמַעְיָה וְאַבְטַלְיוֹן קִבְּלוּ מֵהֶם. שְׁמַעְיָה אוֹמֵר: אֱהוֹב אֶת הַמְּלָאכָה, וּשְׂנָא אֶת הָרַבָּנוּת, וְאַל תִּתְוַדַּע לָרָשׁוּת.

---

(1) These two rabbis were descendants of converts to Judaism, but of a Jewish mother. For that reason, there was no objection in naming the former "*nasi*" (head of the Sanhedrin), and the latter, "*Av Bet Din*" (head of the Supreme Court).

(2) Idleness leads a person to depression and is the cause of many ills.

(3) "Mastery" here signifies the lust for power over others. According to the Talmud, one who loves humility will be exalted, and he who exalts himself, will be humbled.

(4) In my opinion, Shemaya's recommendation refers in particular to the idolatrous governments of his time; that is, the government of Rome and that of Herod. They took advantage of the people known by the authorities, benefiting from them when they were needed, but ignoring them when they were in need of assistance. The authorities often despoiled them of their wealth, and forced them to abandon their religion. Further on (Ch. II, 2), one is advised to be prudent with government authorities, and in Chapter III, 2, to pray for the well being of the king. (Cf. "*Siddur Masliah*", p. 306)

VERSE I:11

1:11. Avtalyon used to say, sages, be careful with your words, for you may condemn yourselves to exile to some place where the waters of learning (1) are impure. There the disciples who follow you will drink (misinterpret your words) and die (spiritually) and God's name will be profaned.

יא. אַבְטַלְיוֹן אוֹמֵר: חֲכָמִים, הִזָּהֲרוּ בְדִבְרֵיכֶם, שֶׁמָּא תָחוּבוּ חוֹבַת גָּלוּת וְתִגְלוּ לִמְקוֹם מַיִם הָרָעִים, וְיִשְׁתּוּ הַתַּלְמִידִים הַבָּאִים אַחֲרֵיכֶם וְיָמוּתוּ, וְנִמְצָא שֵׁם שָׁמַיִם מִתְחַלֵּל.

---

(1) Be careful with your words, and give clear and precise explanations, and above all, see that those who listen to them are God-fearing so that they do not misinterpret them, and are led into heresy. His students, Sadok and Baytos misinterpreted the words of Antigonos of Soho, and deduced that there is neither reward nor punishment beyond the grave, thus, they laid the foundation of the heretical sects in Judaism, the Sadducees and the Baytocees, who rejected the Oral Law. Both sects disappeared when Jerusalem fell, but some of their beliefs survive among the Karaites to this day. Avtalyon was referring here mainly to the Jewish community of Alexandria of that time, which was under Hellenistic influence (50 B.C.E.), and was considered the intellectual capital of the world, but distant from the traditionalist spirit of the Jews who lived in the Holy Land. For this reason, Alexandria was judged by the sages of Palestine to be a place of impure waters and heresy. The disciples, who drank of these waters, would be subject to die spiritually, having distanced themselves from the true spirit of the teachings of the Torah, and profaned the name of God.

VERSE 1:12

1:12. Hillel and Shammai (1) received the tradition from Shemayah and Avtalyon. Hillel was wont to say, be like the disciples of Aaron (2), who love peace and strive for it, love their fellow man (3), and draw them close to Torah.

יב הִלֵּל וְשַׁמַּאי קִבְּלוּ מֵהֶם. הִלֵּל אוֹמֵר: הֱוֵי מִתַּלְמִידָיו שֶׁל אַהֲרֹן, אוֹהֵב שָׁלוֹם וְרוֹדֵף שָׁלוֹם, אוֹהֵב אֶת הַבְּרִיּוֹת וּמְקָרְבָן לַתּוֹרָה.

---

(1) These two rabbis lived in Jerusalem in the first century of the Common Era. They were the first *"tannaim"* (authors of the Mishnah). Hillel was famous for his humility and gentleness, in contrast to Shammai who was severe.

(2) Aaron Ha-Cohen, the brother of Moses the Prophet, loved peace, and strived for it in the following manner: When he saw that two men were angry at each other, he would approach one and tell him, "My son, you don't know how repentant your companion is. He goes about lamenting and saying to himself: Woe is me, how can I lift my head with the shame I feel for having behaved so?" Aaron would talk to him until he removed from his heart all the enmity he had towards the other.

He would talk in the same way to the other, and it would come about that when the two would meet again, each would rush to embrace the other.

Another champion of peace was Rabbi Meir. The Midrash relates that a woman, having arrived home late one Friday afternoon for having attended this rabbi's sermon was refused entry into her home by her husband until she went and spat seven times into Rabbi Meir's face. The woman, in her desolation took refuge in the house of a neighbor to whom she told what had happened. Upon hearing of the incident, Rabbi Meir passed by asking in a loud voice, "Is there around here by chance, some woman who might know how to cure the pain in my eye by *enduco* (a word in Ladino which means 'to alleviate an illness by exhaling through the mouth and emitting saliva')? Hearing this, the neighbor said to the saddened woman, "This is a God given opportunity. Go and do what he asks!" When the woman completed the *enduco*, Rabbi Meir said to her, "Go in peace to your home and tell your husband, 'You commanded me to spit at Rabbi Meir seven times, and I spat at him three times more.'

(3) Similarly, when Aaron, due to his great love for all human beings without exception, would note that someone had transgressed a commandment of the Torah, he would join that person as if he did not know of it. That person would say to himself, "If Aaron had an inkling of my evil deeds; he surely would not show me such friendship." Aaron's attitude would shame the transgressor, and induce the transgressor to rectify his conduct and come closer to adhering to the Torah. The people of Sodom were destroyed because hatred reigned among them. On the other hand, God did not destroy the generation that built the Tower of Babel for the sole reason that there was peace among them. According to the Mishnah (*Bereshit Raba* 38,6), peace is so agreeable in the eyes of God that even if the people of Israel should serve idols (Heaven forbid), but there were peace among them, He would not allow any nation to have dominion over them. On the contrary, even if Israel should fulfill all the commandments of the Torah, but there be discord among them, any nation could annihilate them easily.

VERSE 1:13

1:13. He (Hillel) used to say, he who extends his fame (seeking greatness) is apt to destroy his name (1). He who does not increase his knowledge decreases it (2). He who does not study (or teach) (3) is not worthy of life. He who subverts the crown of the Torah for worldly uses will pass away (4).

יג הוּא הָיָה אוֹמֵר: נְגִיד שְׁמָא אֲבַד שְׁמֵהּ, וּדְלָא מוֹסִיף יָסֵף, וּדְלָא יַלִיף קְטָלָא חַיָּב, וּדְאִשְׁתַּמֵּשׁ בְּתַגָּא חֲלָף.

It seems odd that this paragraph, a following one (Ch. II, 7), and that of Ben Heh Heh (Ch. V, 26) were written in Aramaic. In my opinion, the compiler of the Mishnah probably preferred to write what each rabbi was wont to say as a motto, and in the actual language in which he said it; that is, in Hebrew or Aramaic.

(1) One, who out of ambition seeks to acquire fame runs the risk of losing his good name and himself as well, since the desire creates jealousy, rivals, etc.

(2) He who does not try to increase his knowledge is likely to forget even what he has learned. There are those who translate the word *yesif* as "he will rejoin his people"; that is, he will die before his time, for God gives life so that a person may perfect him or herself continually, and if one does not do so, for what purpose does one need to stay alive!

(3) The ignorant do not deserve life, for they are subject to committing unpardonable sins out of ignorance. Another version tells us that this refers to the teacher who does not wish to teach all he knows, thinking that to do so would diminish his greatness; or, that he does not wish to take the trouble to teach students who have difficulty in learning, and thus leaves them in ignorance. This is considered as if the teacher destroyed the spirit of the student. Such a teacher does not deserve

life. One who makes use of his knowledge for his own ends, or for immoral purposes, or for material gain is subject to lose himself, and to distance himself from his people, and be taken from this world.

The Talmud relates that Rabbi Tarfon, while passing through an orchid ate some abandoned figs. The watchmen arrived and began to beat him, but when he told them who he was, they let him go. Rabbi Tarfon lamented this to his dying day, saying, "Woe is me for I took advantage of the crown of the Torah for my own benefit."

There exist other interpretations of this saying by Hillel: the condemnation refers to the teacher who accepts services from students who are not his, because this is considered deriving benefit from knowledge of the Torah. This is not the case when it deals with the teacher's own students for whom serving the teacher is a form of learning and training.

(4) To utilize the crown of the Torah signifies here to use the ineffable Name of God, the Tetragrammaton.

The true name of God, by means of which He created the world, is different in its pronunciation from the one found in the Bible. It could only be revealed to a middle aged person who was pious, modest, not stubborn, not easily angered, and who never drinks alcoholic beverages (see *Kiddushin* 71). One who knows this name and who preserves it in purity is beloved in heaven and earth; he can bring about extraordinary things; he sees and understands clearly things that for the layperson constitute all kinds of mysteries. He has a good portion in this life and in the world to come, in contrast to one who, knowing the Tetragrammaton, uses it for his own benefit or for profane ends. It is for this reason that Hillel here condemns one who makes improper use of the Holy Name.

The Tetragrammaton is called in Hebrew "*Shem ha-Meforash*," two words that have two meanings: the explicit Name of God, or the separate (exclusive) Name. Said Name composed of four letters can be written with different vowels, as for example: the one composed of the 22 letters of the alphabet, that of 42 letters or words, or that of 72 (elements), which is considered to be the most holy of all.

Translator's note: Rabbi Matzliah Melamed continues with a detailed explanation of how the Name consisting of 72 elements is derived. I choose not to translate this for the following reason: Maimonides states in his *Guide of the Perplexed*, (Ch LXII) that the Name consisting of 22 letters was used as a substitute for the Tetragrammaton, but when "unprincipled men had become acquainted with that name, the Sages concealed also that name, and only communicated it to the worthiest among the priests, that they should pronounce it when they blessed the people in the Temple; for the Tetragrammaton was no longer uttered in the Sanctuary on account of the corruption of the people." The same applied to the Name of 42 letters; hence, I fear that to reveal how the Name of 72 letters was derived, by translating Rabbi Matzliah Melamed's explanation, may be improper.

VERSE 1:14

1:14. He [Hillel] also said, if I am not for myself, who is for me (1), and if I am for myself alone, what am I worth (2)? And if not now (that I have the opportunity), when (3)?

יד הוּא הָיָה אוֹמֵר: אִם אֵין אֲנִי לִי, מִי לִי, וּכְשֶׁאֲנִי לְעַצְמִי, מָה אֲנִי, וְאִם לֹא עַכְשָׁו, אֵימָתַי.

---

(1) This means that if a person does not try to elevate him or herself, no one will do it for him or her. Everyone should acquire merits for him or herself, and not depend upon the merits of others. It is true that we Jews believe in *"zehuth avoth"* (the merit of the patriarchs and our forebears), but this does not mean, in my opinion, that their merits will protect us even if we sin. The merit of Abraham did not redeem Ishmael, his son, and the *"zehuth"* of the patriarch Isaac was not able to redeem Esau, his son. God judges a person according to his own actions and deeds, and if we appeal to the *"zehuth avoth"* of our ancestors, it is only so that they may inspire us to be good and just, as they were.

(2) This phrase has several interpretations: if I care only for my material necessities without consideration for the perfection of my soul, of what worth am I? Or rather, what difference is there between an animal and me? And even when I fulfill some precepts of the Torah, what good am I, considering the innumerable moral duties and commandments that I have not observed?

(3) A person should not say, I cannot do this good deed today, I cannot study Torah today. I will do so tomorrow. Since tomorrow sometimes never arrives, yesterday's opportunity may be lost forever.

Another interpretation tells us that if one does not study and acquire good qualities when young, to do so when one is older is difficult. After a person leaves this world, all hope is lost. In the words of King David (Psalm cxv:17) "The dead cannot praise the Lord...." As long as a person is alive, he has the opportunity to perform good deeds and do penance in order to obtain God's pardon, but once dead, even the just cannot increase the merits they acquired in life.

VERSE 1:15

1:15. Shammai would say, set a fixed time for the study of Torah (1). Say little, but do much (2). Receive all men [people] with friendliness. (3)

טו שַׁמַּאי אוֹמֵר: עֲשֵׂה תּוֹרָתְךָ קֶבַע, אֱמוֹר מְעַט וַעֲשֵׂה הַרְבֵּה, וֶהֱוֵי מְקַבֵּל אֶת כָּל הָאָדָם בְּסֵבֶר פָּנִים יָפוֹת.

---

(1) On Judgment Day, one of the first questions that one will be asked is, "Did you set a time for the study of Torah?" Although one may be engaged in many other activities and have many cares, one is not permitted to neglect the study of Torah. Moreover, one should make the study of Torah one's principal aim in life, and consider other occupations secondary.

(2) A just person speaks little and does much; an evil person does

the opposite. Our patriarch Abraham offered the three angels a piece of bread (Genesis XVII:5), and wound up giving them a virtual banquet (verses 6–8). Efron began by offering Abraham his field gratis (Genesis XXIII:11), and in the end asked for four hundred coins of silver (verse 15), and of good quality.

(3) It seems odd that Shammai, depicted in the Talmud as a severe man, should have given this advice, for he, himself, did not practice it (see *Siddur Masliah haShalem*, p. 560). In my opinion, Shammai gave this advice desiring to change his ways.

This advice seems to say that although we may have personal problems and sadness, we should treat people kindly. Shammai's advice also means that when we do a favor for our fellow man, or we give charity, we should do so in good spirit. If we were to give, against our will, all the gifts in the world, we bring ill feeling to the hearts of those who receive them, and this is not good in the eyes of God. When we give, even if it is not much, but we give wholeheartedly in accordance with our means, this is doubly considered a meritorious deed.

According to the Talmud, the son who gives his father the best food in the world but mistreats him, deserves to go to hell, but he who sustains his father with bread and salt, kindly and sweetly, goes to heaven.

VERSE 1:16

1:16. Rabban Gamliel (1) used to say, get yourself a teacher (2) so that you will be free of doubt. Do not often tithe [a tax of 10%] (3) by rough estimate (4).

טז רַבָּן גַּמְלִיאֵל הָיָה אוֹמֵר: עֲשֵׂה לְךָ רַב, וְהִסְתַּלֵּק מִן הַסָּפֵק, וְאַל תַּרְבֶּה לְעַשֵּׂר אֲמָדוֹת.

---

(1) Rabban Gamliel was the grandson of Hillel, and the first to be called *"rabban"* (master, head of the Sanhedrin). Of extraordinary humanitarian sentiments, he instituted the sacred precepts of visiting

the sick, the burial of foreigners, charity in all forms, even towards gentiles, and the precept of not imposing a decree that the majority of the people cannot carry out. Christianity affirms that the Apostle Paul was a disciple of Rabban Gamliel. It does not surprise me since, apart from its modifications, all that is good in Christianity is nothing more than a repetition (told in other words) of our Holy Bible and of the teachings of our teachers and wise men like Rabban Gamliel.

(2) Verse 1:6 gives the same advice. For this reason, the commentators state that what is written here refers to a judge, to a teacher, or to any leader, so that a person may be acquainted with someone with superior knowledge, and be able to consult him or her when necessary to clear up any doubts.

(3) The 2% that was given to the priests and the 10% to the Levites (see details in *La Ley de Moisés* by the same author, p. 909.)

(4) He wishes to teach us that a person should not be accustomed to act when in doubt.

VERSE 1:17

1:17. Simeon, son of Rabban Gamliel, used to say, all my days I have grown up among the sages, and I have found nothing better for a man than silence (1). What is essential is not study, but action (2), and one who talks too much brings about sin (3).

יז שִׁמְעוֹן בְּנוֹ אוֹמֵר: כָּל יָמַי גָּדַלְתִּי בֵּין הַחֲכָמִים, וְלֹא מָצָאתִי לַגּוּף טוֹב מִשְּׁתִיקָה, וְלֹא הַמִּדְרָשׁ הוּא הָעִקָּר אֶלָּא הַמַּעֲשֶׂה, וְכָל הַמַּרְבֶּה דְבָרִים מֵבִיא חֵטְא.

---

(1) In the Book of Proverbs (XVII:28), it is written, "Even a fool when he holds his peace, is considered wise, and he that shuts his lips is esteemed a man of understanding."

(2) This does not mean that study is less important, for without it, a deed cannot be performed as it should be. What is meant here is that theory should be followed by action, and not remain just theory. (Cf. III:12, 19, 22).

(3) Rabbi Simeon received his inspiration for these words from King Solomon (Proverbs x:19), "In the multitude of words, sin is not lacking, but he who restrains his lips is wise." Much harm can come to a person for speaking more than is necessary. God gave us two ears, but only one tongue in order to suggest to us that we should listen more than we speak.

VERSE 1:18

1:18. Rabban Simeon, son of Gamliel (1), used to say, the world is supported on three pillars – truth, justice, and peace, as it is written in (Zechariah VIII, 16), "Execute the judgment of truth and peace in your gates." (2)

יח רַבָּן שִׁמְעוֹן בֶּן גַּמְלִיאֵל אוֹמֵר: עַל שְׁלֹשָׁה דְבָרִים הָעוֹלָם קַיָּם, עַל הַדִּין וְעַל הָאֱמֶת וְעַל הַשָּׁלוֹם. שֶׁנֶּאֱמַר: אֱמֶת וּמִשְׁפַּט שָׁלוֹם שִׁפְטוּ בְּשַׁעֲרֵיכֶם.

רַבִּי חֲנַנְיָא בֶּן־עֲקַשְׁיָא אוֹמֵר: רָצָה הַקָּדוֹשׁ בָּרוּךְ הוּא לְזַכּוֹת אֶת־יִשְׂרָאֵל, לְפִיכָךְ הִרְבָּה לָהֶם תּוֹרָה וּמִצְוֹת, שֶׁנֶּאֱמַר: יְיָ חָפֵץ לְמַעַן צִדְקוֹ, יַגְדִּיל תּוֹרָה וְיַאְדִּיר.

Rabbi Hanania, son of Akashia (3) used to say, the Holy One, blessed be He, wishing to render Israel the more worthy enlarged for them the Torah and its commandments. For so we may read the words of the prophet Isaiah (XLII:21), "The Lord was pleased for His righteousness' sake to magnify Torah and to make it glorious."

---

(1) Rabban Simeon was the son of Gamliel and the father of Judah ha-Nasi.

(2) In my opinion, the author of this saying does not contradict the three bases cited in Verse 1:2 by Simeon ha-Tzadik who listed first the Torah, from which emanates the practice of justice, truth, and peace, as all that is good for a human being. The three principles mentioned here; that is, justice accompanied by truth and peace constitute the three basic principles for the existence of human society, since if justice reigns, then truth exists, and there is peace in the world. As for the three precepts of Verse 1:2: Torah, worship, and beneficence, these

relate to the relationship between man and God, as well as good relations among human beings.

(3) This rabbi belongs to the third generation of *'tannaim'* (2nd Century C.E.). His words do not form part of this tractate, but are found in the Talmud (*Makot* 3, 16). In view of the fact that they constitute a magnificent statement, it was decided to quote them as a conclusion at the end of the reading of paragraphs from the Talmud, Mishnah, Zohar, etc., and before reciting Kaddish Rabanan, the Rabbis' Kaddish. (See the Commentary at the end of this book.)

Chapter II פרק ב'

VERSE 2:1

2:1. "All Israel has a share in the world to come…"
(1) Rabi (2) used to say, which is the right way (3) that a man should choose. Whichever brings him honors, and honors his fellow man (4). Be careful with a light commandment (5) as with a weighty one, for you do not know the reward (6) of each commandment. Compare any loss you may suffer in fulfilling a commandment against its reward in observing it (7), and compare any benefit that may result from committing a sin against the penalty it carries. Reflect upon three things, and you wilt not come into the power of sin: – Know what is above you – a seeing eye, a hearing ear, and that all your actions are being set down on record (8).

"כָּל יִשְׂרָאֵל יֵשׁ לָהֶם חֵלֶק לָעוֹלָם הַבָּא, שֶׁנֶּאֱמַר: וְעַמֵּךְ כֻּלָּם צַדִּיקִים, לְעוֹלָם יִירְשׁוּ אָרֶץ, נֵצֶר מַטָּעַי מַעֲשֵׂה יָדַי לְהִתְפָּאֵר."

א רַבִּי אוֹמֵר: אֵיזוֹ הִיא דֶרֶךְ יְשָׁרָה שֶׁיָּבוֹר לוֹ הָאָדָם, כֹּל שֶׁהִיא תִפְאֶרֶת לְעוֹשֶׂיהָ וְתִפְאֶרֶת לוֹ מִן הָאָדָם. וֶהֱוֵי זָהִיר בְּמִצְוָה קַלָּה כְּבַחֲמוּרָה, שֶׁאֵין אַתָּה יוֹדֵעַ מַתַּן שְׂכָרָן שֶׁל מִצְוֹת. וֶהֱוֵי מְחַשֵּׁב הֶפְסֵד מִצְוָה כְּנֶגֶד שְׂכָרָהּ, וּשְׂכַר עֲבֵרָה כְּנֶגֶד הֶפְסֵדָהּ. הִסְתַּכֵּל בִּשְׁלֹשָׁה דְבָרִים וְאֵין אַתָּה בָא לִידֵי עֲבֵרָה, דַּע מַה לְּמַעְלָה מִמְּךָ, עַיִן רוֹאָה וְאֹזֶן שׁוֹמַעַת, וְכָל מַעֲשֶׂיךָ בְּסֵפֶר נִכְתָּבִים.

---

(1) See the commentary that precedes Chapter 1.

(2) "Rabi" is an abbreviation for Rabbi Judah ha-Nasi, the son of Rabban Simeon ben Gamliel. He lived in the years 135 – 213 of the Common Era. He was the co-author, compiler, and editor of the Mishnah (the six tome Code of Jewish Civil and Religious Law).

[The Oral Law received by Moses on Mount Sinai was handed down through the ages until transcribed by Rabbi Judah ha-Nasi].

(3) The words *"derech yesharah"* (right way or path) means "correct conduct in life". The word *"halachah"* (legal decision) is derived from this for the verb *"halach"* means to walk or go. "The *"halachah"* is really the right path that a person should choose to follow. A Jew finds his right path by allowing himself to be guided by the teachings of the Torah. However, Rabbi Judah ha-Nasi is speaking here in general terms applicable to all human beings.

(4) By virtue of the fact that a person has free will to choose his own actions, Rabi recommends acting in a manner so that all one's actions bring one honor to oneself and meet with the approval of others. However, the exegete Bertinoro explains it thusly, one should follow moderation in one's conduct; that is, one should be neither overly stingy, nor overly generous. In the first case, his conduct is beneficial to himself because he accumulates wealth, but others do not benefit from it. The second case can lead one to need outside financial assistance, which would not be good for him or her. Therefore, it is recommended that one should follow the golden mean in all aspects of one's comportment with the exception of "pride", in which case, one should follow the other extreme, or rather, maximum humility, and not moderation. (See Ch. IV, 4)

(5) A commandment that does not demand much effort and sacrifice. (Cf. Ch. IV, 2)

(6) A king ordered each of his servants to plant a fruit tree in his garden, but did not specify the amount he would pay for it. Each servant planted the tree that he thought would bring him the greatest compensation. After the planting was over, each servant was surprised to receive a greater or lesser payment than he expected. The king had purposely kept secret the value of each kind of tree so that his garden would have all kinds of trees. In like manner, God did not reveal the reward for each of the precepts of the Torah, so that all would be fulfilled.

(7) Whatever sacrifices, whether material or physical, that you may make to fulfill a commandment is insignificant in comparison with the reward that God will give you in this world and the next for fulfilling it. Likewise, the benefit, the enjoyment, etc. that you may get from a sin is not worth anything when compared to the enormous loss that you will suffer for having committed it.

(8) Upon committing a sin, a person thinks that no one is watching or listening, but if he would take into account that God is present, it is less likely that he would commit it; just as when a person is in the presence of a king or of an important person, he is careful in his speech and behavior. All the more reason why he should be mindful of his actions thinking that he is constantly in the presence of the Creator who sees all, hears all, and records all, (in the figurative sense, since we do not know exactly how, and we do not attribute to Him a corporeal form.)

VERSE 2:2

2:2 Rabban Gamliel, the son of Judah ha-Nasi (the Prince) was wont to say; excellent is the study of Torah together with worldly occupation (1), for their combined exactions do not allow one to think on sin. All study of Torah not combined with work induces sin and in the end

ב רַבָּן גַּמְלִיאֵל בְּנוֹ שֶׁל רַבִּי יְהוּדָה הַנָּשִׂיא אוֹמֵר: יָפֶה תַלְמוּד תּוֹרָה עִם דֶּרֶךְ אֶרֶץ, שֶׁיְּגִיעַת שְׁנֵיהֶם מַשְׁכַּחַת עָוֹן. וְכָל תּוֹרָה שֶׁאֵין עִמָּהּ מְלָאכָה, סוֹפָהּ בְּטֵלָה וְגוֹרֶרֶת עָוֹן. וְכָל הָעוֹסְקִים עִם הַצִּבּוּר, יִהְיוּ עוֹסְקִים עִמָּהֶם לְשֵׁם שָׁמַיִם, שֶׁזְּכוּת אֲבוֹתָם מְסַיַּעְתָּם, וְצִדְקָתָם עוֹמֶדֶת לָעַד. וְאַתֶּם, מַעֲלֶה אֲנִי עֲלֵיכֶם שָׂכָר הַרְבֵּה כְּאִלּוּ עֲשִׂיתֶם.

will bring about sin (2). Let all who labor for the community do so for the glory of God (3); for the merit of their forefathers upholds them and their virtue endures. To you (4) who do communal work, God surely will say, "I attribute to you great rewards as if the work were solely yours."

---

(1) The exegete, Rabbi Obadiah of Bertinoro, translated the phrase *"derech eretz"* (which also signifies human conduct, good moral behavior or upbringing) as work, commercial occupation or profession by means of which one earns a living. In my humble opinion, he was obliged to translate the phrase like this because it is better adapted to the sense of the words that follow.

It is surprising to note the insistence of the sages of the Talmud that a person should have an occupation. Even a Torah scholar should dedicate a certain amount of time to teach others for no one should live exclusively for oneself, or take advantage of another without others deriving benefit from him. For this reason, we find in the Talmud that many of our sages had a trade or profession, as for example: Rabbi Yonatan was a shoemaker, Rabbi Yitzhak was a blacksmith, Hillel was a woodcutter, Rabbi Aba was a tailor, and [in medieval times] Maimonides was a doctor, as were many other rabbis. [This is true even to this day.]

(2) The Talmud says "If one does not teach his son a trade or profession, it is as if he induced him to steal."

(3) And not for personal gain

(4) "You" – those who work for the community.

VERSE 2:3

2:3. Be cautious with those in political authority (1) for they draw a man on for their own ends. They wear the guise of friends when it profits them, but they stand not by a man in the hour of his need.

ג הֱווּ זְהִירִין בָּרָשׁוּת, שֶׁאֵין מְקָרְבִין לוֹ לְאָדָם אֶלָּא לְצֹרֶךְ עַצְמָן, נִרְאִין כְּאוֹהֲבִין בִּשְׁעַת הֲנָאָתָן. וְאֵין עוֹמְדִין לוֹ לְאָדָם בִּשְׁעַת דָּחֳקוֹ.

---

(1) This recommendation refers to the authorities of ancient times (see Ch. 1:10). Nevertheless, it can also apply to the present governments of certain countries.

VERSE 2:4

2:4. He (Rabban Gamliel) was also wont to say, do the will of God as thy will (1), that He may do thy will as His will. Renounce thy will out of love of His will, so that He may annul the will of others against yours.

ד הוּא הָיָה אוֹמֵר: עֲשֵׂה רְצוֹנוֹ כִּרְצוֹנֶךָ, כְּדֵי שֶׁיַּעֲשֶׂה רְצוֹנְךָ כִּרְצוֹנוֹ. בַּטֵּל רְצוֹנְךָ מִפְּנֵי רְצוֹנוֹ, כְּדֵי שֶׁיְּבַטֵּל רְצוֹן אֲחֵרִים מִפְּנֵי רְצוֹנֶךָ.

---

(1) If a person does the will of God, and this is also the will of the person at the same time, it is not considered a great deed. But if this same person does the will of God in spite of it not being his own, this is what is called doing the will of God. As a person becomes accustomed to doing the will of God, he comes to desire only what is pleasing to the Creator, and thus, God grants all his desires, since these are what are pleasing to Him. This means that there is no negotiating between God and man. There is no saying, "I will do what You wish, and You

will grant my wishes." Likewise, when a person annuls his own will to do the will of God, He will deny the wishes of His adversaries who do not carry out His will, which is also the will of God.

VERSE 2:5

2:5. Hillel (1) used to say, do not separate yourself from the community (2). Trust not thyself till (3) the day of thy death. Judge not thy fellow man until thou come to his situation (4).

ה הִלֵּל אוֹמֵר: אַל תִּפְרוֹשׁ מִן הַצִּבּוּר, וְאַל תַּאֲמִין בְּעַצְמְךָ עַד יוֹם מוֹתְךָ, וְאַל תָּדִין אֶת חֲבֵרְךָ עַד שֶׁתַּגִּיעַ לִמְקוֹמוֹ, וְאַל תֹּאמַר דָּבָר שֶׁאִי אֶפְשָׁר לִשְׁמוֹעַ שֶׁסּוֹפוֹ לְהִשָּׁמַע, וְאַל תֹּאמַר לִכְשֶׁאֶפָּנֶה אֶשְׁנֶה, שֶׁמָּא לֹא תִפָּנֶה.

Say naught that is unintelligible for it is to be understood ultimately (5). Say not, "When I have leisure, I will study;" perchance thou wilt have no leisure.

---

(1) He is the same Hillel previously mentioned. The compiler of the Mishnah preferred to place his recommendations here with the intention of writing them before the advice of his disciple Rabban Yohanan Ben Zaccai. [See Ch. II, 9]

(2) To not separate oneself from the community means to become a member of a congregation and of the Jewish community in general. That is, to attend the synagogue, to participate in the services, and in all communal matters. In short, to make common cause with the community in all that happens, and not to be apart from it, especially when it is in distress. All this is possible, in my opinion, if the community is guided by the precepts of our holy Torah, and by the principles of justice and morality.

(3) This means, stay away as far as possible from temptation and sin even if you are very virtuous and have a strong character, for King Solomon who had so much intelligence and wisdom, in the end,

fell into sin, as we read in 1 Kings, xi: 4. "For it came to pass, when Solomon was old, that his (foreign) wives turned away his heart after other gods, and his heart was not perfect with the Lord, his God..." No matter how wise, intelligent, or religious a person may be, he may stray into the wrong path, as did the High Priest who, according to the Talmud, became a Sadducee after many years of service in the Temple. [The Sadducees rejected many of the doctrines of rabbinical Judaism such as the belief in resurrection and retribution in a future life.]

(4) Do not condemn a person who has committed an error, or who has been tempted to sin before you, yourself, have been in similar circumstances, and avoided evil, for perhaps you, too, might have done the same or even worse. One can also say, do not criticize a president, a rabbi, or a leader for acting improperly in your eyes before you, yourself, have reached such a position and acted differently.

(5) Hillel's advice here can have several interpretations: Do not speak ill of your fellow man, and do not tell secrets thinking that no one will hear them, for wise King Solomon said in Ecclesiastes x:20 "...for a bird of the sky shall carry the sound, and that which has wings shall tell the matter."

It can also be interpreted in the following way: Be explicit in your words so that they do not require extraordinary perception and intelligence by others for them to be understood. Your words and your teaching should be clear and intelligible.

Another interpretation tells us: when you do not understand something, do not say, I'll try to understand it later. Instead, you should try to study the matter and understand it as best you can at the moment.

VERSE 2:6

2:6. He would say, a crude man (1) will not be fearful of sin, an ignoramus pious, the timid (2) learned, the irate (3) a teacher; nor the one engrossed in business, a scholar (4). Where there are no men, strive to be a man (5).

וּ הוּא הָיָה אוֹמֵר: אֵין בּוּר יְרֵא חֵטְא, וְלֹא עַם הָאָרֶץ חָסִיד, וְלֹא הַבַּיְשָׁן לָמֵד, וְלֹא הַקַּפְּדָן מְלַמֵּד, וְלֹא כָל הַמַּרְבֶּה בִסְחוֹרָה מַחְכִּים, וּבִמְקוֹם שֶׁאֵין אֲנָשִׁים, הִשְׁתַּדֵּל לִהְיוֹת אִישׁ.

---

(1) The Hebrew word *"bur"* was translated in the Talmud as a parcel of uncultivated land. According to Maimonides, *"bur"* refers to a person lacking education in general, one who lacks moral qualities. An *"Am ha-Aretz"* is one who is not an intellectual, but who has some moral qualities. However, in daily usage among our people, the term *"Am ha-Aretz"* is applied to one who is ignorant in matters of religion.

According to another interpretation, the *"bur"* is one who does not have Torah learning, nor good deeds or bad deeds, since he has no notion of virtue or evil. The *"Am ha-Aretz"* is a person who has knowledge of what is proper conduct, but who is lacking in Torah learning and logic, like one who sees a married woman drowning in a river, and does not attempt to save her so as not to commit the sin of touching her. While in the Talmud (*Berahot* 47:), it says that an *"Am ha-Aretz"* is also one who in spite of having studied the Bible and the Mishnah, has not served (attended to) the sages of the law. *"Hassid"* (pious) signifies a man of saintly character who practices the Torah more than is necessary because he lacks wisdom.

(2) Timidity is a virtue in some cases, but in the case of a student who does not ask questions about what he does not know, or who feigns understanding what has been said out of fear of seeming stupid, such a degree of timidity impedes learning.

(3) The teacher who is bad tempered will not succeed in teaching because the fear he or she instills in students will prevent them from

asking questions. In addition, this kind of teacher loses patience or equanimity.

(4) A person who is occupied constantly, or more than necessary, cannot concentrate one hundred percent on what he or she is reading or studying. That is the reason why Hillel said that such a person cannot be learned, although he or she may be studious. ("*Mahkim*" is derived from "*haham*" (wise) as was said by King Solomon, "*Vayehkam mikol haadam*".)

(5) Where there is fear of taking responsibility, try to be a leader without fear of being called arrogant. Where there is no one to lead the community, try to assume leadership even if that means neglecting somewhat your business or study of the Torah. The Midrash, *Shemuel*, interprets Hillel's thought on this in the following manner: In a place where no one sees you or knows you, don't say, "If I sin here, who is going to see, or who is going to know me?" Even though there is no one who sees you or knows you, be good and god fearing.

VERSE 2:7

2:7. Hillel, upon seeing a skull floating in the water, said to it, because thou didst drown [others], thou hast been drowned, and in turn, they who drowned thee shall themselves be drowned (1). ז אַף הוּא רָאָה גֻלְגֹּלֶת אַחַת שֶׁצָּפָה עַל פְּנֵי הַמָּיִם. אָמַר לָהּ: עַל דַּאֲטֵפְתְּ, אַטְפוּךְ, וְסוֹף מְטִיפַיִךְ יְטוּפוּן.

---

(1) The skull was probably found floating in shallow water, because otherwise it would not float according to Archimedes principle. [the skull is heavier than water.] Rashi explains that it was noticed that the skull had been severed from the body, leading Hillel to assume that it probably belonged to a bandit who had been killed by other bandits, and that is why he said what he said.

The idea emphasized here is that one who receives punishment, does not receive it accidentally, but for the evils he has committed. Hillel was probably inspired by Moses the prophet who, according to the Midrash, saw the skull of Pharaoh floating in the Red Sea and said, "Because you drowned the male children of Israel in the Nile, you were also drowned." This tells us that the Divine Law mentioned in the Talmud (*Sanhedrin* 96:) *"Midaa k'neged midaa"* (a person receives reward and punishment for what he or she has done) governs the world.

These happenings are sometimes visible and can be corroborated by mankind, but others remain hidden. We should not doubt God's justice even when things seem irrational and incomprehensible in our eyes.

VERSE 2:8

ח הוּא הָיָה אוֹמֵר: מַרְבֶּה בָשָׂר, מַרְבֶּה רִמָּה. מַרְבֶּה נְכָסִים, מַרְבֶּה דְאָגָה. מַרְבֶּה נָשִׁים, מַרְבֶּה כְשָׁפִים. מַרְבֶּה שְׁפָחוֹת, מַרְבֶּה זִמָּה. מַרְבֶּה עֲבָדִים, מַרְבֶּה גָזֵל. מַרְבֶּה תוֹרָה, מַרְבֶּה חַיִּים. מַרְבֶּה יְשִׁיבָה, מַרְבֶּה חָכְמָה. מַרְבֶּה עֵצָה, מַרְבֶּה תְבוּנָה. מַרְבֶּה צְדָקָה, מַרְבֶּה שָׁלוֹם. קָנָה שֵׁם טוֹב, קָנָה לְעַצְמוֹ. קָנָה לוֹ דִבְרֵי תוֹרָה, קָנָה לוֹ חַיֵּי הָעוֹלָם הַבָּא.

2:8. He used to say, the more flesh, the more worms (1); the more wealth, the more worry; the more women, the more superstition (2); the more maid servants, the more license; the more men servants, the more thieving. But the more Torah, the more life; the more study, the more wisdom (3); the more counsel, the more understanding; the more virtue, the more peace (4). Gain a good name, and for yourself you have gained it (5); but gain knowledge of the Torah (6), and you have gained the future life.

---

(1) A person who gains weight does not necessarily engender worms,

therefore, in my opinion; this saying refers to the worms that despoil the body after death. According to the Talmud, the bite of a worm is like being pricked with a needle even when a person is dead.

(2) Rivalry among women makes them turn to magic in order to gain the affection of the same man. This refers in particular to the age when a man was permitted to have more than one wife; that is, before the decree of Rabbi Gershon of Metz [circa 1000 c.e.]

(3) In the Talmud (*Taanit* 7,) it says, I have learned much from my teachers, still more from my colleagues, and even much more from my students.

(4) The Hebrew word t*zedakah* meaning justice also signifies charity, for in Judaism; charity is in reality an act of justice that one performs in favor of the poor. Once there is social justice, there is peace in society, as said by the prophet Isaiah (xxxii:17): "And the work of righteousness shall be peace…"

(5) When a person dies, and leaves behind money, goods, and property, these are enjoyed by his heirs, while a good name is the exclusive property of the one who acquires it.

(6) The beneficial effect of the words of the Torah serves one in this world and contributes toward the acquisition of the eternal life. The Torah has been compared to a tree of (eternal) life, and through it, one acquires length of days and years of life and peace (Proverbs iii, 2).

VERSE 2:9

2:9. Rabban Yohanan ben Zaccai received the tradition from Hillel and Shammai. He used to say, hast thou learned Torah abundantly, plume not thyself thereon (1), for thou wast created therefore.

ט רַבָּן יוֹחָנָן בֶּן זַכַּאי קִבֵּל מֵהִלֵּל וּמִשַּׁמַּאי. הוּא הָיָה אוֹמֵר: אִם לָמַדְתָּ תּוֹרָה הַרְבֵּה, אַל תַּחֲזִיק טוֹבָה לְעַצְמְךָ, כִּי לְכַךְ נוֹצָרְתָּ.

---

(1) A person who studies Torah resembles a debtor who is paying his debt. He was created for this end, and therefore, he should not take pride in having done so, just as a debtor who pays his debt is only fulfilling his obligation.

VERSE 2:10

2:10. Rabban Yohanan ben Zaccai (1) had five disciples (2), Rabbi Eliezer ben Hyrcanus, Rabbi Joshua ben Hananya, Rabbi Yose, the priest, Rabbi Simeon ben Nethanel and Rabbi Elazar ben Arah.

י חֲמִשָּׁה תַלְמִידִים הָיוּ לוֹ לְרַבָּן יוֹחָנָן בֶּן זַכַּאי, וְאֵלּוּ הֵן: רַבִּי אֱלִיעֶזֶר בֶּן הָרְקָנוֹס, רַבִּי יְהוֹשֻׁעַ בֶּן חֲנַנְיָא, רַבִּי יוֹסֵי הַכֹּהֵן, רַבִּי שִׁמְעוֹן בֶּן נְתַנְאֵל, וְרַבִּי אֶלְעָזָר בֶּן עֲרָךְ.

---

(1) As previously mentioned, Rabban Yohanan ben Zaccai was a disciple of Hillel. He survived the fall of Jerusalem in the year 70 C.E. and played an important role in organizing Jewish life after that, making the city of Yavneh the center of Torah study. In the Talmud (*Gittin* 56:), it is said that in the interview he had with the king, alluding to Vespasian (although it is more likely that the interview had been with Titus, the governor), Rabban Yohanan ben Zaccai asked

permission to open a rabbinical academy in Yavneh, and received it. As a result of it being granted, he rescued Judaism from destruction.

(2) He had many disciples, but these were the most outstanding.

VERSE 2:11

2:11. He used to portray their qualities thusly: Eliezer ben Hyrcanus is a plastered cistern (1) that loses not a drop. Joshua ben Hananya – happy, she who bore him (2). Yose, the priest, he is pious (3). Simeon ben Nethanel fears sin (4). Elazar ben Arah is as a perennial spring (5).

יא הוּא הָיָה מוֹנֶה שְׁבְחָן: רַבִּי אֱלִיעֶזֶר בֶּן הָרְקָנוֹס, בּוֹר סוּד שֶׁאֵינוֹ מְאַבֵּד טִפָּה. רַבִּי יְהוֹשֻׁעַ בֶּן חֲנַנְיָה, אַשְׁרֵי יוֹלַדְתּוֹ. רַבִּי יוֹסֵי הַכֹּהֵן, חָסִיד. רַבִּי שִׁמְעוֹן בֶּן נְתַנְאֵל, יְרֵא חֵטְא. וְרַבִּי אֶלְעָזָר בֶּן עֲרָךְ, כְּמַעְיָן הַמִּתְגַּבֵּר.

---

(1) The Hebrew word *"sud"* (from *"sayud"* – cemented) is more correct than *"sid"*, otherwise *"bor-sid"* would mean a cistern of lime. What Rabban Yohanan ben Zaccai wished to convey with regard to Rabbi Eliezer was that he was like a cemented cistern; that is; he had an extraordinary memory, and never forgot what he learned. He was outstanding in the teaching of the Tradition, and was the teacher of Rabbi Akiva ben Yosef.

(2) It is told in the Talmud that Rabbi Joshua's mother would walk by the House of Study while she was pregnant so that the students would bless the child she bore within her. It is also said that she would bring Rabbi Joshua, when he was still a child, to the Academy so that his ears would be familiar with words of Torah. Rabbi Joshua was one of the most outstanding representatives of the Jewish people in his time, and famous for his disputations with the Greek philosophers of that age.

(3) The adjective "pious" is applied to one who goes beyond his moral obligation in studying Torah and practicing deeds of kindness.

(4) He refrained from many things, even those that are permitted, for fear of falling into sin.

(5) What is meant is that he added his own deductions to the knowledge that he acquired in his studies, in contrast to the plastered cistern that only contains the water (learning) that it receives.

VERSE 2:12

2:12. He said further, were all the sages of Israel in one scale of the balance and Eliezer ben Hyrcanus in the other; he would outweigh all the rest. But Abba Shaul reported him as saying that were all the sages of Israel together with Eliezer ben Hyrcanus in one scale of the balance and Elazar ben Arah in the other, it is he who would outweigh all the rest (1).

יב הוּא הָיָה אוֹמֵר: אִם יִהְיוּ כָּל חַכְמֵי יִשְׂרָאֵל בְּכַף מֹאזְנַיִם, וֶאֱלִיעֶזֶר בֶּן הָרְקְנוֹס בְּכַף שְׁנִיָּה, מַכְרִיעַ אֶת כֻּלָּם. אַבָּא שָׁאוּל אוֹמֵר מִשְּׁמוֹ: אִם יִהְיוּ כָּל חַכְמֵי יִשְׂרָאֵל בְּכַף מֹאזְנַיִם וְרַבִּי אֱלִיעֶזֶר בֶּן הָרְקְנוֹס אַף עִמָּהֶם, וְרַבִּי אֶלְעָזָר בֶּן עֲרָךְ בְּכַף שְׁנִיָּה, מַכְרִיעַ אֶת כֻּלָּם.

---

(1) According to the exegete Ovadiah of Bertinoro, Rabban Yohanan ben Zaccai praised Rabbi Elazar ben Arah for his intelligence and extraordinary mental powers, saying that he could easily understand the most difficult subjects of study, while Eliezer ben Hyrcanus was praised for his experience and excellent memory. Therefore, there is no contradiction between what was said by Judah ha-Nasi, the compiler of the Mishnah, and what was said by Abba Shaul, his contemporary.

VERSE 2:13

2:13. Rabban ben Zaccai then said to his five disciples: go forth and see which is the best way for a man to keep (1). Rabbi Eliezer said, a good eye (2), Rabbi Joshua said, a good associate (3). Rabbi Yose said, a good neighbor (4). Rabbi Simeon said, foresight (5). Rabbi Elazar said a good heart (6). Said Rabban Yohanan ben Zaccai, I approve the words of Elazar ben Arah the most, because in them the sayings of the rest are included.

יג. אָמַר לָהֶם: צְאוּ וּרְאוּ אֵיזוֹ הִיא דֶרֶךְ טוֹבָה שֶׁיִדְבַּק בָּהּ הָאָדָם. רַבִּי אֱלִיעֶזֶר אוֹמֵר: עַיִן טוֹבָה. רַבִּי יְהוֹשֻׁעַ אוֹמֵר: חָבֵר טוֹב. רַבִּי יוֹסֵי אוֹמֵר: שָׁכֵן טוֹב. רַבִּי שִׁמְעוֹן אוֹמֵר: הָרוֹאֶה אֶת הַנּוֹלָד. רַבִּי אֶלְעָזָר אוֹמֵר: לֵב טוֹב. אָמַר לָהֶם: רוֹאֶה אֲנִי אֶת דִּבְרֵי אֶלְעָזָר בֶּן עֲרָךְ מִדִּבְרֵיכֶם, שֶׁבִּכְלַל דְּבָרָיו דִּבְרֵיכֶם.

---

(1) In order for the answers of the disciples to correspond more or less to the question asked by the master, we should assume that what he meant by his question was, what is the path that a person should choose as the essence of a correct life, or in other words, what is the key to righteous living.

(2) This means not having envy, jealousy, covetousness or bad thoughts that come from what the eye sees. As is said in the *Shema*, "Then shall you not stray after your heart and your eyes whereafter ye are wont to lust."

(3) A good companion and friend recommends what is good, and leads one in the path of righteousness. This can also be interpreted as being oneself a good companion to others.

(4) A person can learn many good things from the comportment of a good neighbor whom he can see day and night. Rabbi Jose wishes

to tell us also that each one of us should become a good neighbor in the neighborhood in which we live, and love all human beings where we may live.

(5) In order to avoid harm and evil consequences.

(6) A person who has a good heart is generous, attracts good friends, and good neighbors. He distances himself from all that is evil. It is for this reason that the master preferred the opinion of Rabbi Elazar above the others.

VERSE 2:14

2:14. Again, he said to them, go forth and see which is the way that a man should shun. Rabbi Eliezer said an evil eye. Rabbi Joshua said an evil associate. Rabbi Yose said an evil neighbor. Rabbi Simeon said to borrow and not repay (1), whether from man or from God (2), as the verse of Psalm XXXVII:21 says, "The wicked borrow and do not repay, but the righteous man gives with a good grace (3)." Rabbi Elazar said an evil heart. Said Rabban Yohanan ben Zaccai, I approve the words of Elazar ben Arah the most, because in them the sayings of rest of you are contained.

יד אָמַר לָהֶם: צְאוּ וּרְאוּ אֵיזוֹ הִיא דֶּרֶךְ רָעָה שֶׁיִּתְרַחֵק מִמֶּנָּה הָאָדָם. רַבִּי אֱלִיעֶזֶר אוֹמֵר: עַיִן רָעָה. רַבִּי יְהוֹשֻׁעַ אוֹמֵר: חָבֵר רָע. רַבִּי יוֹסֵי אוֹמֵר: שָׁכֵן רָע. רַבִּי שִׁמְעוֹן אוֹמֵר: הַלֹּוֶה וְאֵינוֹ מְשַׁלֵּם. אֶחָד הַלֹּוֶה מִן הָאָדָם כְּלֹוֶה מִן הַמָּקוֹם, שֶׁנֶּאֱמַר: לֹוֶה רָשָׁע וְלֹא יְשַׁלֵּם, וְצַדִּיק חוֹנֵן וְנוֹתֵן. רַבִּי אֶלְעָזָר אוֹמֵר: לֵב רָע. אָמַר לָהֶם: רוֹאֶה אֲנִי אֶת דִּבְרֵי אֶלְעָזָר בֶּן עֲרָךְ מִדִּבְרֵיכֶם, שֶׁבִּכְלַל דְּבָרָיו דִּבְרֵיכֶם.

---

(1) It would seem that the master did not need to ask them which is

the way a man should shun, since they would answer the opposite of what they had previously said. Nevertheless, he did so because in reality there exist virtues, which even if one does not practice, one is not considered bad for not practicing them. For example, one can be good without reaching the level of saintliness, but that would not make a person bad. Likewise, if a person is content with his lot, this is considered a good quality, but if a person aspires to have more than he possesses, without hurting anyone, that would not make such a person bad as long as his aspiration is not tainted by envy, covetousness, or evil thoughts. This is what Rabbi Simeon was referring to when he said in his answer, "to borrow and not to repay."

(2) Rabbi Simeon preferred to say these words in contrast to what he said before (to have foresight), for whoever does not have foresight is not capable of avoiding the consequences and results of his conduct. Rabbi Simeon gives as an example, one who borrows knowing beforehand that he will not be able to fulfill his obligation and does not pay, or being in doubt about being able to repay, plays with the fortune of others, with the result that later no one will wish to lend anything to someone who is not considered honest. One who lends money, etc. to another does so confiding in the commandment of God, which obliges the debtor to pay his debts, and not in the debtor himself; therefore, it is considered as if the person were borrowing from God.

In the Talmud Yerushalmi (*Berahot* 2:3, 4) it tells of a certain Jew who always put on *tefilin*, and by virtue of this, people confided in his sense of values. On denying one day, that he had received certain articles, one of his victims said to him, "It is not in you that I placed my confidence, but in God who commanded you to put on the *tefilin*."

(3) The exegete, Ovadiah of Bertinoro explains this Biblical verse in the following way, "The malevolent one borrows and does not repay, but God who is just, takes pity on the creditor and returns to him what he lent." Thus, the debtor remains in debt to God.

VERSE 2:15

2:15. Each of them said three things. Rabbi Eliezer (1) was wont to say, be the honor of thy fellow dear to thee as thine own (2), and be not lightly moved to anger (3). Repent one day before thy death (4). Warm thyself at the fire of the sages, but beware lest thou burn thyself with their glowing brands (5). Their bite can be as the fox, their sting as the scorpion, their hiss as the serpent (6), and all their words as flaming coals.

טו הֵם אָמְרוּ שְׁלֹשָׁה דְבָרִים. רַבִּי אֱלִיעֶזֶר אוֹמֵר: יְהִי כְבוֹד חֲבֵרְךָ חָבִיב עָלֶיךָ כְּשֶׁלָּךְ, וְאַל תְּהִי נוֹחַ לִכְעוֹס. וְשׁוּב יוֹם אֶחָד לִפְנֵי מִיתָתְךָ. וֶהֱוֵי מִתְחַמֵּם כְּנֶגֶד אוּרָן שֶׁל חֲכָמִים, וֶהֱוֵי זָהִיר בְּגַחַלְתָּן שֶׁלֹּא תִכָּוֶה, שֶׁנְּשִׁיכָתָן נְשִׁיכַת שׁוּעָל, וַעֲקִיצָתָן עֲקִיצַת עַקְרָב, וּלְחִישָׁתָן לְחִישַׁת שָׂרָף, וְכָל דִּבְרֵיהֶם כְּגַחֲלֵי אֵשׁ.

---

(1) Rabbi Eliezer ben Hyrcanus, called the Great, began his studies at a relatively late age. He became one of the great teachers of his time, and his name appears innumerable times in the Talmud.

In spite of his greatness, the Talmud (*Bava Metzia* 59) relates that he was shunned by his colleagues because he refused to abide by the decisions of the majority. He spent the last twenty years of his life in sadness for having been treated so harshly. This event is one of the most dramatic in the Talmud.

(2) In any word or deed, we should take care not to stain the honor and reputation of our fellow man. The Talmud proclaims, "He who elevates himself as a result of the fall or degradation of his fellow man, has no part in the world to come.

(3) By virtue of the fact that one generally cannot avoid getting angry in certain circumstances, Rabbi Eliezer recommends that we do not lose our temper easily. A person's character is revealed in three ways: *bekoso* (in his cups); that is, when he is drunk, *bekiso* (in his purse);

that is, in his money dealings, and *bekaso* (in his anger) [*Eruvin* 65:]. Our sages said in Talmud (*Shabbat* 105, "One who loses his temper is as if he were worshipping idols", for one who worships idols is capable of committing barbaric acts, much like a person who, in his anger, loses his mental equilibrium. In the Biblical story of Elijah and the four hundred fifty prophets of the idol Baal, we read that "they cried and cut themselves with knives and lancets till the blood gushed out upon them." (See 1 Kings XVIII:28).

(4) In the Talmud, it is told that when Rabbi Eliezer made this recommendation, they asked him, "Does a person know, by chance, on what day he is going to die so that he may repent the day before?" The rabbi answered them, "All the more reason why we should repent today, for perhaps, we may die tomorrow; and if this should not happen, we should do so tomorrow, for we may die the day after tomorrow. Thus, all our days should be days of repentence." The reason why the day of death is hidden from us is because, if we knew it, we might say to ourselves, "I still have time to perform good deeds, or to repent." [In other words, we need not bother with that now.]

(5) Just as one who is cold should sit a certain distance from the fire so as to be warm without being in danger of burning himself, so should a disciple absorb the learning imparted to him by the teacher, and not become too familiar with him by trying to impress him with his intelligence. The abuse and poor application of intimacy can cause discord instead of benefit, and generally, rabbis do not forgive easily.

(6) The bite of a fox and the sting of a scorpion are the worst of their kind. The *saraf* (a type of poisonous snake) is so called because one feels the burning, even without being bitten, solely because of the breath that comes from the mouth of this serpent.

VERSE 2:16

2:16. Rabbi Joshua would say, a grudging eye (1), evil desire (2), and hatred of one's fellows (3) remove one from human society (4).

טז רַבִּי יְהוֹשֻׁעַ אוֹמֵר: עַיִן הָרַע, וְיֵצֶר הָרַע, וְשִׂנְאַת הַבְּרִיּוֹת, מוֹצִיאִין אֶת הָאָדָם מִן הָעוֹלָם.

---

(1) These three defects can be categorized as egotism. A person who envies others for what they possess and he lacks, finds himself suffering constantly, and this shortens his life.

(2) The evil impulse is in the human heart from youth on. (Genesis VIII: 21) It causes a person to commit all sorts of evils and abuses, endangering one's physical and mental health, and consequently shortens one's life.

(3) This can be called misanthropy. The misanthrope, due to his hatred of others, is condemned to live a lonely life, not having others to offer him the assistance that he may require. This type of person finds himself in a state of constant tension for always being opposed to what others do, and consequently his life is shortened.

(4) This interpretation, which follows the Hebrew, signifies that the person is withdrawn from human society. A selfish person distances himself from his fellows and from society. It is as if he left this world.

VERSE 2:17

2:17. Rabbi Yose used to say, let thy neighbor's money be as precious to thee as thine own (1). Set thyself to learn Torah, for it does not come to thee as an inheritance (2). Let all thy actions be for the glory of God (3).

יז רַבִּי יוֹסֵי אוֹמֵר: יְהִי מָמוֹן חֲבֵרְךָ חָבִיב עָלֶיךָ כְּשֶׁלָּךְ. וְהַתְקֵן עַצְמְךָ לִלְמוֹד תּוֹרָה, שֶׁאֵינָהּ יְרֻשָּׁה לָךְ. וְכָל מַעֲשֶׂיךָ יִהְיוּ לְשֵׁם שָׁמָיִם.

---

(1) In other words, respect the rights and property of others just as you would want yours to be respected. In material matters, if you know that your companion's merchandise is good, consider it your duty to tell him so, but on the other hand, if it is not good, tell those who ask you if it is good, that you do not know. You would not want your merchandise to be called bad. In moral matters, if you know a person is good, proclaim his goodness, and if a person is not good, keep quiet or say that you do not know anything about that person.

(2) No one can make his children heirs to his knowledge. They must study or make an effort to acquire it. Moses and Eli, (1 Samuel, Ch. III), wanted their children to succeed them, but since they were not capable, God chose Joshua to be Moses' successor, and Samuel to be Eli's.

(3) Even eating, drinking, etc., which do not seem to be religious acts, should be done in order to maintain the body's health with the aim of serving God. That is, we should consecrate ourselves eternally to the divine, and nothing should be done with any other purpose but to serve God. Hillel used to tell his disciples that bathing in order to keep the body clean was a religious obligation.

VERSE 2:18

2:18 Rabbi Simeon was wont to say, be scrupulous in reading the Shema and in prayer. When thou prayest, make not thy prayer a fixed form (1), but make it an entreaty and supplication of love before the Almighty. For the prophet Joel has said (II:3), "Gracious and compassionate is He, long suffering and abundant in mercy, and repenting of evil." Be not evil in thine own sight (2).

יח רַבִּי שִׁמְעוֹן אוֹמֵר: הֱוֵי זָהִיר בִּקְרִיאַת שְׁמַע וּבִתְפִלָּה. וּכְשֶׁאַתָּה מִתְפַּלֵּל, אַל תַּעַשׂ תְּפִלָּתְךָ קֶבַע, אֶלָּא רַחֲמִים וְתַחֲנוּנִים לִפְנֵי הַמָּקוֹם, שֶׁנֶּאֱמַר: כִּי חַנּוּן וְרַחוּם הוּא, אֶרֶךְ אַפַּיִם וְרַב חֶסֶד, וְנִחָם עַל הָרָעָה. וְאַל תְּהִי רָשָׁע בִּפְנֵי עַצְמֶךָ.

---

(1) This means that in addition to being careful to recite the Shema, etc. at the proper time, you should make sure that your mouth, heart, and thoughts are directed to God with love, and reverence (see *Berahot* 28:). Prayer without *kavanah* (concentration) is like a body without a soul.

(2) As long as a person has low self esteem, he becomes used to this idea, and anything bad that he does, seems all right to him, for he does it out of second nature. But if a person is really convinced that he has done wrong, not just because others think so, that person will be able to reproach himself for his improper conduct.

VERSE 2:19

2:19. Rabbi Elazar said, be alert to learn Torah. Know what to answer an unbeliever (1). Know before whom thou art laboring, and who is the Master of thy work who will pay thee the wages due thy actions (2).

יט. רַבִּי אֶלְעָזָר אוֹמֵר: הֱוֵי שָׁקוּד לִלְמוֹד תּוֹרָה, וְדַע מַה שֶּׁתָּשִׁיב לְאֶפִּיקוֹרוֹס. וְדַע לִפְנֵי מִי אַתָּה עָמֵל. וְנֶאֱמָן הוּא בַּעַל מְלַאכְתְּךָ שֶׁיְשַׁלֵּם לְךָ שְׂכַר פְּעֻלָּתֶךָ.

---

(1) The Hebrew term for unbeliever, *apicoros*, is derived from Epicurus who was an ancient Greek philosopher who denied the existence of God, and said the universe was a product of chance. Hence, our sages adopted the term "*apicoros*" in the Talmud (*Sanhedrin* 99) to categorize one who denigrates the "*talmidei hahamim*" – the sages of the Law, one who interprets the Torah erroneously, and one who denies the fundamental bases of our faith.

A person who debates an "*apicoros*" should study the Torah deeply beforehand; otherwise, the latter may easily defeat him with his arguments, even though these may be unfounded. It is preferable to have such debates with a non-believing gentile than with Jewish heretics for these are the more dangerous. In any case, one should have sufficient knowledge, and be very careful in debates as well as with questions raised and answers given so that the heart will not be swayed by the opinions of the unbeliever. Nevertheless, it is the duty of sages to defend the honor and the truths of Judaism against those who have strayed or are malevolent.

(2) Upon studying the Torah or performing good deeds, do not think that you are wasting your time or money, for God is faithful in his rewards. In some books, this part of the text is omitted in order not to contradict what Antigonos says in the first chapter that we should not serve God in expectation of receiving a reward.

VERSE 2:20

2:20. Rabbi Tarfon (1) used to say, the day is short, the work is great, the laborers are laggard, the reward is abundant and the Master of the house is urgent (2).

כ רַבִּי טַרְפוֹן אוֹמֵר: הַיּוֹם קָצֵר, וְהַמְלָאכָה מְרֻבָּה, וְהַפּוֹעֲלִים עֲצֵלִים, וְהַשָּׂכָר הַרְבֵּה, וּבַעַל הַבַּיִת דּוֹחֵק.

---

(1) Rabbi Tarfon was one who most fulfilled the fifth commandment to honor one's father and mother. It is told in the Talmud that on one Shabbath on which his mother had torn her shoe, Rabbi Tarfon put his hands under her feet so that she might walk on them until she reached where she was going.

(2) A person's life is short, and the study of Torah is long and arduous, therefore it is necessary to hurry in order to acquire as much as possible from this study. In my opinion, this is also true of other studies such as medicine, etc. However, a person often wastes his time on inane things as if he were lazy, and does not calculate the abundant reward he loses by neglecting to study Torah and perform good deeds. This resembles a king who told his servant, "Count from now until tomorrow all the gold coins that you can count, and they will be yours." Is it possible that the servant would be so foolish as to sleep that night and lose a fortune? The Master of the house; that is the Holy One, blessed be He, from whom a reward is expected, rewards us in life, as is written in Joshua (1:8), "…but thou shall meditate therein day and night… and then thou shalt have good success."

VERSE 2:21

כא הוּא הָיָה אוֹמֵר: לֹא עָלֶיךָ הַמְּלָאכָה לִגְמוֹר, וְלֹא אַתָּה בֶן חוֹרִין לְהִבָּטֵל מִמֶּנָּה. אִם לָמַדְתָּ תּוֹרָה הַרְבֵּה, נוֹתְנִים לְךָ שָׂכָר הַרְבֵּה, וְנֶאֱמָן הוּא בַּעַל מְלַאכְתְּךָ שֶׁיְּשַׁלֵּם לְךָ שְׂכַר פְּעֻלָּתֶךָ, וְדַע שֶׁמַּתַּן שְׂכָרָן שֶׁל צַדִּיקִים לֶעָתִיד לָבוֹא.

2:21. He used to say, it is not incumbent on thee to complete the work, but thou art not free to evade it (1). If thou hast learned much Torah, there will be given thee abundant reward, for the Master of thy work is trustworthy to pay thee the reward of thine activity. But know that the giving of the reward to the righteous is reserved for the time to come (2).

רַבִּי חֲנַנְיָא בֶּן־עֲקַשְׁיָא אוֹמֵר: רָצָה הַקָּדוֹשׁ בָּרוּךְ הוּא לְזַכּוֹת אֶת־יִשְׂרָאֵל, לְפִיכָךְ הִרְבָּה לָהֶם תּוֹרָה וּמִצְוֹת, שֶׁנֶּאֱמַר: יְיָ חָפֵץ לְמַעַן צִדְקוֹ, יַגְדִּיל תּוֹרָה וְיַאְדִּיר.

Rabbi Hanania, son of Akashia used to say, the Holy One, blessed be He, wishing to render Israel the more worthy enlarged for them the Torah and its commandments. For so we may read the words of the prophet Isaiah (XLII:21), "The Lord was pleased for His righteousness' sake to magnify Torah and to make it glorious."

---

(1) In spite of the fact that the days of our life are short and insufficient to be spent in the study of the Torah, don't say, "I will dedicate myself exclusively to this study, and not occupy myself with other activities." If you do so, there is danger that you will tire or become lazy and abandon the study entirely since your body and mind will be weakened by the efforts you make beyond your capabilities. On the

other hand, you cannot say, "Since it is not in me to complete this study, I will give it up or give it little time." God created you for the study of Torah and the observance of His commandments.

(2) The reward that is spoken of here is worthy of belief. The Almighty is faithful in granting it in this life, or in the world of the soul (after death), as well as in the world to come (after the resurrection of the dead).

FROM THE THIRD CHAPTER ON, THE SAGES ARE NOT MENTIONED, EITHER IN CHRONOLOGICAL ORDER, OR IN ORDER OF IMPORTANCE.

Chapter III פרק ג'

VERSE 3:1

"כָּל יִשְׂרָאֵל יֵשׁ לָהֶם חֵלֶק לָעוֹלָם הַבָּא, שֶׁנֶּאֱמַר: וְעַמֵּךְ כֻּלָּם צַדִּיקִים, לְעוֹלָם יִירְשׁוּ אָרֶץ, נֵצֶר מַטָּעַי מַעֲשֵׂה יָדַי לְהִתְפָּאֵר."

א עֲקַבְיָא בֶּן מַהֲלַלְאֵל אוֹמֵר: הִסְתַּכֵּל בִּשְׁלֹשָׁה דְבָרִים וְאֵין אַתָּה בָא לִידֵי עֲבֵרָה. דַּע מֵאַיִן בָּאתָ, וּלְאָן אַתָּה הוֹלֵךְ, וְלִפְנֵי מִי אַתָּה עָתִיד לִתֵּן דִּין וְחֶשְׁבּוֹן. מֵאַיִן בָּאתָ, מִטִּפָּה סְרוּחָה, וּלְאָן אַתָּה הוֹלֵךְ, לִמְקוֹם עָפָר רִמָּה וְתוֹלֵעָה. וְלִפְנֵי מִי אַתָּה עָתִיד לִתֵּן דִּין וְחֶשְׁבּוֹן, לִפְנֵי מֶלֶךְ מַלְכֵי הַמְּלָכִים הַקָּדוֹשׁ בָּרוּךְ הוּא.

"All Israel has a share in the world to come…"(1)

3:1. Akavia ben Mahalalel (2) used to say, ponder on three things and thou wilt not come into the power of sin: know whence thou comest, whither thou art going, and before whom thou art destined to give an accounting. Whence thou comest? From a fetid drop (3). Whither thou art going? To the place of dust and worms. Before Whom thou art destined to give an accounting? Before the supreme King of kings, the Holy One, blessed be He (4).

---

(1) See text and commentary at the beginning of Chapter I.

(2) This sage, a contemporary of Hillel, had been named vice-president of the Sanhedrin after the death of Shammai, but he refused the appointment for he did not wish to change his views on the interpretation of some laws of the Torah recognized by the Sanhedrin. (see Tractate *Eduyot* v, 6). On renouncing the appointment, he said, "I do this so that no one may say that I changed my point of view due to interest in remaining in the post." When he was on his deathbed, his son asked him to recommend him to some of his friends. Akavia

answered, "Your own actions can bring you close to them, and your own actions can distance you from them."

(3) This refers to the sperm from which we are engendered. When we think of this origin, and that our ultimate destiny is to return to dust, etc., we no longer succumb to pride, ambition, and other moral defects, and we learn to be humble.

(4) When a person is called to appear before a high human authority to render an accounting, it is very natural that he feel a certain apprehension in spite of having the possibility of saving himself by hiring an attorney to defend him, or by bribing or deceiving the judge. However, none of this can happen when he or she has to render accounts before the King of kings, God, Who knows the truth, does not accept bribes, nor can be deceived in any way.

VERSE 3:2

3:2. Rabbi Hanina, substitute for the High Priest, would say, "Pray for the welfare of the government (1), for if it were not for the fear (2) of it, men would eat each other up alive."

ב רַבִּי חֲנִינָא סְגַן הַכֹּהֲנִים אוֹמֵר: הֱוֵי מִתְפַּלֵּל בִּשְׁלוֹמָהּ שֶׁל מַלְכוּת, שֶׁאִלְמָלֵא מוֹרָאָהּ, אִישׁ אֶת רֵעֵהוּ חַיִּים בְּלָעוֹ.

---

(1) Rabbi Hanina's advice does not refer solely to the government of Israel, but to any government of a country in which Jews may be living. According to Jeremiah (XXIX:7), "And seek the peace of the city into which I have caused you to be carried, and pray to the Lord for it; for in its peace shall you have peace." In like manner, Ezra, the Scribe recommended that the Jews pray for the life of the king and his sons. (See Ezra, VI:10). Rabbi Hanina was referring to the government of Rome in particular (66 C.E.), as he was a moderate rabbi.

(2) Without the fear of authorities to punish people, thefts, crimes, oppression, etc. would be multiplied, and there would be no one to stop them. It is for this reason that our synagogue ritual includes the prayer for the government, *Hanoten teshua* [said in Sephardic synagogues before taking out the Torah]. The expression that men would eat each other up alive alludes to the behavior of fish in the sea where the larger ones eat the smaller. In the words of the prophet Habakkuk (1:14), "And (Thou) dost make men like the fishes of the sea, like the creeping things, that have no ruler over them."

VERSE 3:3

3:3. Rabbi Hananiah ben Teradyon (1) used to say, when two sit together and no words of Torah pass between them, theirs is the session of scorners' spoken of by the Psalmist. But when two sit together and words of Torah pass between them, God's Shechinah [Divine presence] rests on them (2). For is it not said by the prophet Malachi (III:16), "Then those who feared the Lord spoke to one another; and the Lord hearkened and heard it; and a book of remembrance was written before Him for those who feared the Lord, and took heed of His name." This applies to two. What verse can be adduced to show that the Holy One, blessed be He, determines a reward for even one who sits and occupies himself with the

ג רַבִּי חֲנִינָא בֶּן תְּרַדְיוֹן אוֹמֵר: שְׁנַיִם שֶׁיּוֹשְׁבִין וְאֵין בֵּינֵיהֶן דִּבְרֵי תוֹרָה, הֲרֵי זֶה מוֹשַׁב לֵצִים, שֶׁנֶּאֱמַר: וּבְמוֹשַׁב לֵצִים לֹא יָשָׁב. אֲבָל שְׁנַיִם שֶׁיּוֹשְׁבִין וְיֵשׁ בֵּינֵיהֶם דִּבְרֵי תוֹרָה, שְׁכִינָה שְׁרוּיָה בֵּינֵיהֶם, שֶׁנֶּאֱמַר: אָז נִדְבְּרוּ יִרְאֵי יְיָ אִישׁ אֶל רֵעֵהוּ, וַיַּקְשֵׁב יְיָ וַיִּשְׁמָע, וַיִּכָּתֵב סֵפֶר זִכָּרוֹן לְפָנָיו, לְיִרְאֵי יְיָ וּלְחֹשְׁבֵי שְׁמוֹ. אֵין לִי אֶלָּא שְׁנַיִם, מִנַּיִן שֶׁאֲפִילוּ אֶחָד שֶׁיּוֹשֵׁב וְעוֹסֵק בַּתּוֹרָה, שֶׁהַקָּדוֹשׁ בָּרוּךְ הוּא קוֹבֵעַ לוֹ שָׂכָר, שֶׁנֶּאֱמַר: יֵשֵׁב בָּדָד וְיִדֹּם כִּי נָטַל עָלָיו.

Torah, the verse of Lamentations, "Let him sit alone and muse, for God has laid it on him (3)."

---

(1) Rabbi Hananiah, the father of Beruria, learned wife of the famous Rabbi Meir, was one of the ten martyrs. He was burned to death wrapped in a scroll of the Torah by order of the Emperor Hadrian, after the defeat of the Bar Kokhba rebellion against Rome in the year 135 C.E. His last words before dying were, "The parchment is burning, but its contents rise to the heavens." By this, he meant that the words of the Torah are indestructible.

(2) This signifies that God enlightens us better when there are two who study together, for each can correct his companion on the difficult themes of the Torah, and thus, there is less probability of not understanding them or of committing errors.

(3) The Divine Presence accompanies a person who directs his thoughts towards the Holy Scriptures even when studying alone.

VERSE 3:4

ד רַבִּי שִׁמְעוֹן אוֹמֵר: שְׁלֹשָׁה שֶׁאָכְלוּ עַל שֻׁלְחָן אֶחָד וְלֹא אָמְרוּ עָלָיו דִּבְרֵי תוֹרָה, כְּאִלּוּ אָכְלוּ מִזִּבְחֵי מֵתִים, שֶׁנֶּאֱמַר: כִּי כָּל שֻׁלְחָנוֹת מָלְאוּ קִיא צֹאָה בְּלִי מָקוֹם. אֲבָל שְׁלֹשָׁה שֶׁאָכְלוּ עַל שֻׁלְחָן אֶחָד וְאָמְרוּ עָלָיו דִּבְרֵי תוֹרָה, כְּאִלּוּ אָכְלוּ מִשֻּׁלְחָנוֹ שֶׁל מָקוֹם, שֶׁנֶּאֱמַר: וַיְדַבֵּר אֵלַי, זֶה הַשֻּׁלְחָן אֲשֶׁר לִפְנֵי יְיָ.

3:4. Rabbi Simeon (1) said, three who have eaten together at table and have said over it no words of Torah are as though they had eaten sacrifices to the dead, as is suggested by the verse of Isaiah (xxviii:8), "For all tables without God are full of filthy vomit." (2) But three who have eaten together at table and have said over it words of Torah are as though they had eaten of the table of God, as is suggested by the verse of Ezekiel (XLI:22), "And he said unto me, this is the table that is before the Lord."

---

(1) Rabbi Simeon bar Yohai (a contemporary of Rabbi Akiva (100–160 C.E.), renowned figure of Jewish mysticism, believed to be the author of the Zohar, was a bitter enemy of the tyranny of the Romans who, in his time, occupied the Holy Land. Having been condemned to death by the Romans, he had to flee with his son Elazar, and hid in a cave for thirteen years, living on herbs and wild fruits.

Being a fervent nationalist, Rabbi Simeon affirmed that every Jew is of royal descent. He described the famous solidarity of the Jews in the following parable: In a boat full of passengers, one of them began to drill a whole in the bottom that was beneath where he was seated. The other passengers exclaimed, "What are you doing?" He answered, "What is it to you? I am drilling in my own space." The other passengers replied, "It is true that it is in your own place, but when the water begins to enter the boat, we, too, will drown." In like manner, when a Jew does wrong, this has repercussions on all Jews.

(2) A meal at which there is no mention of the name of God, or at least *ha-motzi*, table hymns, *Bircat ha-mazon*, etc. is considered a meal of idolators. This concept finds its inspiration in Psalm CVI:28, "Then they joined themselves to Ba'al Pe'or [an idol] and ate the sacrifices of the dead." (The word 'dead' alludes to idols that are inanimate.) When the name of God is mentioned and words of Torah are spoken, the table is as if it were the expiatory altar which existed in the Temple, and the food on it as offerings. It says in the Talmud, "All the while that the Temple existed, the expiation of sins was done by means of the altar and the sin offerings, but now that it is destroyed, said expiation is effectuated at the table when words of Torah are spoken and the poor are given to eat and drink. "*Beli makom* here signifies literally "without an empty space", but it can also mean "without the presence of God", and we opt for this second interpretation. One of the reasons why we put bread and salt on the table is because the

words *lehem* (bread) and *melah* (salt) have the same letters whose numerical value is three times the numerical value of the name of God [26 x 3 = 78].

VERSE 3:5

3:5. Rabbi Hanina ben Ha'hinai used to say, he who awakens by night and gives his heart to idle thoughts, or he who walks alone and gives his heart to idle thoughts, endangers his life (1).

ה רַבִּי חֲנִינָא בֶּן חֲכִינַאי אוֹמֵר: הַנֵּעוֹר בַּלַּיְלָה, וְהַמְהַלֵּךְ בַּדֶּרֶךְ יְחִידִי, וּמְפַנֶּה לִבּוֹ לְבַטָּלָה, הֲרֵי זֶה מִתְחַיֵּב בְּנַפְשׁוֹ.

---

(1) Rabbi Hanina's thought has the following meaning: the time spent in idleness or on vain things, especially at night, is considered a grave sin because of the consequences that it brings, such as, temptations, bad thoughts, etc., while filling this time with Torah study purifies the thoughts and the soul. Rabbi Hanina says the same of a person who walks alone aimlessly for he is exposed to many dangers such as evildoers, etc. Solitude and idleness leave the door open to bad happenings, to temptations and bad thoughts, which does not happen when the mind is directed towards the study of Torah, as is written in Proverbs VI:22, "When thou walkest, it shall lead thee; when thou liest down, it shall keep thee; and when thou awakest, it shall talk with thee, for the commandment is a lamp, and Torah is light, and reproofs of correction are the way of life…"

VERSE 3:6

3:6. Rabbi Nehunya ben Hakanah (1) was wont to say, whosoever accepts the yoke of Torah (2) has removed from him the yoke of government (3) and the yoke of worldly affairs (4); but he who casts off the yoke of Torah will find himself bearing the yokes of government and of worldly affairs (5).

ו רַבִּי נְחוּנְיָא בֶּן הַקָּנָה אוֹמֵר: כָּל הַמְקַבֵּל עָלָיו עֹל תּוֹרָה, מַעֲבִירִין מִמֶּנּוּ עֹל מַלְכוּת וְעֹל דֶּרֶךְ אֶרֶץ. וְכָל הַפּוֹרֵק מִמֶּנּוּ עֹל תּוֹרָה, נוֹתְנִין עָלָיו עֹל מַלְכוּת וְעֹל דֶּרֶךְ אֶרֶץ.

---

(1) This rabbi and mystic is the author of the well known prayer "*Ana Behoah*", which is read during *Shahrith* (morning prayers), and contains the 42 letter holy name of God. Among his virtues are found the following when he would say, "I never took to bed with me the error I committed toward someone which I did not repair, nor did I end the day without pardoning one who oppressed me.

(2) The yoke of the Torah is not the same as that of the oppression of slavery, but a symbol of obedience and the duty of observing the commandments of the Torah.

(3) This concept of Rabbi Nehunya's is based on what is said in the Talmud (*Bava Batra* 8.) that government taxes and tributes were not to be collected from rabbis and their students. Nowadays in the modern State of Israel, rabbis and Orthodox Jews are given many concessions including dispensation from serving in the military. In Turkey, the country of origin of the author of this book, the rabbis were exempt from military service during World War 1.

(4) A devoted student of Torah attains, through faith, the blessing of God in his work and in all his activities. He is satisfied with the economic status that God has given him; he has no vain worries, evil im-

pulses, mundane compromises that are meaningless; nor is he bound by purely material pursuits.

(5) In contrast to Rabban Gamliel (see Ch. II, 2) who advised having a trade or profession in addition to studying the Torah, Rabbi Nehunya thought that one should dedicate himself exclusively to the study of Torah. This divergence of opinions is found in the Talmud between Rabbi Simeon Bar Yohai and Rabbi Ishmael. The former interpreted literally the verse in Joshua 1:8, "The Book of the Torah shall not depart out of thy mouth, but thou shalt meditate therein day and night…"; that is, one should dedicate the 24 hours of the day to the study of Torah. However, Rabbi Ishmael divided the day into three parts: eight hours for work, eight hours for study, and eight hours for sleep. Those who followed the opinion of Rabbi Simeon bar Yohai failed, while those who followed Rabbi Ishmael triumphed.

One who casts off the yoke of the Torah, or rather, one who rebels against God's commandments, or who considers them a heavy yoke is made by God to fall under the heavy yoke of government and of mundane affairs with greater rigor.

VERSE 3:7

3:7. Rabbi Halafta ben Dosa of Kfar Hananya used to say, ten who sit down and occupy themselves with the Torah, the Shechinah rests among them, as is suggested by the verse of Psalms (LXXXII:1, "God stands in the holy congregation (1)." What Biblical verse can we interpret to show that this is so

ז רַבִּי חֲלַפְתָּא בֶּן דּוֹסָא אִישׁ כְּפַר חֲנַנְיָא אוֹמֵר: עֲשָׂרָה שֶׁיּוֹשְׁבִין וְעוֹסְקִין בַּתּוֹרָה, שְׁכִינָה שְׁרוּיָה בֵּינֵיהֶם, שֶׁנֶּאֱמַר: אֱלֹהִים נִצָּב בַּעֲדַת אֵל. וּמִנַּיִן אֲפִילוּ חֲמִשָּׁה, שֶׁנֶּאֱמַר: וַאֲגֻדָּתוֹ עַל אֶרֶץ יְסָדָהּ. וּמִנַּיִן אֲפִילוּ שְׁלֹשָׁה, שֶׁנֶּאֱמַר: בְּקֶרֶב אֱלֹהִים יִשְׁפֹּט. וּמִנַּיִן אֲפִילוּ שְׁנַיִם, שֶׁנֶּאֱמַר: אָז נִדְבְּרוּ יִרְאֵי יְיָ אִישׁ אֶל רֵעֵהוּ, וַיַּקְשֵׁב יְיָ וַיִּשְׁמָע. וּמִנַּיִן אֲפִילוּ אֶחָד, שֶׁנֶּאֱמַר: בְּכָל הַמָּקוֹם אֲשֶׁר אַזְכִּיר אֶת שְׁמִי אָבוֹא אֵלֶיךָ וּבֵרַכְתִּיךָ.

of five? The verse of Amos (IX:6), "And He has established His group (2) over the earth." What verse suggests it also of three? The verse of Psalm LXXXII, What verse suggests it even of two? The verse of Malachi (III:16), "Then those who fear the Lord spoke with one another, and God hearkened and heard it." (4) What verse suggests it even of one? The verse of Exodus (XX:21), "In all places where I cause my name to be pronounced, I will come to thee, and I will bless thee."

---

(1) The words of Rabbi Halafta have almost the same meaning as of those of the Verses III:3–4, only here the number of persons is extended to ten. The Hebrew word *adat* of Psalm LXXXII:1, which we translated as "congregation" really means a group of at least ten persons. This number is derived from Numbers XIV:27, when God, referring to the ten spies of the Holy Land, said, "How long shall I bear with this evil congregation…?"

The reason why he used the word *nitzav* (standing) for the group of ten persons is in accordance with what is written in the Talmud: "When there are ten people, the Divine Presence is among them even before they get together. And when there are less than ten, the Lord presents Himself after they are gathered." From this we derive that a congregation should have a minimum of ten men older than thirteen years of age. It was from this that the sages of the Law were inspired to insist that public services should be held in the presence of ten men, which is called a *minyan* (quorum). If in the dialogue between God and the patriarch Abraham with regard to the wicked city of Sodom (Genesis XVIII:23–33), ten righteous men could have saved the inhabitants, what great power a *minyan* can have when it prays in favor of an entire community!

(2) Rabbi Halafta associates the Hebrew word *agudah*, which we translate as "group", to the five fingers of the hand, meaning that the Divine Presence descends from heaven when there is a group of five people studying the Torah. In like manner, we see that the word

agudah (association) refers also to the five elements of matter, the five senses, the five commandments on each of the tablets of the Law, the five books of the Torah, etc. God created the heavens and the earth with the Hebrew letter /*he*/ as is commented upon in the Talmud, the word *behibaream* – *behe beroam* (He created them with /*he*/).

(3) A *Bet Din* (rabbinic tribunal) is comprised of a minimum of three members.

(4) We deduce from the words "He listened" and "He heard" that God was present.

VERSE 3:8

3:8. Rabbi Elazar of Bartota (1) would say, Give (unto God) what is His, because you and what is yours is His (2). King David said the same. As he is quoted in 1 Chronicles XXIX:14, "For all things come of Thee…"

ח רַבִּי אֶלְעָזָר אִישׁ בַּרְתּוֹתָא אוֹמֵר: תֶּן לוֹ מִשֶּׁלּוֹ, שֶׁאַתָּה וְשֶׁלְּךָ שֶׁלּוֹ. וְכֵן בְּדָוִד הוּא אוֹמֵר: כִּי מִמְּךָ הַכֹּל, וּמִיָּדְךָ נָתַנּוּ לָךְ.

---

(1) Bartota is a place in Galilee.

(2) This means that we should serve God physically as well as morally and materially, since all that is ours (body, soul, possessions, etc.) come from God, and we do not give anything we believe to be ours, but rather what God has granted each of us according to His will.

The author of this saying would comply perfectly with what is written in the Talmud: "*Nae doresh, ve nae mecayem*" (a good preacher and a good doer). He was so generous that those who collected money for charity would not dare knock on his door for fear that he would give beyond his means, as was his custom (see *Taanit* 24).

VERSE 3:9

3:9. Rabbi Jacob used to say, one who is studying (1) Torah as he walks by the way, and who interrupts to say, "How beautiful is this tree, or this fallow ground," is as though he risked his life. (For the words of the Shema declare, "Thou shalt speak of them when thou walkest by the way.")

ט רַבִּי יַעֲקֹב אוֹמֵר: הַמְהַלֵּךְ בַּדֶּרֶךְ וְשׁוֹנֶה, וּמַפְסִיק מִמִּשְׁנָתוֹ וְאוֹמֵר: מַה נָּאֶה אִילָן זֶה וּמַה נָּאֶה נִיר זֶה, מַעֲלֶה עָלָיו הַכָּתוּב כְּאִלּוּ מִתְחַיֵּב בְּנַפְשׁוֹ.

---

(1) The Talmud recommends that one not study deep subjects while on one's way. Likewise, one is not permitted to interrupt the reading of the Torah for profane matters, even if one is not walking on a road. For me, the act of praising a tree or a field should not be considered a sin, since one is praising the works of the Creator.

The reason why "by the way" was written is because, as was previously mentioned (see Verse III:5), one is liable to encounter, above all if one is alone, all kinds of dangers by the way or road, which are not likely to occur when we are protected by words of Torah. This thought is based on what is said in the Talmud, that the study of Torah keeps all evil occurrences from happening. Thus, a person who interrupts the study of Torah is mortally at fault. It can also be said that the act of interrupting the study of Torah on such occasions causes a person to become accustomed to frequent interruptions, which is considered a sin. It is not the act of praising the works of Creation that is sinful. Indeed, the rabbis prescribed blessings for each work of beauty in the universe.

VERSE 3:10

3:10. Rabbi Dosthai bar Yannai would say in Rabbi Meir's name, one who forgets anything of his Torah learning (1) is as though he committed a mortal sin. This is suggested by the verse of Deuteronomy (IV:9), "Only take heed to thyself and guard thy soul diligently lest thou forget the things which thy eyes have seen." If one should think that this applies even when the learning has been too difficult, the verse continues, "and lest they depart from thy heart all the days of thy life," i.e. it is as though one risked one's life only when one deliberately removes God's words from one's heart.

י. רַבִּי דוֹסְתַּאי בַּר יַנַּאי מִשּׁוּם רַבִּי מֵאִיר אוֹמֵר: כָּל הַשּׁוֹכֵחַ דָּבָר אֶחָד מִמִּשְׁנָתוֹ, מַעֲלֶה עָלָיו הַכָּתוּב כְּאִלּוּ מִתְחַיֵּב בְּנַפְשׁוֹ, שֶׁנֶּאֱמַר: רַק הִשָּׁמֶר לְךָ וּשְׁמֹר נַפְשְׁךָ מְאֹד, פֶּן תִּשְׁכַּח אֶת הַדְּבָרִים אֲשֶׁר רָאוּ עֵינֶיךָ. יָכוֹל אֲפִילוּ תָקְפָה עָלָיו מִשְׁנָתוֹ, תַּלְמוּד לוֹמַר: וּפֶן יָסוּרוּ מִלְּבָבְךָ כֹּל יְמֵי חַיֶּיךָ. הָא אֵינוֹ מִתְחַיֵּב בְּנַפְשׁוֹ עַד שֶׁיֵּשֵׁב וִיסִירֵם מִלִּבּוֹ.

---

(1) In my opinion, it is not a matter here of forgetting, but of not reviewing what one has studied of the Torah; hence, one is bound to forget what he has learned and commit errors of judgment, permitting what is prohibited and vice versa. Therefore, such a person is considered to have committed a grave sin. By reviewing what we have studied in the Torah, we not only do not forget what we have learned, but, each time we review, our study becomes more profound, and we gain new insights. Otherwise, "He, who abandons the study of Torah for one day, loses two days of learning." (Rashi)

VERSE 3:11

3:11. Rabbi Hanina ben Dosa (1) used to say, everyone for whom dread of sin takes precedence over learning, has learning that will endure; but everyone whose learning takes precedence over his dread of sin, has learning that will not endure (2).

יא רַבִּי חֲנִינָא בֶּן דּוֹסָא אוֹמֵר: כֹּל שֶׁיִּרְאַת חֶטְאוֹ קוֹדֶמֶת לְחָכְמָתוֹ, חָכְמָתוֹ מִתְקַיֶּמֶת. וְכֹל שֶׁחָכְמָתוֹ קוֹדֶמֶת לְיִרְאַת חֶטְאוֹ, אֵין חָכְמָתוֹ מִתְקַיֶּמֶת.

---

(1) The Talmud relates that this rabbi, considered a mystic and miracle worker, was so poor that he lacked even the food that he needed to sustain himself. His poverty was so great that one day his wife said to him, "Ask for some of the good that we will have in the future life." Suddenly, Oh wonders! They saw a golden table leg extended from on high and they took it. That same night, they saw in a dream that all the righteous in paradise ate on golden tables with four legs, while theirs had only three. In the morning, they prayed to God that He take back the leg, and a hand from on high received it.

(2) These principles of Rabbi Hanina are based on the promise that the Israelites made at the foot of Mt. Sinai (Exodus xxiv:8) "All that the Lord has said, we will do, and obey." In other words, they would first do what God commanded, and then they would study it. It is also based on that statement in Psalm cxi:10, "The fear of the Lord is the beginning of wisdom."

A person should first become accustomed to observing the Lord's commandments even when he does not understand the reasons why they were instituted, and later study them as much as he can. One who acts in such a way affirms his knowledge better than one who studies and observes only those laws that seem logical and good to him. Such a person is more inclined to forget and to sin.

Now then, how can a person dread sin if he has no knowledge [of what is considered sinful]? It has been previously said (Ch. II, 6), that one lacking in knowledge [of Torah] and in moral principles cannot have any fear of sin. Therefore, we might say that Rabbi Hanina is not referring to someone who is entirely ignorant, but to one who has some knowledge of Torah, but is unaware of the reason for this or that precept, and still complies with it so that his learning may be firmly established through faith.

VERSE 3:12

3:12. He also used to say, everyone whose actions are greater than his learning, his learning will endure; but everyone whose learning is greater than his actions, his learning will not endure (1).

יב הוּא הָיָה אוֹמֵר: כֹּל שֶׁמַּעֲשָׂיו מְרֻבִּין מֵחָכְמָתוֹ, חָכְמָתוֹ מִתְקַיֶּמֶת. וְכֹל שֶׁחָכְמָתוֹ מְרֻבָּה מִמַּעֲשָׂיו, אֵין חָכְמָתוֹ מִתְקַיֶּמֶת.

---

(1) This principle is based on what was said in Chapter 1:17, in the sense that the study of Torah is not as fundamental as the practice of its precepts. A person whose works surpass his learning tries to study more and more, and thus increase his knowledge; whereas one whose learning surpasses his works diminishes his learning because he does not put into practice what he has studied.

VERSE 3:13

3:13. He used to say also, in everyone in whom the spirit of his fellow man takes pleasure, the spirit of God also takes pleasure; but everyone in whom the spirit of his fellow man does not take pleasure, the spirit of God takes no pleasure in him (1).

יג. הוּא הָיָה אוֹמֵר: כֹּל שֶׁרוּחַ הַבְּרִיּוֹת נוֹחָה הֵימֶנּוּ, רוּחַ הַמָּקוֹם נוֹחָה הֵימֶנּוּ. וְכֹל שֶׁאֵין רוּחַ הַבְּרִיּוֹת נוֹחָה הֵימֶנּוּ, אֵין רוּחַ הַמָּקוֹם נוֹחָה הֵימֶנּוּ.

---

(1) In my opinion, this thought of Rabbi Hanina wishes to explain that if a person is beloved by his fellow men, the name of God is glorified, for it is said of such a person, "Blessed be God who created such a good person." Otherwise, if he is bad, some might say, "How did God create such an evil person?" Thus, the name of God is profaned. We can also explain it in this way, anyone who is pleasing to people in any way, would be considered pleasing also to God. When a person observes the Torah and keeps God's commandments, he is merciful and loves truth. It is not possible for such a person not to find favor in the eyes of man. (See 1 Samuel 11:26 and Proverbs 111:1–4).

On the other hand, it is known that no human being can please everyone without exception. Therefore, we are dealing here with a good person in the true sense of the word; that is, good in the eyes of the majority of people.

VERSE 3:14

3:14. Rabbi Dosa ben Harkinas said, morning sleep (1), noonday wine (2), children's talk (3) and frequenting the synagogues of the ignorant (4) takes a man from the world of life (5).

יד רַבִּי דוֹסָא בֶּן הָרְכִּינַס אוֹמֵר: שֵׁנָה שֶׁל שַׁחֲרִית, וְיַיִן שֶׁל צָהֳרַיִם, וְשִׂיחַת הַיְלָדִים, וִישִׁיבַת בָּתֵּי כְנֵסִיּוֹת שֶׁל עַמֵּי הָאָרֶץ, מוֹצִיאִין אֶת הָאָדָם מִן הָעוֹלָם.

---

(1) This refers to a lazy person; according to the words of King Solomon (Proverbs xxvi:13): "as a door turns on its hinges, so does a lazy person turn in his bed." Naturally, he is not referring to a person who for reasons of health needs sleep in the morning.

(2) The hours of the day were made to be dedicated to work and to study (of the Torah). David said this in Psalm civ:23, "Man goes forth to his work and to his labor until the evening." Drinking wine or liquor at noon or in the morning weakens the mind, preventing one from attending to his duties and causing him, at times, to commit irresponsible acts. In reference to this, King Solomon said (Ecclesiastes x:17), "Happy art thou, Oh land, when thy king is a man of dignity, and thy princes eat in due season for strength and not for drunkenness.

The Midrash relates that on the night before the dedication of the Temple, King Solomon took the keys of the sanctuary, and left them under his pillow and slept until the fourth hour after sunrise. It was then that Bat-Sheva, his mother, entered the royal apartment, awakened him and chastised him, saying (Proverbs xxxi:4), "It is not for kings to drink wine, nor for princes to say, where is strong drink, lest they drink and forget the Law…"

(3) "Children's talk" refers to prolonged conversations with children and also playing with them, which results in wasting time on insig-

nificant things; thus, taking time away from the study of Torah or important activities. Nevertheless, we can say that when a father or any other adult dedicates a certain amount of time to teach good morals to his children or to answer the questions they raise, this is not considered idle chatter with children. On the contrary, these are things a father should do with his children.

(4) Here, this refers to gatherings with ignorant people who waste time in trivial talk or jeering like those who gather at street-corners, marketplaces, cafés, etc. King David was referring to this type of people when he said (Psalm 1:1), "Blessed is the man who does not walk in the counsel of the wicked, nor stands in the way of sinners, nor sits in the seat of scorners, but his delight is in the Torah of the Lord, and in His Torah he meditates day and night."

The meaning of "*am ha-arets*" in this case, refers to the common man who has limited or no knowledge of Torah. The Talmud (*Sanhedrin* 52) advises students of the Torah to avoid conversations, and above all, arguments, with an "*am ha-aretz*" and states, "When a "*talmid haham*" (a wise man learned in the Torah) meets an "*am ha-aretz*" the latter compares him to a golden pitcher all the time that the wise man is silent. When the sage begins to speak with the common man, the sage appears in his eyes like a silver pitcher, and when the sage becomes friendly with him, the sage is reduced to a pitcher of clay.

(5) See Chapter II, 16 of this Commentary.

VERSE 3:15

טו רַבִּי אֶלְעָזָר הַמּוֹדָעִי אוֹמֵר: הַמְחַלֵּל אֶת הַקֳּדָשִׁים, וְהַמְבַזֶּה אֶת הַמּוֹעֲדוֹת, וְהַמַּלְבִּין פְּנֵי חֲבֵרוֹ בָרַבִּים, וְהַמֵּפֵר בְּרִיתוֹ שֶׁל אַבְרָהָם אָבִינוּ, וְהַמְגַלֶּה פָנִים בַּתּוֹרָה שֶׁלֹּא כַהֲלָכָה, אַף עַל פִּי שֶׁיֵּשׁ בְּיָדוֹ תּוֹרָה וּמַעֲשִׂים טוֹבִים, אֵין לוֹ חֵלֶק לָעוֹלָם הַבָּא.

3:15. Rabbi Elazar of Modiin (1) would say, the following have no share in the future world even though they be possessed of Torah and good deeds: one who profanes holy things (2), one who despises the festivals (3), one who puts his fellow man to shame in public (4), one who obliterates the covenant of our father Abraham (5), and one who arbitrarily interprets the Torah in conflict with the Halachah (6).

---

(1) This rabbi was killed by Bar Kochba, the leader of the revolt against the Romans, because of the false accusation made by a (good?) Samaritan, who was in contact with the enemy during the siege of the city of Betar in the year 132 C.E. Rabbi Akiva was the one who openly supported Bar Kochba, and for this he became a martyr at the hands of the Romans.

(2) Each of the offerings that were made at the Temple had their respective regulations such as: the time that they were to be offered and to be eaten, the portion that was to be set aside for the priests, etc. Here this refers to the lack of compliance with these regulations. This also can refer to one who makes inappropriate use of the holy objects in a synagogue, or of the monies set aside for charity, etc.

(3) He who despises the festivals is one who does not respect or observe the festival days mentioned in the Torah, who does not honor them by eating special foods or wearing better clothing than he would normally wear during the ordinary days of the week, etc. However,

since in times past it was inconceivable that a Jew would behave in this way during the festivals, the commentators said that this refers to the semi-festivals, called in Hebrew "*Hol ha-moed*. One who does not honor these days is guilty unless he is obliged to work on *hol ha-moed* out of extreme necessity.

(4) It is written in the Talmud (*Bava Metzia* 5:) "When someone shames his neighbor in public, it is as if he shed blood." Elsewhere, the Talmud tells us (*Berahot* 43), referring to the passage regarding Yehudah and Tamar (Genesis XXXVIII:13–23), "It is better for a person to allow himself to be burned in a hot oven than to shame his fellow man in public."

(5) In view of the fact that circumcision is called the covenant of our patriarch Abraham, the father that does not have his son circumcised, or if the son, on reaching maturity, does not have himself circumcised, breaks the covenant. The condemnation refers also to Jewish youths in the time of the occupation of the Holy Land by the ancient Greeks who tried to hide (by any means possible) the signs of circumcision when they appeared naked in the sports arena in order to show that they weren't Jewish, or as a sign of their hellenization.

(6) Examples of not interpreting the commandments of the Torah in accordance with the meaning given them by the rabbinical sages are: saying that God's intention with regard to this or that precept is what one thinks. One example is to believe that the commandment not to kindle fire on the Sabbath means that God did not want us to start arguments or disputes on that day. Another is to say that in ancient times it was an arduous task to kindle fire and it was prohibited to do so for that reason, but now that matches have been invented, it should be permitted to strike a match and light a fire. Another example of an erroneous interpretation is to affirm that the eating of pork was prohibited because formerly there was no way of destroying the germs of trichnosis, but now there is, so we are now allowed to eat pork

VERSE 3:16

3:16. Rabbi Ishmael (1) used to say, be pliant to those in political authority and flexible under oppression. Receive every man with good cheer. (2)

טז רַבִּי יִשְׁמָעֵאל אוֹמֵר: הֱוֵי קַל לְרֹאשׁ וְנוֹחַ לְתִשְׁחֹרֶת, וֶהֱוֵי מְקַבֵּל אֶת כָּל הָאָדָם בְּשִׂמְחָה.

---

(1) Rabbi Ishmael ben Elisha was the grandson of the High Priest who bore the same name. He was known to have been guided by the literal sense of the Scriptures, and not its mystical meaning. Rabbi Ishmael is the author of the thirteen principles of logic by which the Torah may be expounded. As a young man, he was taken prisoner to Rome after the fall of Jerusalem, and then ransomed by Rabbi Yehoshua ben Hananiah. He died a martyr during the persecutions of the Emperor Hadrian in the year 135 C.E. Among his famous sayings is the following, "All the daughters of Israel are beautiful, but poverty is what makes them appear plain."

Rabbi Ishmael recommends having the greatest respect and obedience towards a teacher, a rabbi or a superior in knowledge, and to serve them, especially in their old age. Likewise, when a superior has black hair, that is, he is still young, be serene and formal with him, and not be thoughtless, since it is dangerous to lord it over one who is in power. This is my opinion with regard to the Hebrew word *"tishhoret"* used here. Nevertheless, in *Tana Debe Eliyahu, Raba* 1, this word is translated as a person or place of oppression.

(2) Greet with like pleasure the humble and the great, the young and the old, the freeman and the slave, the superior and the inferior without distinction of race or creed. (Cf. Chapter 1:15).

VERSE 3:17

3:17. Rabbi Akiva (1) would say, merrymaking and frivolity lead a man to immorality (2). Tradition is a safeguarding fence to the Torah (3), tithes are fence to wealth (4); vows a fence to abstinence (5); silence a fence to wisdom (6).

יז רַבִּי עֲקִיבָא אוֹמֵר: שְׂחוֹק וְקַלּוּת רֹאשׁ מַרְגִּילִין אֶת הָאָדָם לְעֶרְוָה. מָסֹרֶת סְיָג לַתּוֹרָה, מַעַשְׂרוֹת סְיָג לָעֹשֶׁר, נְדָרִים סְיָג לַפְּרִישׁוּת, סְיָג לַחָכְמָה שְׁתִיקָה.

---

(1) Rabbi Akiva (60–135 C.E.) was one of the greatest Torah sages of his time. Rabbi Meir and Rabbi Yehudah ha-Nasi were among his numerous (24,000) disciples. Rabbi Yehudah ha-Nasi compiled and was the co-author of the Mishnah. He affirmed that one should look for the deep meaning of each word, each letter, and each sign of the Torah because they are beyond the everyday language of man. According to legend, Rabbi Akiva began his study of the Torah at the age of 40, and married the daughter of his rich patron who refused to acknowledge or materially help his son-in-law until he became one of the greatest teachers of his time. Akiva's faith in the Almighty was so great that even in hard times, he would say, "All that God does is for our own good." During the revolt against the Roman invaders of the Holy Land, he joined the hero, Bar Kochba in the year 135 C.E. and died a martyr for his faith and for his people.

(2) Sometimes, out of modesty, neither a man nor a woman can express their sexual desires, but through frivolity, laughter and off color jokes, they may become intimate and even immoral.

(3) This refers to the Oral Law as well as to the explanation given to the Torah and to the entire Bible by the exegetes whose commentaries are based on the Tradition (See Chapter 1:1).

(4) This opinion is based on the commentary on the two words writ-

ten in Deuteronomy xix, 22 *"aser, teaser"* (tithe, you shall tithe) and commented upon in the Talmud as follows: *"Aser bishvil shetitasher"* (Give the tithe so that you may be enriched.) God helps increase the wealth of a person accustomed to giving charity (the tithe formerly given to the Levite was a form of charity). Such a person does not throw his money away on vain things, and thus conserves his wealth, as is said in the Talmud, *"Melah mamon haser (hessed)."* meaning that just as salt is what helps conserve meat, so is charity the salt that conserves wealth. In other words, money spent on beneficence does not reduce capital, but conserves it.

(5) This refers, in my opinion, to abstaining from bad things in particular. When a person is under the evil impulse to do something wrong, and makes a vow not to do it, the vow serves to stop him from doing it. As for vows in general, our rabbis are of the opinion that one should not be accustomed to making them for fear of not being able to fulfill them. It is recommended in the Talmud as follows: "It is better not to make vows than to promise and not comply."

(6) God created two ears and only one mouth in order to teach us that we should hear more than we should speak, above all, when we find ourselves in the presence of people wiser than us from whom we can learn by listening to them. (Cf. Chapter 1:17) A person who speaks more than is necessary is likely to be a gossip and a slanderer. This is called in Hebrew *lashon ha-ra* (an evil tongue). In reality, it is difficult to completely avoid *avak lashon ha-ra*, which is evil talk to a minor degree. Every human being has within him or her this moral defect, albeit only slightly. For this reason King Solomon warns us (Proverbs x:19), "In the multitude of words, sin is not lacking, but he who restrains his lips is wise."

VERSE 3:18

3:18. He (Rabbi Akiva) used to say, beloved is man (1) for he is created in the image of God (2). Yet still greater love is that God made him know that he was created in the image of God, as it is written in Genesis IX:6, "For in the image of God made he man." Beloved are Israel that they are called children of God, but greater yet is the love that this has been made known to them in the verse of Deuteronomy XIV:1, "You are the children of the Lord your God." Beloved are Israel that there has been given to them a coveted instrument (3) by which the world was created; but greater yet is the love that has been made known to them as is written in the verse of Proverbs IV:2, "For I give you good doctrine, forsake not My Torah."

יח הוּא הָיָה אוֹמֵר: חָבִיב אָדָם שֶׁנִּבְרָא בְּצֶלֶם, חִבָּה יְתֵרָה נוֹדַעַת לוֹ שֶׁנִּבְרָא בְּצֶלֶם, שֶׁנֶּאֱמַר: כִּי בְּצֶלֶם אֱלֹהִים עָשָׂה אֶת הָאָדָם. חֲבִיבִין יִשְׂרָאֵל שֶׁנִּקְרְאוּ בָנִים לַמָּקוֹם, חִבָּה יְתֵרָה נוֹדַעַת לָהֶם שֶׁנִּקְרְאוּ בָנִים לַמָּקוֹם, שֶׁנֶּאֱמַר: בָּנִים אַתֶּם לַיְיָ אֱלֹהֵיכֶם. חֲבִיבִין יִשְׂרָאֵל שֶׁנִּתַּן לָהֶם כְּלִי חֶמְדָּה, חִבָּה יְתֵרָה נוֹדַעַת לָהֶם שֶׁנִּתַּן לָהֶם כְּלִי חֶמְדָּה, שֶׁנֶּאֱמַר: כִּי לֶקַח טוֹב נָתַתִּי לָכֶם, תּוֹרָתִי אַל תַּעֲזֹבוּ.

---

(1) The word *adam* (man) includes all human beings regardless of race or creed, as is written in the Torah (see Genesis 1:27). "So God created Mankind in his own image,"

(2) The word *tzelem* (image), according to Maimonides' *Guide of the Perplexed*, signifies the spiritual likeness, and not the physical, for God has no corporeal image and His essence is beyond the reach of human intelligence. It is this image that distinguishes man from the beast, also created by God, but without intelligence, nor understanding or free will such as humans possess. It is a manifestation of God's love for His chosen people that the Holy Scriptures specify that Mankind

was created in His image and that the children of Israel were called the children of God and were given the Torah.

(3) It is the Torah, the divine Law of God on earth, which guides our life, protects our daily existence, and sheds its blessings on all humanity. The Torah is the master plan by which the physical and spiritual faculties of man are developed, a better world is formed and solidified, and a perfect union between humans and God is created. Just as gold is longed for and coveted, the words of Torah are even more coveted, as King David affirms in Psalm XIX:11, "More to be desired are they (the judgments of the Lord) than gold, even much fine gold."

VERSE 3:19

3:19. All is foreseen, yet freewill is given to man (1). The world is judged with Divine kindness (2), but all is proportioned (3) to one's work.

יט הַכֹּל צָפוּי, וְהָרְשׁוּת נְתוּנָה, וּבְטוֹב הָעוֹלָם נָדוֹן, וְהַכֹּל לְפִי רֹב הַמַּעֲשֶׂה.

---

(1) In reality, it is difficult for us humans to understand the fact that all is foreseen, and that nevertheless, man has free will. It seems like a contradiction. However, since the past, present, and future are known by God, we can thus say that all is foreseen by Him, in spite of the fact that our intelligence cannot conceive such things. That it why it is written in Deuteronomy XXIX:28, "The secret things belong to the Lord, our God," It is also written in Isaiah LV:8, "For My thoughts are not your thoughts, neither are your ways, My ways, says the Lord."

(2) God judges the world with His attribute of mercy, even for evildoers, as is written in Psalm CXLV:9, "The Lord is good to all: and His tender mercies are over all his works." (This includes animals, etc.) However, He is kinder to those who have good deeds to their credit, but when a person has as many good deeds as bad ones, God considers that person good rather than bad.

(3) Although each of the good deeds that a person performs has a greater or lesser value, when some of them are practiced to a greater degree, they are more meritorious. For example, one who distributes five hundred dollars among several poor people has greater merit than one who donates such a sum to only one person.

VERSE 3:20

3:20. He would also say, all is given in pledge (1), and the net (2) is spread over all living, The shop is open, the hand writes (3), and any who wish to borrow may come and borrow (4). However, the collectors go around daily (5) all the time and exact payment with or without consent (6), for they have the warrant on which they rely, since the judgment is a true judgment. All is prepared for the banquet (7).

כ הוּא הָיָה אוֹמֵר: הַכֹּל נָתוּן בָּעֵרָבוֹן, וּמְצוּדָה פְּרוּסָה עַל כָּל הַחַיִּים. הַחֲנוּת פְּתוּחָה, וְהַחֶנְוָנִי מַקִּיף, וְהַפִּנְקָס פָּתוּחַ, וְהַיָּד כּוֹתֶבֶת, וְכָל הָרוֹצֶה לִלְווֹת יָבוֹא וְיִלְוֶה, וְהַגַּבָּאִים מַחֲזִירִין תָּדִיר בְּכָל יוֹם, וְנִפְרָעִין מִן הָאָדָם מִדַּעְתּוֹ וְשֶׁלֹּא מִדַּעְתּוֹ, וְיֵשׁ לָהֶם עַל מַה שֶּׁיִּסְמוֹכוּ, וְהַדִּין דִּין אֱמֶת, וְהַכֹּל מְתֻקָּן לִסְעוּדָה.

---

(1) Rabbi Akiva compares the world to a pawnshop, and human beings are the clients. All that a person possesses is given on loan to be used for good; in other words, one is indebted to God and one is responsible for the good or bad use that one makes of what he receives. Nothing is his own, and God will demand an accounting of all, and there is no escape for his body and soul are surety on loan.

(2) Just as fish are caught in a net or lured by bait, weak people are entrapped by the follies and the vanitites of this world without being able to escape the consequences. (Doing penance in time before death may bring about salvation.)

(3) By virtue of the fact that God has granted man the freedom to choose good or evil, everyone can take whatever he wishes from this world, which is compared to a marketplace where one can find all that is desired for the welfare and happiness of a human being. The owner of the market (God) grants credit; that is, He does not punish a bad person immediately, giving him time to repent

(4) This is said in a figurative sense for God does not need record books to remember anything (Cf. Ch. II:1). There is no forgetting before Him. However, the sins of the past are not counted when a person repents.

(5) "Collectors" here refer to evil consequences, suffering of all kinds that a person undergoes for his bad deeds; or even death, for a person is under the control of God who watches over what use we make of what we receive from Him.

(6) In other words, God collects from a person whether he is conscious of it or not, but all that befalls him is nothing more than retribution for what he has done. I imagine that each of us has a destiny that only God in His Infinite Wisdom and His Divine Mercy decides upon. We, with our limited intelligence, cannot ever explain it. However, at the same time, we have free will to plant in the field of our lives anything we propose. But like the earth, the yield of what one has planted is roses or thorns. However, I also believe that it is in the power of man to eliminate the thorns by means of repentence and return to the proper path before it is too late.

(7) According to Rabbi Kalonymos of Rome, the day of the banquet refers to the day of death when each of us will occupy the place we deserve in the world to come in accordance with our conduct on earth. The just will enjoy the reward they merit for their good deeds, as is said in Isaiah III:10, "Say of the righteous, that it shall be well with them, for they shall eat the fruit of their doings." The righteous one took from the marketplace (this world) good things for his home (the eternal dwelling place of his soul), making good use of them, and he deserves to enjoy them as in a banquet. As for the evildoers and sin-

ners who acquired bad things (or made bad use of good things), they will experience the bitterness of their foul deeds.

VERSE 3:21

3:21. Rabbi Elazar ben Azaryah (1) used to say, where there is no Torah, there is no way of life, (2) and where there is no way of life, there is no Torah. Where there is no wisdom, there is no reverence (3),

כא רַבִּי אֶלְעָזָר בֶּן עֲזַרְיָה אוֹמֵר: אִם אֵין תּוֹרָה, אֵין דֶּרֶךְ אֶרֶץ. אִם אֵין דֶּרֶךְ אֶרֶץ, אֵין תּוֹרָה. אִם אֵין חָכְמָה, אֵין יִרְאָה. אִם אֵין יִרְאָה, אֵין חָכְמָה. אִם אֵין דַעַת, אֵין בִּינָה. אִם אֵין בִּינָה, אֵין דַעַת. אִם אֵין קֶמַח, אֵין תּוֹרָה. אִם אֵין תּוֹרָה, אֵין קֶמַח.

and where there is no reverence, there is no wisdom. Where there is no knowledge, there is no understanding (4), and where there is no understanding there is no knowledge. Where there is no food, there is no Torah (5), and where there is no Torah, there is no food.

---

(1) Rabbi Elazar ben Azarya (70–135 C.E.), the author of this and the following paragraph, was elected *Av bet Din* (the head of the religious tribunal) when he was only 13, some say 18 years of age. (See *Berahot* 28) In the fifth paragraph of the *Haggadah* of Passover, he, himself, says, "I have the appearance of a man of seventy." He said this because his colleagues did not respect him because of his extreme youth; hence, he prayed and on the following morning, when he awoke, he found thirteen white hairs in his beard making him appear like an old man of seventy.

In the time of the Roman persecutions during the Second Century of the Common Era, before the Bar Kochba revolt in 135 C.E., he donated his great fortune for the welfare of his people.

(2) In view of the fact that the highest principles of ethics are found in

the Torah, one who is lacking in knowledge of it is likely to fail in behaving properly and getting along with others, even when such a person is by nature a decent person. Likewise, if a person is not naturally inclined to conduct himself properly, the knowledge of the Torah will not suffice for him to be perfect in the fulfillment of its precepts.

(3) A person who does not possess sufficient knowledge to appreciate the greatness of the Creator cannot have reverence for, nor be in awe of Him. Likewise, one who does not fear the Lord, cannot have wisdom for it is written in Psalm CXI:10, "The fear of the Lord is the beginning of wisdom."

(4) A person who lacks knowledge of Torah or any other body of knowledge cannot grow nor add to his knowledge if he is incapable of doing so.

(5) A person who is not adequately fed, or who is concerned for his sustenance and that of his family cannot dedicate himself to nor concentrate on the study of Torah. And when there is no Torah, there may be bread, but of what use is only material nourishment? God created food so that man would feed himself and nourish his spirit for the primary purpose of the study of Torah and of positive things.

VERSE 3:22

כב הוּא הָיָה אוֹמֵר: כֹּל שֶׁחָכְמָתוֹ מְרֻבָּה מִמַּעֲשָׂיו, לְמָה הוּא דוֹמֶה, לְאִילָן שֶׁעֲנָפָיו מְרֻבִּין וְשָׁרָשָׁיו מֻעָטִין, וְהָרוּחַ בָּאָה וְעוֹקַרְתּוֹ וְהוֹפַכְתּוֹ עַל פָּנָיו, שֶׁנֶּאֱמַר: וְהָיָה כְּעַרְעָר בָּעֲרָבָה, וְלֹא יִרְאֶה כִּי יָבוֹא טוֹב, וְשָׁכַן חֲרֵרִים בַּמִּדְבָּר, אֶרֶץ מְלֵחָה וְלֹא תֵשֵׁב. אֲבָל כֹּל שֶׁמַּעֲשָׂיו מְרֻבִּין מֵחָכְמָתוֹ, לְמָה הוּא דוֹמֶה, לְאִילָן שֶׁעֲנָפָיו מֻעָטִין וְשָׁרָשָׁיו מְרֻבִּין, שֶׁאֲפִילוּ כָּל הָרוּחוֹת שֶׁבָּעוֹלָם בָּאוֹת וְנוֹשְׁבוֹת בּוֹ אֵין מְזִיזִין אוֹתוֹ מִמְּקוֹמוֹ, שֶׁנֶּאֱמַר: וְהָיָה כְּעֵץ שָׁתוּל עַל מַיִם, וְעַל יוּבַל יְשַׁלַּח שָׁרָשָׁיו, וְלֹא יִרְאֶה כִּי יָבֹא חֹם, וְהָיָה עָלֵהוּ רַעֲנָן, וּבִשְׁנַת בַּצֹּרֶת לֹא יִדְאָג, וְלֹא יָמִישׁ מֵעֲשׂוֹת פֶּרִי.

3:22. He, Rabbi Elazar, would say, one whose knowledge surpasses his works, to what is he likened (1)? – to a tree with abundant boughs and scanty roots. The wind blows, uproots it and it lies a prone log, even as is said by the prophet Jeremiah (xvii:6), "For he shall be like the juniper tree in the desert, and shall not see when good comes; he shall inhabit the parched places in the wilderness, a salt land and not inhabited." However, he whose works exceed his wisdom, to what is he likened? – to a tree with sparse boughs but abundant roots. Though all the winds in the world come and blow against it, they cannot budge it from its place. "For he shall be like a tree planted by the waters, and that spreads out its roots by the river, and shall not see when the heat comes, but its leaf shall be green, and shall not be anxious in the year of drought, nor shall it cease from yielding fruit." (Jeremiah xvii:8)

---

(1) A similar thought was previously expressed by Rabbi Hanina ben Dosa (See Verse iii:12), only that here the idea is accompanied by examples from verses [from Jeremiah]. Study has no value if it is not

applied to life. However, study and wisdom are of absolute necessity in order to direct the character of a person toward good. In other words, Rabbi Elazar ben Azariah wishes to tell us that what is essential is not theory but practice, and that both together constitute the ideal for a person.

VERSE 3:23

3:23. Rabbi Elazar Hisma (1) used to say, offerings of birds and rules of cleansing from personal impurity – such are essential precepts [of the Torah] (2), but astronomical and mathematical computations (3) – these are incidentals. (4)

כג רַבִּי אֱלִיעֶזֶר (בֶּן) חִסְמָא אוֹמֵר, קִנִּין וּפִתְחֵי נִדָּה, הֵן הֵן גּוּפֵי הֲלָכוֹת. תְּקוּפוֹת וְגִמַטְרִיָּאוֹת, פַּרְפְּרָאוֹת לַחָכְמָה.

רַבִּי חֲנַנְיָא בֶּן עֲקַשְׁיָא אוֹמֵר: רָצָה הַקָּדוֹשׁ בָּרוּךְ הוּא לְזַכּוֹת אֶת יִשְׂרָאֵל, לְפִיכָךְ הִרְבָּה לָהֶם תּוֹרָה וּמִצְוֹת, שֶׁנֶּאֱמַר: יְיָ חָפֵץ לְמַעַן צִדְקוֹ, יַגְדִּיל תּוֹרָה וְיַאְדִּיר.

Rabbi Hanania, son of Akashia used to say, the Holy One, blessed be He, wishing to render Israel the more worthy enlarged for them the Torah and its commandments. For so we may read the words of the prophet Isaiah (XLII:21), "The Lord was pleased for His righteousness' sake to magnify Torah and to make it glorious." (5)

---

(1) The name of this rabbi is written in some books as Eliezer Hisma, in others, as Elazar Hisma, and in still others as Elazar ben Hisma. In the Mishnah (*Vayikra Raba*, 23), it is told that he was mocked for his lack of experience as a rabbi, and however, on one occasion, he surpassed his teacher, Rabbi Akiva, when he taught him how he should act in

such a case. Those who mocked him later came to admire him for his knowledge exclaiming, "Is this the same Elazar Hisma, the tongue tied one? "*Hisma* is derived from the Hebrew verb *hasom* meaning "to cover the mouth", according to the verse in Deuteronomy xxv:4, "Thou shalt not muzzle (*lo-tehesom*) the ox when he treads out the corn."

(2) Rabbi Elazar, famous for his knowledge of physics and astronomy, wishes to tell us here that in spite of the fact that Temple offerings are no longer permitted due to the destruction of the Temple, we should still study the laws relating to the offerings of birds (See Leviticus Ch. XII, XIII, and XV and the tractate *Kinnin*), These are also precepts of the Torah which make it difficult to decide what is the law when one of these obligatory offerings is confused with one that is not., etc. Likewise, he recommends us to study the laws relating to menstruation (See Leviticus Ch. XV and the tractate *Nida*), above all, in cases of irregularities. These laws also constitute the essence of the Oral Law handed down from Moses through generation after generation, and should not be neglected.

(3) Astronomy and *gematria* [computations derived from the numerical value of the letters of a Hebrew word] require a deep knowledge of mathematics and sharpen the mind of those who study them. *Gematria* is one of the means of revealing the hidden meaning of the Torah; for example, Genesis, Ch. XLII:2 reads, "And he (Jacob) said, behold, I have heard there is corn in Egypt: go down there, and buy for us from there…" The Hebrew word "*redu*" (go down) has the numerical equivalent of 210 alluding to the 210 years of slavery his descendants would eventually suffer there. (Though they dwelt in Egypt for 400 years, the period of bondage lasted only 210 years.) *Gematria* is applied to words that are different from one another but are related by virtue of having the same numerical value. For example, the opening words of the Torah "*Bereshit bara*" (In the beginning, God created …) have the same numerical value (1, 116) as the words "*Berosh Hashanah nivra*" (It was created on Rosh ha-Shanah) meaning that the world was created on the New Year. By "*gematria*", Rabbi Elazar also means the science of mathematics. As mentioned, he was

so expert in this science that the Mishnah (*Horayot* IV, 19) exaggerates in attributing to him the ability to calculate the number of drops of water in the sea.

(4) By incidentals [the Hebrew refers to them as dessert eaten after the meal.], he means that our primary study should be that of the Torah, and that afterwards we can dedicate ourselves to the study of astronomy and *gematria*. The Torah should always be considered the principal nourishment for the soul, just as bread, as is said in Proverbs IX:5 "Come, eat of my bread…"

(5) Rabbi Hanania ben Akashia…(Cf. end of Ch. 1)

Chapter IV / פרק ד'

VERSE 4:1

"כָּל יִשְׂרָאֵל יֵשׁ לָהֶם חֵלֶק לָעוֹלָם הַבָּא, שֶׁנֶּאֱמַר: וְעַמֵּךְ כֻּלָּם צַדִּיקִים, לְעוֹלָם יִירְשׁוּ אָרֶץ, נֵצֶר מַטָּעַי מַעֲשֵׂה יָדַי לְהִתְפָּאֵר."

א בֶּן זוֹמָא אוֹמֵר, אֵיזֶהוּ חָכָם, הַלּוֹמֵד מִכָּל אָדָם, שֶׁנֶּאֱמַר: מִכָּל מְלַמְּדַי הִשְׂכַּלְתִּי. אֵיזֶהוּ גִבּוֹר, הַכּוֹבֵשׁ אֶת יִצְרוֹ, שֶׁנֶּאֱמַר: טוֹב אֶרֶךְ אַפַּיִם מִגִּבּוֹר, וּמֹשֵׁל בְּרוּחוֹ מִלֹּכֵד עִיר. אֵיזֶהוּ עָשִׁיר, הַשָּׂמֵחַ בְּחֶלְקוֹ, שֶׁנֶּאֱמַר: יְגִיעַ כַּפֶּיךָ כִּי תֹאכֵל אַשְׁרֶיךָ וְטוֹב לָךְ. אַשְׁרֶיךָ בָּעוֹלָם הַזֶּה, וְטוֹב לָךְ לָעוֹלָם הַבָּא. אֵיזֶהוּ מְכֻבָּד, הַמְכַבֵּד אֶת הַבְּרִיּוֹת, שֶׁנֶּאֱמַר: כִּי מְכַבְּדַי אֲכַבֵּד, וּבֹזַי יֵקַלּוּ.

"All Israel has a share in the world to come…" (1)
4:1. Ben Zoma (2) used to say, who is wise? He who learns from all men (3), as is said in Psalms CXIX:99, "From all my teachers I have gained wisdom." Who is strong? He who controls his passions (4), as is said in the Book of Proverbs XVI:32, "Better is the slow to anger than the mighty, and the one who rules his spirit than he who captures a city (5)." Who is rich? He who rejoices in his lot (6), as is said in Psalms CXXVIII:2, "For thou shalt eat the labour of thy hands; happy shalt thou be, and it shall be well with thee in this world and in the world to come." (7) Who is honored? He who honors his fellow men (8), as is said in 1 Samuel II:30, "For I honor those who honor Me, and those who despise Me shall be lightly esteemed."

---

(1) See the commentary that precedes Chapter 1.

(2) The first name of this rabbi and that of the following Mishnah (Ben Azzai) is Simeon. In light of the fact that both died prematurely

before receiving rabbinical ordination, the Mishnah refers to them only by the name of their fathers [Ben Zoma – son of Zoma, and Ben Azzai – son of Azzai] for that was the ancient custom. This was so even though both were quite learned in matters of Torah and Kabbalah. Ben Zoma, Ben Azzai, Elisha ben Avuya, and Rabbi Akiva had dedicated themselves to the study of the mystical process of Creation, to the mystery of the nature of God, and to other speculations of mysticism, which led to the following consequences: Ben Zoma and Ben Azzai died young; Elisha ben Avuya, the teacher of the famous Rabbi Meir, became a heretic; Rabbi Akiva remained firm in his beliefs even after penetrating all the secrets that are difficult to be understood and upheld by the fragile human mind. He became one of the most famous masters of Judaism and of the occult sciences.

(3) The true sage is one who does not miss a chance to learn from anyone, be he superior or inferior, older or younger, and who does not feel diminished by accepting good and constructive ideas and opinions. This is particularly more valid when it deals with Torah learning, as King David said, "From all my teachers I acquired understanding, because Thy testimonies were my daily meditation." (Psalm CXIX:99)

(4) Here this refers to a person who has a strong impulse to do something bad, but nevertheless restrains himself. It does not refer to a person of a gentle nature and character who does not need to make an effort to retain self- control. One of the greatest examples of self-control is the ability to repress the hatred we feel towards an enemy and to make a friend of him or her

(5) This pertains to a king who, after conquering a city whose inhabitants wished to kill him, restrains his desire for vengeance and does not kill them. Rashi interprets the first verse of the *Parasha* "*Ki Tetze*" (Deuteronomy XXI:10) "When thou goest forth to war against thy enemies…" these enemies are the evil urges; they are the worse adversaries of man, and are stronger and more powerful than physical enemies.

(6) A person who is truly rich makes good use of the little or the

abundance that God has granted him and enjoys it in the best way possible. Neither the rich who are discontent, nor the poor who lament their poverty achieve happiness. This does not mean, however, that the poor should not try to improve their situation.

A play on the Hebrew word *ashir* spelled 'ayin', 'shin', 'yod' 'resh', is made into an acrostic 'ayin' – *enayim* – eyes; 'shin' –*shinayim* – teeth, 'yod' – *yadayim* – hands, 'resh' – *raglayim* – feet, tells us that one who has all these four parts of the body in good condition enjoys good health and should consider himself rich.

(7) According to the Talmud, this verse teaches us that one who supports himself by a trade or profession, etc. is greater in merit than one who, in spite of being god fearing, expects others to support him. This is deduced from the verse referring to one who fears God, which says, "Happy is the one who fears the Lord", and does not mention the words "it shall be well with thee" as in the case of one who "shall eat the labor of thy hands" (supports himself by the labor of his hands).

(8) This quote which comes after "Who is wise, strong, or rich?" tells us that one who possesses any of these three qualities is often honored by others. Now then, what should a person do to deserve to be honored for oneself, and not for the wisdom, strength or riches that one may possess? He should also honor his fellow man. The famous Cuban poet and patriot, Jose Marti, was probably inspired by this when he said, *"Honrar, honra."* – To honor, brings honor.

When a person honors others, he is in reality honoring himself, for in this way, he leads others to honor him. One who honors his fellow man, created like him in the spiritual image of God, is in fact honoring the Creator who honors those who honor Him. On the other hand, one who despises his fellow human beings despises the Creator who created them. However, God does not scorn the scorners directly. They despise themselves. (See 1 Samuel, Ch. 11:30).

Ben Zoma used to preach the importance of honoring one's fellow man without exception saying, "We human beings depend on one another. Imagine if I had to plant the wheat, harvest it, grind it, convert it into flour, knead the bread, and bake it. In the meanwhile, I get up in the morning and find all that I need ready for me. Even if it were for this alone, we have to honor all human beings."

VERSE 4:2

ב בֶּן עַזַּאי אוֹמֵר: הֱוֵי רָץ לְמִצְוָה קַלָּה, וּבוֹרֵחַ מִן הָעֲבֵרָה. שֶׁמִּצְוָה גּוֹרֶרֶת מִצְוָה, וַעֲבֵרָה גוֹרֶרֶת עֲבֵרָה, שֶׁשְּׂכַר מִצְוָה מִצְוָה, וּשְׂכַר עֲבֵרָה עֲבֵרָה.

4:2. Ben Azzai (1) would say, be eager to observe a light commandment (2) and flee from transgression, for one commandment (*mitzvah* – also, blessing) induces another (3), one transgression induces another; the reward of one *mitzvah* is another *mitzvah*, while the retribution of a transgression is another.

---

(1) Simeon Ben Azzai was one of the most outstanding disciples of Rabbi Yohanan Ben Zaccai in Yavneh (135 B.C.). Besides his wisdom, he was gifted with an extraordinary human character. His love for God and study were so great that he remained unmarried in order to dedicate himself completely to Torah and mysticism. But even so, he criticized those who did not enter into marriage at the proper age. For this reason, Maimonides in his *Sefer Ha-Mitzvoth* tells us, "Only a man like Ben Azzai can remain single if he so desires."

(2) When a person rushes to perform a good deed, even if it be a minor one, this will lead him to perform deeds of greater importance. Likewise, when a person does not avoid a minor transgression, he will be predisposed to commit greater sins.

(3) One who performs a good deed and experiences satisfaction in having done so will feel a desire to do others. But on the contrary, one who commits a sin and is not sorry for having done so will surely commit another. It is for this reason that the words "flee from transgression" were used. They mean that one should flee from temptation so that it will be more difficult to succumb to it.

The Mishnah explains the first verse of the Book of Psalms in the following way, First a person walks in the path of the wicked, then in the way of sinners, and afterwards sits in the seat of scorners.

VERSE 4:3

4:3. He also used to say, despise no man (1), and hold nothing impossible, for there is no man but has his day, and no thing but has its place (2).

ג הוּא הָיָה אוֹמֵר: אַל תְּהִי בָז לְכָל אָדָם, וְאַל תְּהִי מַפְלִיג לְכָל דָּבָר, שֶׁאֵין לְךָ אָדָם שֶׁאֵין לוֹ שָׁעָה, וְאֵין לְךָ דָבָר שֶׁאֵין לוֹ מָקוֹם.

---

(1) Don't say of even one who is poor, humble, weak, small, etc., "What harm or good can this person do me? God gives everyone his chance. As for the things that a person often considers impossible to happen, it is necessary to judge them cautiously, to investigate a matter and examine it thoroughly before deciding that it is out of the realm of reality.

(2) The text mentions the word *maflig*, which means to set aside and to keep distant. This means that if there be the slightest suspicion that such a thing can happen, don't think, "Such a thing is unlikely to happen, and there's no need to worry about it."

VERSE 4:4

4:4. Rabbi Levitas, the man of Yavneh, was wont to quote, "Be exceedingly humble (1) for the end of man is the worm (2)."

ד רַבִּי לְוִיטַס אִישׁ יַבְנֶה אוֹמֵר: מְאֹד מְאֹד הֱוֵי שְׁפַל רוּחַ, שֶׁתִּקְוַת אֱנוֹשׁ רִמָּה.

---

(1) At the beginning of the second chapter of this tract, Rabi (Yehudah

ha-Nasi) says that one should adopt the middle position in all cases. And here it says that pride or arrogance is such a bad defect that one should go to the extreme opposite and be humble in spirit. In the Talmud (*Sota* 4:) it is says that anyone who is arrogant is considered an idol worshipper and a denier of the Lord. In my humble opinion, the author of this thought on advising us to be humble and not arrogant and belittling of others, does not recommend that we humble ourselves, especially when dealing with evil or ignorant people who scorn the Torah and those who study it.

(2) Just to think that in the end we will be food for the worms and turn into dust, we can avoid being proud, vain, ostentatious, and other similar things.

VERSE 4:5

4:5. Rabbi Yoḥanan ben Berokah used to say, whosoever profanes God's name (1) in secret (2) will pay the penalty in public;

ה רַבִּי יוֹחָנָן בֶּן בְּרוֹקָא אוֹמֵר: כָּל הַמְחַלֵּל שֵׁם שָׁמַיִם בַּסֵּתֶר, נִפְרָעִין מִמֶּנּוּ בַּגָּלוּי. אֶחָד שׁוֹגֵג וְאֶחָד מֵזִיד בְּחִלּוּל הַשֵּׁם.

and profanation of God's name is equally evil whether committed involuntarily or willfully (3).

---

(1) To profane the Name of God means to perform acts or to speak against the principles of the Torah, denying the Absolute Wisdom and Providence of God (Cf. 1:11).

(2) I believe the profanation of the Name of God in secret implies a sin committed together with another person, as for example incest and other similar things. Although the transgression may have taken place in secret, the consequences will come to be known in public.

(3) Although the punishment will be carried out in public, the degree will not be as great for one who profanes the Holy Name without intention or purpose.

VERSE 4:6

4:6. Rabbi Ishamel, his son, used to say, he who learns in order to teach will be enabled both to learn and teach; but he who learns in order to practice will be enabled to learn, to teach, and to practice (1).

ו רַבִּי יִשְׁמָעֵאל בַּר רַבִּי יוֹסֵי אוֹמֵר: הַלּוֹמֵד תּוֹרָה עַל מְנָת לְלַמֵּד, מַסְפִּיקִין בְּיָדוֹ לִלְמוֹד וּלְלַמֵּד. וְהַלּוֹמֵד עַל מְנָת לַעֲשׂוֹת, מַסְפִּיקִין בְּיָדוֹ לִלְמוֹד וּלְלַמֵּד לִשְׁמוֹר וְלַעֲשׂוֹת.

---

(1) Study is always important, in any event, because it often leads to practice. Therefore, one should consider study of primary importance.

The Talmud comments that the Amoraim (the authors of the Gemara, which is the detailed study of the Mishnah) Abbaye and Rava were descendants of Eli, one of the Judges of Israel. In 1 Samuel, 11:32, Eli is told, "…and there shall not be an old man in thy house" [because of the sins of his sons]. For this reason Abaye and Rava were destined to die young, but Abaye, who practiced beneficence as ordained in the Torah, lived to the age of sixty. Rava, on the other hand, died at forty.

VERSE 4:7

4:7. Rabbi Zadok would say, do not separate yourself from the community, and when you judge do not play the role of the lawyer. Do not make the Torah a crown for self-aggrandizement, or a spade to dig with (1). Similarly, Hillel used to say; he who makes worldly use of the crown of the Torah will perish. Thus, you should also know that all who use the Torah for their own benefit hasten their departure from this life.

ז רַבִּי צָדוֹק אוֹמֵר: אַל תִּפְרוֹשׁ מִן הַצִּבּוּר, וְאַל תַּעַשׂ עַצְמְךָ כְּעוֹרְכֵי הַדַּיָּנִין, וְאַל תַּעֲשֶׂהָ עֲטָרָה לְהִתְגַּדֵּל בָּהּ, וְלֹא קַרְדֹּם לַחְפֹּר בָּהּ. וְכָךְ הָיָה הִלֵּל אוֹמֵר: וּדְאִשְׁתַּמֵּשׁ בְּתַגָּא חֲלָף. הָא לָמַדְתָּ, כָּל הַנֶּהֱנֶה מִדִּבְרֵי תוֹרָה, נוֹטֵל חַיָּיו מִן הָעוֹלָם.

---

(1) In some books, the first and second thoughts of this paragraph were attributed to Hillel and Yehudah ben Tabay respectively instead of Rabbi Zadok (See Ch. II, 5 and 8).

To study the Torah exclusively in order to be qualified to be a rabbi and to receive payment or honors wherefrom was always against the teaching of Moses who said, "I have not taken one ass from them," (Numbers XVI: 15). Also, the prophet Samuel said, "…answer me before the Lord, and before the anointed: whose ox have I taken, or whose ass have I taken?" (I Samuel XII: 3). This thought is deduced also from the following words of Moses, "I have taught you statutes and judgments, even as the Lord, my God, commanded me." (Deuteronomy IV: 5) What Moses meant was that God had ordered him to teach them [the people of Israel] without pay, and just as he taught without remuneration, so should you teach the Torah without receiving any pay. Therefore, one should not make of the Torah a spade to dig with; that is, an instrument or means of support, since it is prohibited to take advantage of the sanctity of the Torah. However, it is permitted for teachers and educators of religion to receive a salary and support themselves through their profession for the salary they receive is for caring for children and not for teaching them the Torah. Likewise, rabbis who serve a congregation are permitted to receive a salary and communities are obligated to pay them well, even beyond their needs so that they may not have financial worries, and; thus, be able to dedicate themselves to their sacred duties. According to the Talmud, a rabbi should be exempt from taxes and community levies, even if he himself is rich. If a rabbi is a merchant, everyone should buy his goods before those of others so that he may have more time free to study the Torah and teach it free. To honor a rabbi is equivalent to honoring the Torah and not the man [or woman in Reform or Conservative synagogues that have woman rabbis]. In reality, many sages of the Talmud refused to accept remuneration for their services to the community, and supported themselves through some other occupation like Rabbi Yonatan who was a shoemaker, Rabbi Yitzhak who was a blacksmith, and others. Such rabbis did not wish to benefit from their religious services out of their own will and character and not because of the prohibition against receiving compensation. (See the explanation given by Rabbi Ovadiah of Bertinoro in this Mishnah.)

VERSE 4:8

4:8. Rabbi Yose (1) used to say, everyone who honors the Torah (2) will himself be honored by men, and everyone who dishonors the Torah will be dishonored by men.

ח רַבִּי יוֹסֵי אוֹמֵר: כָּל הַמְכַבֵּד אֶת הַתּוֹרָה, גּוּפוֹ מְכֻבָּד עַל הַבְּרִיּוֹת. וְכָל הַמְחַלֵּל אֶת הַתּוֹרָה, גּוּפוֹ מְחֻלָּל עַל הַבְּרִיּוֹת.

---

(1) Rabbi Yose ben Halafta, the author of this thought, was a disciple of the famous Rabbi Akiva. He is also the author of the *Seder Olam*, a chronology of the people of Israel from the Creation to the revolt of Bar Kochba (135 C.E.).

(2) To honor the Torah has several interpretations: to honor the very content of the Torah, to observe its commandments, to honor sages of the Law, their written works, not to hold in equal esteem any other book or existing code of law, to consider most holy the Sefer Torah (written on parchment), even more than the Books of the Prophets and the Writings, to place the Torah and holy books in clean, high, and adequate places, etc. It can also be said of a person who has studied the Torah and leads an exemplary life, as stated in the Talmud (*Yoma* 86), "Look upon so and so who studied the Torah, how appropriate and righteous is his behavior. Blessed be the parents who raised him, blessed the teacher who taught him the Torah." Such a person is honoring the Torah.

VERSE 4:9

4:9. Rabbi Ishmael, his son, used to say, he who shuns the office of judge (1) escapes enmity, theft and perjury, while he who presumptuously lays down the law (2) is arrogant, a fool and a knave.

ט רַבִּי יִשְׁמָעֵאל בְּנוֹ אוֹמֵר: הַחוֹשֵׂךְ עַצְמוֹ מִן הַדִּין, פּוֹרֵק מִמֶּנּוּ אֵיבָה וְגֵזֶל וּשְׁבוּעַת שָׁוְא. וְהַגַּס לִבּוֹ בְּהוֹרָאָה, שׁוֹטֶה רָשָׁע וְגַס רוּחַ.

---

(1) He who shuns the office of judge, there being others more qualified than he to occupy the post, or who being judge, tries to mediate between both sides so that they reach an amicable agreement, avoids enmity, since the condemned generally hate the judge who condemned them. He is free of theft, not directly, but in case he had condemned an innocent party, the latter would have had to pay what was not rightly due. A judge is also subject to hearing false statements from the litigants. The Talmud (*Sanhedrin* 7:) writes with reference to a judge who would say each time he was to pass judgment, "I go to my death. Would that at the final judgment, I not be found worse than at the beginning."

(2) This refers to a person who is self confident and rushes to render judgment, pretending to be an expert in the matter, and does not take into account that all cases have to be carefully studied to the minutest detail, and that not all cases are similar. The reason why the Talmud says that one who is presumptuous in his judgment is a fool, a knave, and arrogant, is due to the fact that such a person does not take into account that in his haste he can make a mistake, thus, condemning the innocent without fear of God.

VERSE 4:10

4:10. He used to say, judge not alone (1), for there is but One who may judge alone. Say not, "Accept my opinion," (2) for they have the right to decide, not thou.

י הוּא הָיָה אוֹמֵר: אַל תְּהִי דָן יְחִידִי, שֶׁאֵין דָּן יְחִידִי אֶלָּא אֶחָד. וְאַל תֹּאמַר קַבְּלוּ דַעְתִּי, שֶׁהֵן רַשָּׁאִין וְלֹא אָתָּה.

---

(1) According to the Law, a judge who is alone and an expert in the subject can pass judgment on property matters, although it is not recommended. But the Mishnah refers here to judges who do not have sufficient experience, or to litigants who do not wish to be judged by only one judge. This is why Jewish courts are normally composed of at least three judges.

(2) This can refer to the judge who insists that his colleagues decide according to his opinion. It can also refer to the judge who imposes himself as such before the litigants. It can likewise apply to a leader of an organization or anyone else who forces others to adopt his decisions. It is permissible to convince others by means of arguments and proofs with the aim of reinforcing one's own opinion, but always allowing the majority to decide.

VERSE 4:11

4:11. Rabbi Jonathan would say, everyone who fulfills the Torah in poverty will in the end fulfill it in wealth, and everyone who disregards the Torah in wealth will in the end disregard it in poverty (1).

יא רַבִּי יוֹנָתָן אוֹמֵר: כָּל הַמְקַיֵּם אֶת הַתּוֹרָה מֵעֹנִי, סוֹפוֹ לְקַיְּמָהּ מֵעשֶׁר. וְכָל הַמְבַטֵּל אֶת הַתּוֹרָה מֵעשֶׁר, סוֹפוֹ לְבַטְּלָהּ מֵעֹנִי.

---

(1) A poor person who works hard to provide for his material needs and still dedicates some time to study the Torah and observe its commandments will be helped by God to do so also in wealth. But on the contrary, a rich man who is solely concerned with his business, diversions, social obligations, etc., and does not find time to study and observe the precepts of the Torah, will not be able to do so in poverty. It can likewise be said that what one is not accustomed to doing when young, will be difficult to do in old age.

Rabbi Meir (see the following Mishnah), one of the outstanding disciples of Rabbi Akiva, was a famous scribe who lived in poverty, earning only three *selaim* per week (one *sela* was worth approximately 30 grams of silver). He would spend his salary this way: one *sela* for food, one for clothing, and the last he would distribute among Torah students who were even poorer than he. When asked what he would do for the future of his children, he answered, "If they are righteous, they will not want for anything, for thus said King David in Psalm XXXVII:25, "I have not seen a just man forsaken, and his seed begging bread." The Midrash (*Kohelet Raba* 2, 18) adds this thought, if they (the children) are not [just], why should I leave what is mine to the enemies of God?

Rabbi Meir had the virtue of acquiring knowledge from anyone, regardless of his behavior. One such person was the sage Elisha ben Avuya, a rabbi who became a heretic due to what befell a man who, wishing to comply with the precept of the Torah cited in Deuteronomy xxii:6–7, with regard to what it says about birds' nests, fell from a tree and died prematurely. Deut. xxii:6–7 states, "If a bird's nest chances to be before thee in the way in any tree or on the ground… thou shalt not take the mother bird together with the young, but thou shalt surely let the mother go… and thou mayest prolong thy days." The man died in the fall wishing to protect the birds. instead of prolonging his life.

Rabbi Meir died in Asia Minor. He had previously asked to be buried at the edge of the sea, "So that the waves which wash the land of my fathers also wash my bones." His name is mentioned more than 800 times in the Talmud. He was so intelligent that with his arguments, he was capable of making one convinced that the impure was pure, and that the pure was impure.

VERSE 4:12

יב רַבִּי מֵאִיר אוֹמֵר: הֱוֵי מְמַעֵט בְּעֵסֶק, וַעֲסוֹק בַּתּוֹרָה. וֶהֱוֵי שְׁפַל רוּחַ בִּפְנֵי כָל אָדָם. וְאִם בָּטַלְתָּ מִן הַתּוֹרָה, יֶשׁ לְךָ בְּטֵלִים הַרְבֵּה כְּנֶגְדֶּךָ. וְאִם עָמַלְתָּ בַּתּוֹרָה, יֵשׁ (לוֹ) שָׂכָר הַרְבֵּה לִתֵּן לָךְ.

4:12. Rabbi Meir used to say, engage less in thy business (1), and occupy thyself with the Torah. Be humble of spirit before all men (2). If thou hast neglected the Torah, there are many more impediments before thee (3); but if thou hast labored in the Torah, God (4) has rich reward to give thee.

---

(1) Rabbi Meir advises that a man's principal task should be the study of Torah, and work secondary, dedicating to it only the time necessary to provide for one's needs and those of his family. (Cf. ii, 6) However, Simeon Bar Yohai recommended dedicating all one's time exclusively to the study of Torah, which not everyone can do.

(2) Rabbi Meir is telling us that one should be humble not only before the aged and those superior in intelligence, but even before

lesser persons. This quality keeps a man from pride, and allows him to learn from even those younger and less learned than himself. (Cf. II:1 and IV:4.)

(3) Neglecting the study of Torah, even temporarily, leads one little by little to become accustomed to abandoning it. Many things in this world absorb a person's time without providing spiritual benefit and leave little time for the study of Torah, which is of primary importance.

(4) God rewards those who study and observe the Torah directly and not through intermediaries. The messengers of God (the angels) follow strictly His orders and are not authorized to give a greater reward than is due, while the Creator, being the Lord of the universe, can grant even more. In my opinion, we should also pray to God that the punishment we deserve for our sins come directly from Him, and not through intermediaries because He, being a merciful God, will have more pity on us and will not requite us as we deserve. For this same reason, King David, when he sinned and deserved to be punished said to the prophet Gad, "I am in great distress; let us fall now into the hand of the Lord, for His mercies are great; and let me not fall into the hand of man." (II Samuel XXIV: 14).

VERSE 4:13

4:13. Rabbi Eliezer ben Yaakov would say, one who does a good deed, acquires for himself a defending angel (1); and one who commits a transgression, acquires an accuser. Repentence and good deeds (2) are protection against misfortune.

יג. רַבִּי אֱלִיעֶזֶר בֶּן יַעֲקֹב אוֹמֵר: הָעוֹשֶׂה מִצְוָה אַחַת, קוֹנֶה לוֹ פְּרַקְלִיט אֶחָד. וְהָעוֹבֵר עֲבֵרָה אַחַת, קוֹנֶה לוֹ קַטֵיגוֹר אֶחָד. תְּשׁוּבָה וּמַעֲשִׂים טוֹבִים, כִּתְרִיס בִּפְנֵי הַפֻּרְעָנוּת.

(1) The Mishnah (*Shemot Raba* 32) says: A person who performs a mitzvah (a good deed), creates an angel who protects him. In my opinion, this means that the good deed itself defends the person and will intercede in his favor on Judgment Day. The opposite will happen to one who commits a transgression.

(2) Beginning with the principle that the calamities, misfortunes, and punishments that befall a person derive from the sins that he commits, the remedy, Rabbi Eliezer tells us, is repentence and good deeds. God does not grant His pardon unless there exists true repentence followed by good deeds. These two things are compared here to the protection offered by a shield or armor. The word *teris* used in the Hebrew meaning the sally port of a fortress has also the meaning of shield or armor.

VERSE 4:14

יד רַבִּי יוֹחָנָן הַסַּנְדְּלָר אוֹמֵר: כָּל כְּנֵסִיָּה שֶׁהִיא לְשֵׁם שָׁמַיִם, סוֹפָהּ לְהִתְקַיֵּם. וְשֶׁאֵינָהּ לְשֵׁם שָׁמַיִם, אֵין סוֹפָהּ לְהִתְקַיֵּם.

4:14. Rabbi Yohanan, the cobbler, used to say, every gatherings with sacred aims (1) will, in the end, endure, but one that is not called for a holy mission will not ultimately endure.

---

(1) Any gathering, or assembly brought together for a noble, positive, or charitable cause, or for the search for truth for the common good, even if it does not have a religious image, will endure because God supports positive goals. When people get together to study Torah, or to perform a mitzvah, as well as to combat an illness, an evil, etc. such an assembly is classified as *l'Shem Shamayim* (for the sake of Heaven). On the contrary, a council like the one called by Korah to destroy the work of Moses, an assemblage of people made apparently for religious purposes, but whose real intention is to gain fame or for the moral or material benefit of those that establish them, cannot be considered

l'Shem Shamayim. Consequently, they will not endure and they are condemned to finally disappear.

VERSE 4:15

4:15. Rabbi Eleazar ben Shamua used to say, Let the honor of your disciples be as precious to you as your own (1), and the honor of your colleague be like the respect you have for your teacher, and the respect for your teacher like the reverence you have for God (2).

טו רַבִּי אֶלְעָזָר בֶּן שַׁמּוּעַ אוֹמֵר: יְהִי כְּבוֹד תַּלְמִידְךָ חָבִיב עָלֶיךָ כְּשֶׁלָּךְ, וּכְבוֹד חֲבֵרְךָ כְּמוֹרָא רַבָּךְ, וּמוֹרָא רַבָּךְ כְּמוֹרָא שָׁמָיִם.

---

(1) This advice was inspired by the behavior of Moses, the Prophet, with his disciple, Joshua, by Aaron with his colleague, Moses, and by Joshua with his teacher, Moses. In the Torah (Exodus XVII:9), it is told that Moses, addressing himself to Joshua, said, "Choose us out men and go out, fight with Amalek." Moses, in saying, "choose us" rather than "choose for me" was treating Joshua as an equal. In Number XII:11, Aaron, in spite of being Moses' brother, in addressing him, says, "Alas, my lord, I pray thee, lay no sin upon us." And in Numbers XI:28, Joshua, who was Moses' disciple, says to him, "My lord Moses, restrain them." (In Hebrew, this could also mean annihilate them); thus, comparing Moses to God who is the only One who would have the right to annihilate the rebels.

(2) This does not mean that the teacher should be considered the equal of God. It is only that in honoring rabbis who teach Torah, one is honoring God, the Giver of the Torah.

VERSE 4:16

4:16. Rabbi Yehudah (ben Ilay) would say, "Be careful in your study of the Torah, because an error in teaching is considered an intentional sin (1).

טז רַבִּי יְהוּדָה אוֹמֵר: הֱוֵי זָהִיר בַּתַּלְמוּד, שֶׁשִּׁגְגַת תַּלְמוּד עוֹלָה זָדוֹן.

---

(1) There are two ways of explaining this paragraph: one refers to one who studies the Torah and teaches it incorrectly on purpose; the other, refers to the teacher who teaches a student incorrectly and the latter transmits [the error] to others, giving rise to allowing what is forbidden and vice-versa. The Holy One, Blessed be He, considered negligence of the teacher an intentional sin. Therefore, Rabbi Yehudah recommends that teachers and sages of the Law constantly review what they learned so they do not fall into error, out of forgetfulness, which is considered a great mistake because of the possible consequences of teaching an erroneous doctrine. To cause others to sin is a more serious sin than committing one yourself.

VERSE 4:17

4:17. Rabbi Simeon bar Yohai used to say, there are three crowns: the crown of Torah, the crown of priesthood and the crown of royalty, but the crown of a good name is greater than all (1).

יז רַבִּי שִׁמְעוֹן אוֹמֵר: שְׁלֹשָׁה כְתָרִים הֵם, כֶּתֶר תּוֹרָה וְכֶתֶר כְּהֻנָּה וְכֶתֶר מַלְכוּת, וְכֶתֶר שֵׁם טוֹב עוֹלֶה עַל גַּבֵּיהֶן.

---

(1) The Torah recommends that we honor those who possess the first three crowns or titles worthy of being honored. In Leviticus XIX: 32 it says, "Thou shalt rise up before the hoary head, and honor the face of the old man (*zaken*)." The word *zaken* is explained in the Talmud

as *ze shekana hohmah* alluding to the man who although young has acquired the wisdom of the Torah. With reference to the priesthood, it is written in Leviticus XXI:8, "...he shall be holy to thee"; that is, you shall honor him. As for royalty, it says in Deuteronomy XVII:15, "...thou mayest appoint a king over thee", which signifies that you should also honor him.

The crown of priesthood is not attainable by anyone, but a descendant of the House of Aaron. Likewise kingship, for the king must be a descendant of the House of David (Jeremiah XXI:12). However, it is within the power of anyone to obtain the crown of Torah. One need not belong to a special caste; one only needs to be God-fearing. The crown of Torah is greater than that of priesthood and that of a king for the following reason, these two crowns are inherited, but one acquires the crown of Torah through his own merits. However, there exists a fourth crown, the crown of a good name, which is superior to all the others due to the fact that it is a prerequisite to the other three. For example, the Torah sage who does not have a good reputation is not appreciated, and likewise the king or the priest. Nevertheless, the Torah recommends that we honor the king, the priest, or one learned in the Law such as a rabbi for their knowledge of the Torah or for their position.

King Solomon (Ecclesiastes VII:1) said, "A good name is better than precious ointment;" for a good name crosses boundaries, even that of the grave, while the fragrance of a perfume or precious ointment is limited in terms of time and space. "A good name is rather to be chosen than great riches." (Proverbs XXII:1).

VERSE 4:18

4:18. Rabbi Nehorai (1) said, Emigrate to a place where there is Torah learning (2) and don't say that it should look for you, or that your companions should transmit it to you (3): and don't rely upon your own understanding (4).

יח רַבִּי נְהוֹרַאי אוֹמֵר: הֱוֵי גּוֹלֶה לִמְקוֹם תּוֹרָה, וְאַל תֹּאמַר שֶׁהִיא תָבוֹא אַחֲרֶיךָ, שֶׁחֲבֵרֶיךָ יְקַיְּמוּהָ בְּיָדֶךָ. וְאֶל בִּינָתְךָ אַל תִּשָּׁעֵן.

---

(1) There are those who believe that Rabbi Nehorai was the same Rabbi Eleazar ben Arah or Rabbi Meir, previously mentioned. It is said rather that he is actually Rabbi Meir because the words "Meir" and "Nehorai" both derive from "light" or "clarity."

(2) In case there are no Torah sages where you live, you have to travel, even to another place of exile where there are Torah sages. Do not wait until they come to where you are, since when one studies in the company of sages or, at least, colleagues, many doubts are clarified through the questions and answers that mutually arise.

(3) This can be explained in two ways: The student of a master should not say, "My companions, who listened to the teacher's lesson, will pass it on to me." It is not the same to hear the lesson from the students, as it is to hear it directly from the teacher. Another explanation is the advice to the master's disciple who may think he is intelligent, not to say, "I don't need my companions", since when there is an interchange of opinions, knowledge is enhanced.

(4) To learn from books is not the same as hearing the interpretations of the sages in person for in this way errors of interpretation are avoided. One learns something new that the teacher may add to what is written in the book. Doubts are clarified and what is believed to be true, but isn't can be corrected. That is why King Solomon himself recommends, "Do not rely on your own judgment." (Proverbs 11:3)

VERSE 4:19

4:19. Rabbi Yannai would say, It is beyond our understanding why the evildoers prosper (sometimes), nor do we know why the just (sometimes) suffer (1).

יט רַבִּי יַנַּאי אוֹמֵר: אֵין בְּיָדֵינוּ לֹא מִשַּׁלְוַת הָרְשָׁעִים וְאַף לֹא מִיִּסּוּרֵי הַצַּדִּיקִים.

---

(1) Rabbi Yannai means by this that only God knows the reason why the evildoer who deserves to be punished for his bad deeds prospers, while the righteous person who deserves to be rewarded for his or her good deeds suffers.

Our understanding in this regard is very limited. The commentators tried, each in his way, to interpret the eternal question regarding the well being of the evildoer and the suffering of the just. Among their explanations are found the following: God rewards the evil one in this world for the few good deeds he may have performed. This being the reason that such a person enjoys rewards in this world, but will have no part in the world to come, unless he repents in time. On the other hand, the just suffer for the few errors they may have committed in order to be purified in this world and thus be prepared to receive the reward for their good deeds and righteousness in the world to come.

It appears that the words of Rabbi Yannai can, in my opinion, also signify that we, as simple human beings, wrongly judge the paths of God. Sometimes a person who seems bad on the outside, can have a pure and good soul, and have performed good deeds. On the other hand, that person who seems to us to be a righteous person does not possess the purity of soul that he appears to have. Therefore, it is beyond our understanding to judge the ways of God and say, "This one who deserves to be rewarded is being punished or vice-versa, because only He knows what is inside a person and the reality of things."

VERSE 4:20

4:20. Rabbi Mathiah ben Harash (1) would say, be the first to greet all men (2), and be the tail of a lion rather than the head of a fox (3).

כ רַבִּי מַתְיָא בֶּן חָרָשׁ אוֹמֵר: הֱוֵי מַקְדִּים בִּשְׁלוֹם כָּל אָדָם. וֶהֱוֵי זָנָב לָאֲרָיוֹת, וְאַל תְּהִי רֹאשׁ לְשׁוּעָלִים.

---

(1) It is said of this rabbi that after the fall of Betar, the last bastion of Bar Kohba (135 C.E.), that he fled the Holy Land and settled in Rome.

(2) To greet anyone, great or small, wise or ignorant, Jewish or not, a superior or an inferior is a manifestation of humility and love for all human beings created by God, and contributes to gaining the good will and affection of all. Rabbi Mathiah addressed this advice particularly to the Jews living in the Diaspora as he did.

(3) To be the tail of a lion means to frequent those superior in knowledge of Torah, the sciences, culture, etc. even though one is lower in standing than they. For though one may be considered the tail of a lion (a sage), he belongs to the category of lions. This advice goes against the proverb that says, "It is better to be the head of a mouse than the tail of a lion." To be the tail of a lion is better than being the head of foxes, that is, those who are inferior to you and are ignorant, and from whom one can learn nothing. They contribute to your lack of progress in gaining knowledge and learning and, backwardness in behavior and other similar faults.

VERSE 4:21

4:21. Rabbi Yaakov (ben Korshay) (1) used to say, This world is like an antechamber before the World to Come; prepare yourself in the antechamber so that you may be able to enter the main room (2).

כא רַבִּי יַעֲקֹב אוֹמֵר: הָעוֹלָם הַזֶּה דּוֹמֶה לִפְרוֹזְדוֹר בִּפְנֵי הָעוֹלָם הַבָּא. הַתְקֵן עַצְמְךָ בַּפְּרוֹזְדוֹר, כְּדֵי שֶׁתִּכָּנֵס לַטְּרַקְלִין.

---

(1) This rabbi is the same as the one mentioned in Chapter II:9. It is said that he was one of the teachers of Yehudah ha-Nasi.

(2) This world is like a passage leading to the Future World. It is not an eternally permanent place. Our sages compare it to Friday when a Jew makes preparations for the arrival of the Sabbath; that is, the Future World in which there are neither good nor bad deeds. In order to merit the rewards reserved for the just beyond the grave, it is necessary to perform good deeds, observe the precepts of the Torah or do penance, with the aim of purifying and preparing the soul to enter the World to Come. It is like attending to your appearance in the vestibule before entering the throne room of the king. The prophet Amos (IV:12) exhorts us saying, "Prepare to meet thy God."

VERSE 4:22

4:22. Rabbi Yacov ben Korsshay would also say, An hour spent in repentance and performing good deeds in this world is worth more than all the life in the World to Come (1), and an hour of spiritual bliss in the World to Come is worth more than an entire lifetime in this world.

כב הוּא הָיָה אוֹמֵר: יָפָה שָׁעָה אַחַת בִּתְשׁוּבָה וּמַעֲשִׂים טוֹבִים בָּעוֹלָם הַזֶּה, מִכָּל חַיֵּי הָעוֹלָם הַבָּא. וְיָפָה שָׁעָה אַחַת שֶׁל קוֹרַת רוּחַ בָּעוֹלָם הַבָּא, מִכָּל חַיֵּי הָעוֹלָם הַזֶּה.

---

(1) This means that the happiness that one feels upon performing a good deed in this world is greater than the pleasure of its reward in the Future World, and not that the Future World is inferior to this one, as it may seem to imply on first reading. In my opinion, the idea has the following meaning, In view of the fact that one cannot perform neither good nor bad deeds, nor repent in the Future World, since these things are done in this world to merit the reward for the good that we do, an hour of this earthly existence is considered precious. It is to be taken advantage of by performing good deeds and fulfilling the precepts of the Torah. Therefore, it is more valuable than an eternal life in the World to Come. On the other hand, an hour of spiritual peace in the World to Come surpasses the pleasure that one may enjoy in an entire lifetime in this world. In life on earth, there is neither perfect tranquility nor eternal spiritual bliss.

VERSE 4:23

4:23. Rabbi Simeon ben Elazar (1) used to say, do not placate your companion in his (or her) moment of anger (2), and do not console him in the hour that his dead lies before him (3); neither question him when he is making a vow (4) nor try to see him in his hour of humiliation (5).

כג רַבִּי שִׁמְעוֹן בֶּן אֶלְעָזָר אוֹמֵר: אַל תְּרַצֶּה אֶת חֲבֵרְךָ בִּשְׁעַת כַּעֲסוֹ, וְאַל תְּנַחֲמֵהוּ בְּשָׁעָה שֶׁמֵּתוֹ מֻטָּל לְפָנָיו, וְאַל תִּשְׁאַל לוֹ בִּשְׁעַת נִדְרוֹ, וְאַל תִּשְׁתַּדֵּל לִרְאוֹתוֹ בִּשְׁעַת קַלְקָלָתוֹ.

---

(1) This rabbi was a disciple of Rabbi Meir. The following is found among his famous sayings, If a young man orders you to build and an old man orders you to destroy, follow the advice of the old man for the destruction ordained by the old is constructive, while the construction of the young is destructive.

(2) This advice was given to Moses by God when He was angry at the Israelites for worshipping the golden calf (Exodus XXXII:10), "…now therefore let me alone, that my wrath may burn against them," When a person is excessively enraged pacifying words are useless. On the contrary, these can sometimes intensify the anger. For this reason it is better to wait until the anger has passed. Our sages of Talmud in *Yebamot* 65 recommend that we speak only at the right time, and refrain from speaking at an inappropriate moment.

(3) When one tries to console someone who still has the body of a beloved being before him, whatever words said heighten the sadness and creates negative reactions, even though the one saying them has good intentions. In such cases, silence is recommended. The consolation of the bereaved should take place only after the burial. This is elucidated further in the Siddur Ha-Mercaz by Rabbi Matzliah Melamed.

(4) It is not advisable to ask compromising questions of a person making a promise or a vow. An example of this might be, "When you are swearing not to make peace with Mr. So and So, do you mean this for your whole life?". In that moment of anger, the person might say yes, which could have been avoided had the question not been asked. Moreover, the annulment of the vow according to the ritual (*Hatarat Nedarim*) could be made easier.

(5) When a person has committed a bad deed, it is not the appropriate moment to confront him or her, for the shame, the humiliation, the torture, and the sadness he or she may feel is sufficient to make that person want to avoid contact with people. However, there are people who repent what they have done and look for help in order to repair the harm. These deserve to be helped, and not left to fall. There is an old proverb that says, "One who falls has no friends."

VERSE 4:24

4:24. Samuel the Small (1) cited various verses (2), from Proverbs xxiv:17–18, "Do not rejoice when thy enemy falls, and do not let thy heart be glad when he stumbles: lest the Lord see it, and it displease Him, and turn away His wrath from him." (3).

כד שְׁמוּאֵל הַקָּטָן אוֹמֵר: בִּנְפֹל אוֹיִבְךָ אַל תִּשְׂמָח, וּבִכָּשְׁלוֹ אַל יָגֵל לִבֶּךָ, פֶּן יִרְאֶה יְיָ וְרַע בְּעֵינָיו, וְהֵשִׁיב מֵעָלָיו אַפּוֹ.

---

(1) This tannaite (student and teacher) who lived at the end of the first century C.E. in Yavneh was called the small not for his height, but for his humility. According to the Talmud Yerushalmi (*Sota* 9, 14), he was almost the equal of the prophet Samuel in sanctity. The authorship of the prayer against traducers and apostates called "*lamalshinim*", which forms part of the *Amidah*, is attributed to him.

(2) These verses come as proof of what was said above; that is, not to

visit a person during his hour of misfortune, above all, if he is your enemy. Also, in the Book of Job xxxi:29, Job defends his innocence by saying, "Did I rejoice at the destruction of him who hates me, or did I exult when evil found him?" Nevertheless, if the one who visits the fallen one is a true friend and a good-hearted person, I dare say that he can do so [visit the fallen] with the aim of lending moral or material support.

(3) Generally, a person is happy when his enemy is disgraced, but God does not desire the suffering of the wicked; rather, He desires their return to the path of righteousness. For this reason, if we rejoice, He may withdraw His anger from our enemy and turn it against us. It is only permitted to rejoice when a murderer like Hitler (*yimmah shemo* – may his name be blotted out) disappears, so that we are free of him. But if our enmity against someone is due to personal reasons, we should in no way be happy when that person suffers some misfortune. He should certainly not see us rejoice because he will surely feel badly to be seen in such condition and his suffering will increase.

VERSE 4:25

4:25. Elisha ben Avuya (1) said, One who learns as a child, what does he resemble? Ink written on new paper (2). And one who learns when he is old, what is he like? He is like ink written on rubbed paper.

כה אֱלִישָׁע בֶּן אֲבוּיָה אוֹמֵר: הַלּוֹמֵד יֶלֶד, לְמָה הוּא דוֹמֶה, לִדְיוֹ כְתוּבָה עַל נְיָר חָדָשׁ. וְהַלּוֹמֵד זָקֵן, לְמָה הוּא דוֹמֶה, לִדְיוֹ כְתוּבָה עַל נְיָר מָחוּק.

---

(1) Elisha ben Avuya, who was a teacher of the famous Rabbi Meir, became a heretic as we have mentioned earlier. For this reason, he is called in the Talmud Elisha Aher (Elisha, the Other) in order to set him apart from the other Elishas who were believers in Judaism.

However, there are versions that affirm that this rabbi returned to his original faith in his last moments before death. That is why his words are included in the Pirkei Avoth. Others say that because he had been at first a teacher of Rabbi Meir and later his friend, the latter influenced others not to exclude his words. Nevertheless, in some prayer books that contain the Pirkei Avoth, this paragraph is omitted. I believe that Elisha ben Avuya's words were expressed before he became a heretic. The same can be said with regard to King Solomon who worshipped idols in his old age, yet his books, The *Song of Songs*, *Ecclesiastes*, and *Proverbs*, form part of the Bible, for having been written previously.

(2) The author of *Tiferet Yisrael* explains that new paper also means paper that is blank and clean without anything written on it. Anything written on such paper can be easily read even though the ink dries out in time. That is why the Talmud says that something learned as a child with a fresh mind is not easily forgotten, which is not true when one learns at an advanced age. In spite of the fact that an older person generally understands more than a child, he is always liable to forget what he has learned. That is as if the lesson had been written on rubbed paper that bears traces of what had been written on it before it was erased. When the ink dries the words disappear completely and cannot be read.

Other commentators explain this in the following way, all that is learned in childhood is as if were engraved on stone. Hence, it is difficult to erase what has been written on it, while everything that is learned in old age is as if it were written in the sand.

VERSE 4:26

4:26. Rabbi Yose ben Yehudah of Kefar Bavli (1) would say, one who learns from the young, what is he like? Like one who eats unripe grapes and drinks wine [directly] from the winepress. But one who learns from the elderly, what is he like? Like one who eats ripe grapes and drinks wine that has aged.

כו רַבִּי יוֹסֵי בַּר יְהוּדָה אִישׁ כְּפַר הַבַּבְלִי אוֹמֵר: הַלּוֹמֵד מִן הַקְּטַנִּים, לְמָה הוּא דוֹמֶה, לְאוֹכֵל עֲנָבִים קֵהוֹת, וְשׁוֹתֶה יַיִן מִגִּתּוֹ. וְהַלּוֹמֵד מִן הַזְּקֵנִים, לְמָה הוּא דוֹמֶה, לְאוֹכֵל עֲנָבִים בְּשׁוּלוֹת, וְשׁוֹתֶה יַיִן יָשָׁן.

---

(1) Rabbi Yose came from a town in Gallilee called Babylonian village (Kefar Bavli). He compares the young person, who in spite of his studies does not have enough experience to transmit his teaching, to unripe grapes, unlike a mature teacher. Unripe grapes are bitter to the teeth, and wine when still in the winepress is not yet aged; such is the teaching of the young. Ripe grapes are tasty to the palate, and aged wine, which is beneficial to the health, represent the words of the elderly and their teaching, which go accompanied with life experience gained through the years.

VERSE 4:27

4:27. Rabbi Meir (1) used to say, do not look at the barrel, but its contents. There are new barrels that contain old wine and old barrels that have not even contained new wine.

כז רַבִּי מֵאִיר אוֹמֵר: אַל תִּסְתַּכֵּל בַּקַּנְקַן, אֶלָּא בְּמַה שֶּׁיֵּשׁ בּוֹ, יֵשׁ קַנְקַן חָדָשׁ מָלֵא יָשָׁן, וְיָשָׁן שֶׁאֲפִילוּ חָדָשׁ אֵין בּוֹ.

---

(1) It is not known for certain whether the author of this saying was Rabbi Meir or Rabbi Yehudah ha-Nasi. Some books mention the first, while others the second. The words seem to contradict what was said in the previous Mishnah. Here it says that the age of the teacher should not form the basis of judging his capacity as such. Youth is not always synonymous with inexperience and age with wisdom. One should not take into account the age of the teacher to judge his intellectual capacity, because there can be young teachers full of maturity resembling the new barrels filled with aged wine.

In my opinion, all are in agreement that one should study with a teacher whose learning is solid and clear, without considering his age, but nevertheless, an older teacher with years of experience is generally to be preferred over a young one, although there may be exceptions.

VERSE 4:28

4:28. Rabbi Elazar HaKappar said, envy (1), desire (2), and conceit (3) remove a person from the world.

כח רַבִּי אֶלְעָזָר הַקַפָּר אוֹמֵר: הַקִנְאָה וְהַתַּאֲוָה וְהַכָּבוֹד מוֹצִיאִין אֶת הָאָדָם מִן הָעוֹלָם.

---

(1) The envy spoken of here refers to that which arises from the desire to possess more wealth, more honors, etc. than others. It also alludes to the person who is pained and displeased by the success of others. However, the desire to be as intelligent, studious, noble, and well educated as someone else is a positive quality and not something bad. On the contrary, it is recommended since it helps a person to improve himself.

(2) Here, desire refers to gluttony, lust and other carnal desires, which are unhealthy when excessive.

(3) Conceit implies running after honors and the ambition to have

them with or without having earned them. The Midrash (*Tanhuma, Vayikra* 4) says, "He who runs after honors, honors flee from him. But on the contrary, he who flees from honors, honors run after him."

These three defects contribute to the shortening of the life of a person. This is due to the sadness and the arguments that they bring. They take a person from this world; that is, living in peace with society, and lead to one's personal physical and moral decay.

VERSE 4:29

4:29. He (Rabbi Elazar) used to say, Those who are born are destined to die (1) and the dead to come to life (2); the living are to be judged (3) so that they shall know, make known, and be known (4) that He is God, He is the Former (5), He is the Creator, the One who understands, He is the Judge (6), He is the Witness and the Plaintiff. He is who will judge in the future. Blessed be He in whose presence there exists no iniquity, forgetting, preferences, or receipt of bribes (7), for all is His. And know that all is in accordance with the calculation (8), and do not allow your evil inclination to give you hope that the grave will be your place of refuge (that there is no afterlife), for it is not by your will that (9) you are formed, and not by your will were you born; you live not by your will,

כט הוּא הָיָה אוֹמֵר: הַיִּלוֹדִים לָמוּת, וְהַמֵּתִים לִחְיוֹת, וְהַחַיִּים לִדּוֹן, לֵידַע לְהוֹדִיעַ וּלְהִוָּדַע שֶׁהוּא אֵל, הוּא הַיּוֹצֵר, הוּא הַבּוֹרֵא, הוּא הַמֵּבִין, הוּא הַדַּיָּן, הוּא הָעֵד, הוּא בַּעַל דִּין, הוּא עָתִיד לָדוּן. בָּרוּךְ הוּא, שֶׁאֵין לְפָנָיו לֹא עַוְלָה, וְלֹא שִׁכְחָה, וְלֹא מַשּׂוֹא פָנִים, וְלֹא מִקַּח שֹׁחַד, שֶׁהַכֹּל שֶׁלּוֹ. וְדַע שֶׁהַכֹּל לְפִי הַחֶשְׁבּוֹן. וְאַל יַבְטִיחֲךָ יִצְרְךָ שֶׁהַשְּׁאוֹל בֵּית מָנוֹס לָךְ, שֶׁעַל כָּרְחֲךָ אַתָּה נוֹצָר, וְעַל כָּרְחֲךָ אַתָּה נוֹלָד, וְעַל כָּרְחֲךָ אַתָּה חַי, וְעַל כָּרְחֲךָ אַתָּה מֵת, וְעַל כָּרְחֲךָ אַתָּה עָתִיד לִתֵּן דִּין וְחֶשְׁבּוֹן לִפְנֵי מֶלֶךְ מַלְכֵי הַמְּלָכִים הַקָּדוֹשׁ בָּרוּךְ הוּא.

and against your will, you die. Against your will, you will have to appear in judgment and reckoning before the King of Kings, the Holy One, Blessed be He.

רַבִּי חֲנַנְיָא בֶּן עֲקַשְׁיָא אוֹמֵר: רָצָה הַקָּדוֹשׁ בָּרוּךְ הוּא לְזַכּוֹת אֶת יִשְׂרָאֵל, לְפִיכָךְ הִרְבָּה לָהֶם תּוֹרָה וּמִצְוֹת, שֶׁנֶּאֱמַר: יְיָ חָפֵץ לְמַעַן צִדְקוֹ, יַגְדִּיל תּוֹרָה וְיַאְדִּיר.

Rabbi Hanania, son of Akashia used to say, the Holy One, blessed be He, wishing to render Israel the more worthy enlarged for them the Torah and its commandments. For so we may read the words of the prophet Isaiah (XLII:21), "The Lord was pleased for His righteousness' sake to magnify Torah and to make it glorious." (10)

---

(1) Rabbi Elazar wishes to remind us that by virtue of the fact that all who are born will necessarily have to die, we should therefore follow the paths of God in this world, and be guided by the teachings of the Torah and righteousness.

(2) One of the thirteen principles of the Jewish faith is the belief in the resurrection of the dead. According to the Prophet Daniel (XII:2) "And many of those who sleep in the dust of the earth shall awake, some to everlasting life, and some to shame and everlasting contempt." Therefore, a person should behave in such a way that he or she may belong to the category of those who will awake to eternal life.

(3) Those resurrected will be judged on the Day of Final Judgment; also, those who may be alive at that time.

(4) So that they may know from others, and when they know, they should make it known to others now, but in the future, this will not be necessary because everyone will know it inherently, as told in Jeremiah XXXI:33, "and they shall teach no more every man his neighbor, and

every man, his brother, saying Know the Lord: for they shall all know Me, from the least of them to the greatest of them."

(5) He is the One who formed the human being, just as a potter gives form to clay, and He is its Creator. He knows all secrets and nothing can be hidden from Him, as is said in the Book of Psalms XXXIII:15, "He looks upon all the inhabitants of the earth: He who fashions their hearts alike, who considers all their deeds."

(6) By virtue of the fact that He knows all of a human being's actions, He calls one to judgment; He, being the Judge, and at the same time the Witness (Malachi III:5) "And I will come near to you to judgment, and I will be a swift witness." He will be the Plaintiff to make claims against you sometimes in this world, and He is the One who will pass judgment in the World to Come.

(7) As is written in II Chronicles XIX:7, "for there is no iniquity with the Lord our God, nor respect of persons, nor taking of gifts." This means that even for the just He makes no exception, but rewards all good deeds and punishes all evil.

(8) Faults [sins] even little ones reach a high level when they are many.

(9) According to the Kabbalah, the soul does not desire to leave its repose in Heaven and come into this world. This is done against its will, just as a baby resists leaving its mother's womb, and is born by force, which is why it comes out crying. Likewise, there are people who wish for death because of their suffering and other diverse reasons, yet God does not take them from life; others desire to continue living, but cannot escape death when their time comes. Finally, whether one wishes to or not, a person will have to give an account of all that one did in this world before the Supreme King of Kings, God.

(10) See the commentary at the end of Chapter 1.

Chapter v פרק ה'

VERSE 5:1

"All Israel has a share in the World to Come…" (1)

5:1. The world was created with ten (divine) decrees (2). What does this teach us? That God could have created it with only one decree (3), (but He did not). This was so in order to punish the wicked who destroy the world created with ten decrees, and to reward the just who sustain the world created with ten decrees.

"כָּל יִשְׂרָאֵל יֵשׁ לָהֶם חֵלֶק לָעוֹלָם הַבָּא, שֶׁנֶּאֱמַר: וְעַמֵּךְ כֻּלָּם צַדִּיקִים, לְעוֹלָם יִירְשׁוּ אָרֶץ, נֵצֶר מַטָּעַי מַעֲשֵׂה יָדַי לְהִתְפָּאֵר."

א בַּעֲשָׂרָה מַאֲמָרוֹת נִבְרָא הָעוֹלָם. וּמַה תַּלְמוּד לוֹמַר, וַהֲלֹא בְּמַאֲמָר אֶחָד יָכוֹל לְהִבָּרְאוֹת, אֶלָּא לְהִפָּרַע מִן הָרְשָׁעִים שֶׁמְּאַבְּדִין אֶת הָעוֹלָם שֶׁנִּבְרָא בַּעֲשָׂרָה מַאֲמָרוֹת, וְלִתֵּן שָׂכָר טוֹב לַצַּדִּיקִים שֶׁמְּקַיְּמִין אֶת הָעוֹלָם שֶׁנִּבְרָא בַּעֲשָׂרָה מַאֲמָרוֹת.

---

(1) See commentary at the beginning of Chapter I.

(2) The Talmud (*Rosh haShanah* 32) mentions the nine *vayomer* (and God said) that are in the first and second chapters of Genesis as nine expressions of the Creation of the world, and the word *Bereshit* (in the beginning) as the tenth expression, considering it an expression of God as is written in Psalm xxxiii:6, "By the word of the Lord were the heavens made; and all the host of them by the breath of His mouth." These *vayomer* are found in Chapter I of Genesis, verses 3, 6, 9, 11, 14, 20, 26, 29 and in Chapter II, verse 18. Adding to these the word *Bereshit,* as we explained, the total comes to ten. Meanwhile, there are other commentators who come to this figure differently by including other expressions of Creation in which *vayomer* is not written, as for example, "And God created the great crocodiles, and every living creature that moves, which the waters brought forth abundantly."

(Genesis 1:21) There are also commentators who include the *vayomer* of Ch. II: 18, "And the Lord God said, it is not good that man should be alone," in other words, the sacred institution of marriage. The mystics affirm that these ten expressions of Creation represent the ten emanations (*sefirot*) by means of which God, the *Ein Sof* (the Infinite One), reveals Himself to human beings.

(3) God used the word *vayomer* (and He said) for each act of Creation when He could have created the world saying this word only once by saying "And God said, let the heavens, the earth, the seas, etc. be made." Nevertheless, He created the world in ten stages, describing the details of each one, with the aim of showing the great importance of the work, and to warn the wicked that their actions destroy the world that was created by ten decrees. To destroy what was created in only one day is not as serious as destroying what was made in several.

VERSE 5:2

5:2. There were ten generations from Adam to Noah (1) so that we should know how slow God is to anger (2). All these generations continued to provoke His wrath until He brought upon them the waters of the flood.

ב עֲשָׂרָה דוֹרוֹת מֵאָדָם וְעַד נֹחַ, לְהוֹדִיעַ כַּמָּה אֶרֶךְ אַפַּיִם לְפָנָיו, שֶׁכָּל הַדּוֹרוֹת הָיוּ מַכְעִיסִין וּבָאִין, עַד שֶׁהֵבִיא עֲלֵיהֶם אֶת מֵי הַמַּבּוּל.

---

(1) These ten generations are: Adam, Seth, Enosh, Kenan, Mahalel, Yered, Enoch, Methuselah, Lemekh and Noah. The Bible generally counts the most outstanding son as the successor and as a new generation. This is the reason why Cain and Abel, who were the first and second sons of Adam, were not counted, while on the other hand, Seth, who was the third son, represents the next generation after Adam.

(2) "Slow to anger" ["long suffering" in some translations] is one of the thirteen attributes of God as revealed to Moses in Exodus XXXIV:6.

(These attributes are repeated in the prayers for the Day of Atonement.) Wickedness in its diverse aspects was the sin of these ten generations, and God was slow to anger until He brought the flood in the tenth generation.

VERSE 5:3

5:3. There were ten generations between Noah and Abraham (1). This shows how patient God was in His wrath, for each of these generations continued to provoke His anger until our father Abraham appeared and received the reward that all of them could have earned (2).

ג עֲשָׂרָה דוֹרוֹת מִנֹּחַ וְעַד אַבְרָהָם, לְהוֹדִיעַ כַּמָּה אֶרֶךְ אַפַּיִם לְפָנָיו, שֶׁכָּל הַדּוֹרוֹת הָיוּ מַכְעִיסִין וּבָאִין, עַד שֶׁבָּא אַבְרָהָם אָבִינוּ וְקִבֵּל שְׂכַר כֻּלָּם.

---

(1) The ten generations from Noah to Abraham (without counting Noah) are: Shem (even though Japheth was the eldest of Noah's son), Arpachshad, Shelach, Eber, Peleg, Reu, Serug, Nachor, Terach, and Abraham. In the first ten generations, God did not bring the flood upon them, according to the Midrash, until seven days after the death of Methuselah, the Just, because He takes into consideration the merit of the just so as not to inflict calamities, even to the wicked, as we find in the episode of Sodom and Gomorrah (Genesis XVIII:24–33).

(2) The ten generations between Noah and Abraham were also wicked, but they were saved from destruction because of Abraham's merit, who in spite of having followed corrupt generations and having lived with his father Terach who was an idol worshipper, he was not influenced by the evil example of the people of his age. On the contrary, he practiced justice, and guided the world to the path of truth and repentence, saving them all. Consequently, he merited the reward due to these ten generations (if they had been good).

VERSE 5:4

5:4. Our patriarch Abraham was subjected to ten tests and withstood them all, giving proof of the great depth of his love (of God) (1).

ד עֲשָׂרָה נִסְיוֹנוֹת נִתְנַסָּה אַבְרָהָם אָבִינוּ וְעָמַד בְּכֻלָּם, לְהוֹדִיעַ כַּמָּה חִבָּתוֹ שֶׁל אַבְרָהָם אָבִינוּ.

---

(1) These ten tests were:
 i. When, according to the Midrash, King Nimrod cast him into the burning furnace in the city of Ur of the Chaldees.
 ii. When God told him, "Get thee out of thy country…" (Genesis XII:1).
 iii. When there was famine in the land of Canaan and Abraham went down to Egypt (Genesis XII:10).
 iv. When God tested him regarding his wife Sarah (Genesis XII:11–20).
 v. Upon the occasion of the war against Amrafel and his allies (Genesis XIV:14–20).
 vi. At the covenant made [with God] by the dividing the animals and birds in half (Genesis XV:9–11).
 vii. When God tested him by asking him to be circumcised at an advanced age (Genesis XVII:9–27).
 viii and ix. When God told him, "Cast out this bondwoman [Hagar] and her son [Ishmael] (Genesis XXI:10).
 x. When God told him, "Take now thy son, thy only son, Isaac… and offer him there [Moriah] for a burnt offering" (Genesis XXII:2). Some commentators list other tests instead of these ten, but all agree that there were ten.

The reason why God tested Abraham is explained in the Midrash in this way: Psalm XI:5, it says, "the Lord tries the righteous", for the righteous accept suffering with love, while the wicked rebel whenever anything goes wrong. That is why it is written in the Torah, "And thou shalt remember all the way which the Lord, thy God, led thee these forty years in the wilderness to humble thee, and to prove thee, to know what is in thy heart, whether thou wouldst keep His commandments, or no."(Deut. VIII:2) If a person accepts with love the tests of the Lord, He will reward that person eventually, as is written in Deut. VIII:16, "And that He might prove thee to do thee good at the latter end."

The patriarch Abraham was called "friend" of God (Isaiah XLI:8), and therefore, withstood all the tests, demonstrating in this way his great love of God.

With regard to the tenth test, it seems strange at first sight that God should test whether Abraham would withstand the trial of sacrificing Isaac or not. Besides, in Genesis XXII:12, the Lord calls out to him [when he is about to slay Isaac] and says, "for now I know that thou fearest God, seeing that thou hast not withheld thy son, thy only son from Me." The answer to this is found in the various explanations of the commentators, such as, Maimonides, Saadia Gaon, and others. The test mentioned here consists not in the carrying out of an act in itself, but the intention to do so. This serves as an example of how we should behave in such a case. The expression, "For now I know…" signifies that for this act you earned the merit to be called "God fearing", and humanity will know the degree to which the fear of God should extend.

There is no one in the world who is not put to a test by God. He tries the rich in their behavior towards the poor, and the poor in their willingness to accept suffering without rebelling. He tries the righteous like Abraham knowing beforehand that he would do His bidding, only to show humanity the virtue of the just person.

VERSE 5:5

5:5. Ten miracles were wrought for our forefathers in Egypt (1), and ten others at the Red Sea (2). The Holy One, Blessed be He, inflicted ten (3) plagues upon the Egyptians in Egypt (4) and ten at the Red Sea (5).

ה עֲשָׂרָה נִסִּים נַעֲשׂוּ לַאֲבוֹתֵינוּ בְּמִצְרַיִם, וַעֲשָׂרָה עַל הַיָּם. עֶשֶׂר מַכּוֹת הֵבִיא הַקָּדוֹשׁ בָּרוּךְ הוּא עַל הַמִּצְרִים בְּמִצְרַיִם, וְעֶשֶׂר עַל הַיָּם.

---

(1) These ten miracles consist also in the fact that the Hebrews were not harmed by the diverse calamities that God inflicted upon the Egyptians.

(2) The ten miracles that occurred at the Red Sea are as follows:

 I. the waters divided (Exodus XIV:21)

 II. The sea became like a tent cover, and the Hebrews entered into it. (Exodus XIV:22)

 III. The bottom of the sea became dry ground, without clay or mud. (Exodus XIV:22)

 IV. The sea turned to clay and mud when the Egyptians passed. (Exodus XIV:24–5)

 V. The waters of the sea dried and broke into pieces. (Psalm LXXIV:15)

 VI. The waters of the sea dried up and broke into hard dry crags that broke the heads of the Egyptians, compared to sea monsters. (Psalm LXXIV:14)

 VII. The sea was divided into twelve paths so that each of the twelve tribes would pass through them. (Psalm CXXXVI:13)

 VIII. The waters of the sea were transparent so that the tribes could see each other through them. (See the commentary of Rabbi Ovadiah of Bertinoro on Psalm XVIII:12.)

 IX. The sea-water became fresh and sweet so that the Hebrews could drink (this is derived from the Hebrew word *nozelim* (Exodus XV:8)

x. After the children of Israel drank the water, it congealed and turned into heaps of ice (ibid).

(3) In most books, Verse v:6 begins here. For this reason, number six of this book corresponds to number 7 in those others, etc.

(4) As is known, the ten plagues are: blood, frogs, vermin, wild beasts, cattle plague, boils, hail, locusts, darkness, and the smiting of the first born. (All these are spoken of in the Book of Exodus from Chapter vii:19 to xii:31.)

(5) These are the ten plagues that were inflicted upon the Egyptians in the Red Sea:
  i. Horse and rider were thrown into the sea. (Exodus xv:1)
  ii. Pharaoh's chariots and those of his army were thrown into the sea. (Exodus xv:4)
  iii. His chosen captains were drowned in the sea. (Exodus xv:4)
  iv. The depths of the sea covered them. (Exodus xv:5)
  v. They sank into the bottom of the sea like stones.
  vi. He [the Lord] triumphed over the enemy. (Exodus xv:1)
  vii. He overthrew those who rose up against Him. (Exodus xv:7)
  viii. He sent forth His anger and consumed them as stubble. (ibid.)
  ix. The sea covered them. (Exodus xv:10)
  x. "they sank as lead in the mighty waters." (ibid.)

In the Passover Haggadah, however, the number of all the miracles is considerably increased.

VERSE 5:6

5:6. Our ancestors tried the Holy One, Blessed be He, ten times in the desert (1), as is told in Numbers xiv:22, "…all those men who have seen My glory… and yet have tempted Me now these ten times, and have not hearkened to My voice."

וֹ עֲשָׂרָה נִסְיוֹנוֹת נִסּוּ אֲבוֹתֵינוּ אֶת הַמָּקוֹם בָּרוּךְ הוּא בַּמִּדְבָּר, שֶׁנֶּאֱמַר: וַיְנַסּוּ אֹתִי זֶה עֶשֶׂר פְּעָמִים, וְלֹא שָׁמְעוּ בְּקוֹלִי.

---

(1) Of these ten trials, the doubt of the Hebrews in the existence of God is not one of them. Their doubt was whether God was with them or not. (Exodus xvii:7) "Is the Lord among us or not?"

The ten trials were:

I. They made the Golden Calf (Exodus xxxii:4)

II. They complained that they had no water at a place called Rephidim. (Exodus xvii:3)

III. They rebelled when they came to the Red Sea. (Psalm cvi:7)

IV. In the place that is between Paran and Tofel, when ten of the twelve spies sent by Moses came back with a false report. (Numbers xiii:32)

V. At Tofel, with regard to the Manna left over until the following day despite the advice of Moses not to eat it (Exodus xvi:20)

VI. In the place called Lavan, Korah rebelled against Moses. (Number xvi: 1,2)

VII. At Kivroth-Hattaava, when the people lusted for meat and God sent quails. (Numbers xi:33,4)

VIII, IX, and X. At Tavera, at Massa, and at Kivroth-Hattaava, the people provoked the Lord to anger. (Deut. ix:22)

Some commentators count differently or in another order. Nevertheless, there is no doubt that the case of the false report of the spies is the tenth trial, for it was at this incident that God said, "…all those men who have seen My glory, and My miracles, which I did in Egypt and in the wilderness, and yet have tempted me now these ten times, and have not hearkened to my voice." (Numbers xiv:22)

VERSE 5:7

ז עֲשָׂרָה נִסִּים נַעֲשׂוּ לַאֲבוֹתֵינוּ בְּבֵית הַמִּקְדָּשׁ: לֹא הִפִּילָה אִשָּׁה מֵרֵיחַ בְּשַׂר הַקֹּדֶשׁ, וְלֹא הִסְרִיחַ בְּשַׂר הַקֹּדֶשׁ מֵעוֹלָם, וְלֹא נִרְאָה זְבוּב בְּבֵית הַמִּטְבְּחַיִם, וְלֹא אֵרַע קֶרִי לְכֹהֵן גָּדוֹל בְּיוֹם הַכִּפּוּרִים, וְלֹא כִבּוּ הַגְּשָׁמִים אֵשׁ שֶׁל עֲצֵי הַמַּעֲרָכָה, וְלֹא נִצְּחָה הָרוּחַ אֶת עַמּוּד הֶעָשָׁן, וְלֹא נִמְצָא פְסוּל בָּעֹמֶר וּבִשְׁתֵּי הַלֶּחֶם וּבְלֶחֶם הַפָּנִים, עוֹמְדִים צְפוּפִים וּמִשְׁתַּחֲוִים רְוָחִים, וְלֹא הִזִּיק נָחָשׁ וְעַקְרָב בִּירוּשָׁלַיִם מֵעוֹלָם, וְלֹא אָמַר אָדָם לַחֲבֵרוֹ: צַר לִי הַמָּקוֹם שֶׁאָלִין בִּירוּשָׁלָיִם.

5:7. Ten miracles were performed for our forefathers in the Holy Temple (1): No woman ever miscarried as a result of the odor of the animals being sacrificed (2), The flesh of these animals never rotted (3), No fly was ever seen in the place where they were slaughtered (4), The High Priest never became ritually unfit on the Day of Atonement (5), The rain never put out the fire (6) of the wood arranged on the altar; nor did the wind disperse the column of smoke above the altar (7), No defect was found in the offering of the Omer of barley (8), nor in the bread offering (9), nor in the twelve loaves prepared for the wheat harvest of Shavuoth (10), Though the worshippers stood close to each other on foot, they had sufficient room (11), all could prostrate themselves comfortably; they were never bitten by snakes or scorpions (12), No one in Jerusalem ever said to his companion, "The place is crowded, where will I find a place to stay?" (13).

---

(1) Many miracles were performed for our forefathers as proof of the Divine Presence, but we cite here only the ten that were beneficial to the people of Israel in those times. They are not mentioned in the Torah, nor specifically alluded to. These ten miracles are evidence

of the love of the people for the Temple and for the Holy City of Jerusalem.

(2) It is known that pregnant women, when they smell foods, generally have an urge to taste them, and if they do not do so, they sometimes run the risk of having a miscarriage. Therefore, pregnant women did not enter the Sanctuary so that this would not happen to them. But if they somehow smelled the meat offerings sacrificed on the altar, nothing happened to them. When a pregnant woman feels affected by the smell of meat, the Talmud (*Yoma* 2) prescribes giving her something to eat even on Yom Kippur. I believe the reason for this miracle is that the meat of the sacrifice could only be eaten by the Kohanim (the priests). Therefore it did not affect pregnant women, or anyone who could have been harmed by not eating the roasted meat after smelling it.

(3) This refers to the organs of the sacrificial animals that burned from afternoon to night and often were not entirely consumed. They remained for many hours without smelling bad in spite of the hot climate. This can also refer to the parts of the meat that pertained to the priests who could eat them even after twenty-four hours.

(4) Flies are generally attracted to places where there is meat, blood, etc. Nevertheless, not a single fly was seen in the area of the Sanctuary where animals were slaughtered.

(5) If the High Priest had had a nocturnal emission, he would have been impure and unqualified to participate in the holy services of Yom Kippur. If so, everyone would be aware of the cause of his ritual impurity and the High Priest would be shamed.

The Talmud relates that the High Priest Ishmael, son of Kimhi, had his clothes soiled by the phlegm that came from the mouth of a notable with whom he was speaking. The stain resembled that of semen. Thus, Ishmael's brother substituted for him, but their mother considered them both as functioning High Priests for that day. She was sure of what she was doing, and when the rabbis asked her, "What right do you have for doing so?" she answered, "My merits reach the degree that not even the beams of my house have ever seen the hairs of my head." [A married woman has to keep her hair covered at all times in Orthodox Judaism.]

(6) In spite of the fact that the altar used for the sacrifices was in an open place without overhead covering.

(7) The smoke rising from the fire that burned the offerings on the altar rose vertically and the wind did not disperse it or push it downward. Thus, the smoke did not bother the eyes of the priests who were present. Likewise, the smoke resulting from the burning of the incense on the golden altar went directly and without any interference within the Holy of Holies of the Temple.

(8) An *omer* is a bundle of sheaves of barley whose volume equals 395 cubic centimeters [approx. 5 cu. yds]. It was harvested on the first day of Passover at night (the second night of Passover). On the second day of Passover an offering was made of this *omer* of barley so that God should bless the new harvest (of wheat). If any defect were found in this offering, it would not have been possible to substitute for it. (See Leviticus XXIII:9–11).

(9) These two loaves of bread, baked from the newly harvested wheat, were offered on the festival of Shavuoth in order to permit the use of the new wheat harvest of the year (See Leviticus XXIV:6). Made from wheat flour, these breads were eaten by the priests. And in order to show that the God of Israel is a spiritual divinity that does not physically eat, they would raise the table with the bread upon it every Sabbath before replacing it so that the people could see that none was missing (See Leviticus XXIV:5). King David, although he was not a priest, was obliged to eat of this bread when he was fleeing King Saul (1 Samuel XXI:7).

These three things: the *omer*, the two loaves of bread for the festival of Shavuoth, and the twelve loaves offered on the Sabbath were never found to be rancid, which is considered a miracle. The reason was that the sheaves of the *omer* harvested on the second night of Passover could not be substituted for. They were in the appropriate quantity for the meal offering; the loaves were baked on the eve of Shavuoth and offered on the following day. Likewise, the twelve loaves of the memorial offering were prepared on the eve of the Sabbath.

(11) The word "compact", in Hebrew *tzefufim* is derived from 'to float on water' and tells us that in the festivities, the people stood so close together that the feet of many of them floated in the air. Meanwhile, at the moment that each had to lie prostrate on Yom Kippur on hearing the holy name of God, it seemed that there was a distance of four cubits [A cubit is the length of the forearm from the elbow to the tip of the middle finger] between each person. This miracle occurred so that no one could hear the confession that the person lying alongside was making at that time. (See the prayer of *ve ha-Kohanim* of the Yom Kippur ritual.)

(12) The serpent and the scorpion were cited here as examples of evils. What is meant here is that no one suffered any accident in Jerusalem in the time of the Temple. The Talmud adds, "In case something bad happened to someone outside of the Holy City, he would be cured on seeing its walls."

(13) The Hebrew word *makom* meaning place, is also used as one of the names of God, giving us to understand that God is everywhere. Therefore, the interpretation of this sentence can also be the following, "No one said to his companion, 'God, (*Makom*) has no room for me here; thus, I am obliged to leave Jerusalem.'"

The literal meaning of "the place is crowded…" is that in spite of the fact that Jerusalem was overpopulated, especially during the festivities, no one complained of overcrowding or lack of lodging. Each accommodated himself as best he could, and with joy in his heart for being in the Holy City. The same feeling exists today among those who dwell in Jerusalem or any other city in Israel.

VERSE 5:8

5:8 Ten things were created (1) on the eve of the first Sabbath at twilight: the mouth of the earth (2) (to swallow Korah), the mouth of the well (3) of water in the desert, the mouth of the donkey (4) that spoke to Bilam), the rainbow (5) (of Noah), the *mana* (6) (that the Hebrews ate in the desert), the rod (7) (of Moses), the *shamir* (8) (the worm that split rocks), the form of the letters (9) (of the aleph bet); and the inscription (10) (of the tablets of the Law), the very tablets themselves of the law given at Mt. Sinai (11). There are those who say, also the harmful spirits (12), and the sepulcher of Moses (13), and the ram (14), the sacrificial offering of our patriarch Abraham. There are others who add also the tongs (15), since tongs are needed to make other tongs.

ח עֲשָׂרָה דְבָרִים נִבְרְאוּ בְּעֶרֶב שַׁבָּת בֵּין הַשְּׁמָשׁוֹת, וְאֵלוּ הֵן: פִּי הָאָרֶץ, וּפִי הַבְּאֵר, וּפִי הָאָתוֹן, וְהַקֶּשֶׁת, וְהַמָּן, וְהַמַּטֶּה, וְהַשָּׁמִיר, וְהַכְּתָב, וְהַמִּכְתָּב וְהַלּוּחוֹת. וְיֵשׁ אוֹמְרִים: אַף הַמַּזִּיקִין, וּקְבוּרָתוֹ שֶׁל מֹשֶׁה, וְאֵילוֹ שֶׁל אַבְרָהָם אָבִינוּ. וְיֵשׁ אוֹמְרִים: אַף צְבַת בִּצְבַת עֲשׂוּיָה.

---

(1) All that exists in the universe was created in the six days of Creation described in Genesis, and nothing afterwards, as King Solomon says in Ecclesiastes 1:9, "That which has been, it is that which shall be; and that which has been done is that which shall be done; and there is nothing new under the sun." Although many of the things created in the six days of Creation are not mentioned, we cite here only ten of them created on Friday afternoon before the beginning of the Sabbath, because they include so many other miracles.

(2) The mouth of the earth; that is, the power that God gave beforehand for the earth to open at that place to swallow Korah and his as-

sembly of rebels, and to close afterwards, as if it were a large beast that opens its mouth and swallows its prey. (See Numbers XVI:31.)

(3) The mouth of the well that, according to legend, was the rock that Moses struck in Horeb from which water flowed (Exodus XVII:6) allowing the Israelites to drink from it during their forty years in the desert until the death of Miriam, the Prophetess. The existence of this miraculous well was due to her merit. (see Numbers XXI:16)

(4) In my opinion, the donkey created on the eve of the sixth day of Creation is not the same as the one that spoke to Bilam. That donkey to which God gave the power of speech at this time was a descendant of the first [donkey created] for it is inconceivable that the first could have lived so many years.

(5) The first rainbow was created on the afternoon of the sixth day of Creation, but was not seen until the time of Noah. It was a sign of a covenant between God and the inhabitants of the earth that there would no longer be a flood to destroy all living beings, even though they might merit it. (Genesis IX:13–17)

(6) The *mana* which served as food for the people of Israel during their forty years of wandering in the desert (Exodus XVI:15) is not the same as that which some say falls in the same place to this day. That *mana* had many characteristics: it melted in the heat of the sun, it curdled, it could be ground in a mortar, and it could be baked. Left from one day to the next, it went bad, while on gathering a double portion on Friday, it did not spoil on the Sabbath. On Friday, much more of it fell than on the other days of the week.

(7) The rod that Moses used to perform so many miracles (See Exodus IV:17) belonged, according to some commentators, to Adam. It was made of sapphire and on it was engraved the ineffable name of God (the tetragrammaton). According to legend, this rod had been passed down to Yithro, the father-in-law of Moses, who planted it and it grew roots. In view of the fact that this seems impossible for a rod of stone, some exegetes were forced to say that Yithro's rod was the wooden

rod of Aaron, Moses' brother, that sprouted and brought forth buds and almonds (Numbers XVII:23). It was not the rod of Moses that was made of sapphire.

(8) According to the Talmud (*Sotah* 48) and the Midrash, this *shamir*, this worm, was the size of a grain of barley, and when it was placed upon the markings traced on stones, it would split them according to the sketch. It was in this way that King Solomon cut the stones with which the Temple of Solomon was built, since it was prohibited to use metal tools for this purpose. (See Exodus XX:22 and I Kings: VI:7.) Metal is symbolical of violence and destruction, and the Temple symbolizes among other things peace, unity, reconciliation, and the prolongation of life. The *shamir* was used also to raise in relief the names of the tribes of Israel engraved on the twelve precious stones of the breastplate of the high priest. It was done in the following way: lines around the letters were traced, and the *shamir* was passed along them, leaving the letters raised in relief. The existence of the *shamir* disappeared with the destruction of the Temple.

(9) The form of the letters that were inscribed on the first tablets of the Law that Moses broke (Exodus XXXII:19) [when he saw the people worshipping the golden calf]. These tablets served as a model for the second set carved by him.

(10) The inscription made by God, which could be miraculously read on both sides (See Exodus XXXII:15). According to another opinion, the inscription refers to the tool by means of which the tablets were engraved.

(11) The Tablets of the Law refers to the first tablets that Moses broke when he descended from Mount Sinai upon seeing the children of Israel worshipping the golden calf. These tablets were of sapphire and had been engraved by God (See Exodus XXXII:16.) The dimensions of the tablets were six handbreadths [2½″ to 4″] high, six wide, and three thick. When Moses broke them, they were placed in the Holy Ark, where a container of *mana* and Aaron's rod were also stored. The second tablets were engraved by Moses (See Exodus XXXIV:1).

(12) The Midrash relates that these spirits were being created with a physical likeness on the sixth day of Creation, but they were not completed because the hour of the sanctification of the Sabbath had arrived, and so God ceased his labor. Thus, they remained bodiless spirits and became evil. They are the ones who punish the wicked in hell and sometimes, in this world. Nevertheless, there exists a divergence of opinion among the Jewish sages regarding the existence of the evil spirits, commonly called demons (*ruhot raim, shedim seirim*, etc.) Rabbi Abraham Ibn Ezra (1104–1167) was one of those who categorically rejected the belief in the existence of demons.

I believe the demons are nothing more than the forces of temptation and the evil impulse, which form part of the soul of a human being since childhood, as is written in Genesis VIII:21, "…for the impulse of man's heart is evil from his youth." It is these forces that become evil spirits when they come to dominate a human being.

(13) According to tradition, Moses' burying place is found in a cavern that was created on the sixth day of Genesis. This cavern was hidden by God since the death of Moses, and it is thus, that no one has been able to find it. (See Deut. XXXIV:6.)

(14) In my opinion, this ram is not the same as the one created in Genesis, but one of its descendants, designated since Creation for this purpose (See Genesis XXII:13).

(15) In view of the fact that in order to manufacture a pair of tongs, generally, another one is needed to grasp the one that is being made, there are those who believe that the first tongs must have been made by God. However, this opinion has been refuted in the Talmud (See Ovadiah of Bertinoro) in that it is said that the first tongs could have been made by means of a mould made by man. According to the first opinion, the first tongs were made by God in order to fashion the holy objects of metal that were used in the Temple.

VERSE 5:9

ט שִׁבְעָה דְבָרִים בְּגֹלֶם וְשִׁבְעָה בְּחָכָם. חָכָם אֵינוֹ מְדַבֵּר לִפְנֵי מִי שֶׁגָּדוֹל מִמֶּנּוּ בְּחָכְמָה וּבְמִנְיָן, וְאֵינוֹ נִכְנָס לְתוֹךְ דִּבְרֵי חֲבֵרוֹ, וְאֵינוֹ נִבְהָל לְהָשִׁיב, שׁוֹאֵל כְּעִנְיָן וּמֵשִׁיב כַּהֲלָכָה, וְאוֹמֵר עַל רִאשׁוֹן רִאשׁוֹן וְעַל אַחֲרוֹן אַחֲרוֹן, וְעַל מַה שֶּׁלֹּא שָׁמַע אוֹמֵר לֹא שָׁמַעְתִּי, וּמוֹדֶה עַל הָאֱמֶת. וְחִלּוּפֵיהֶן בַּגֹּלֶם.

5:9. There are seven characteristics of the fool (1), and seven of the wise man. The wise man does not speak before one who is superior to him in knowledge (2); he does not interrupt when his fellow man (3) is speaking; he does not rush to answer (4); he asks questions about the topic that is being discussed, and he answers appropriately (5); he speaks about the first point first, and the last, last (6); regarding what he has not heard (learned), he says, "I have not heard (learned) that." (7); he admits the truth (8). It is characteristic of the fool to do all the opposite.

---

(1) Here are described the seven categories of persons who, by their manner of carrying on a conversation, identify what they are. The Hebrew word *golem*, translated here as a stupid or foolish person, is different from the Hebrew word *bur* or *am ha-arets*. The literal meaning of *golem* is an unformed or amorphous mass. Jewish mysticism of the Middle Ages believed in the possibility of giving the breath of life to a human form made of clay or wood, and called it a *Golem*. The poet Ibn Gabirol created a female *Golem* who attended him. The most famous *Golem* was created by Rabbi Loew of Prague in the year 1600. The word *golem* is applied to a person who may have moral and intellectual qualities, but is deficient in other ways, disorganized, and not polished.

A *bur* is a person who does not possess intellectual or moral virtues, and who lacks a normal upbringing, but nevertheless, has no wickedness in his heart. In other words, the *bur* is neither good nor bad.

As for the *am ha-arets*, this is a person who may have good moral virtues, but is lacking in knowledge of Torah, Talmud, or any other Jewish learning. The majority of the leaders of Jewish communities are, in my experience, *am ha-arets*. They devote themselves to social and beneficent works for the general welfare, but at the same time, they cause problems for rabbis, due to erroneous concepts that some of them have in this regard. On the other hand, there also exist, although rarely, synagogue presidents and community leaders who are knowledgeable of Jewish law. Others, in spite of being *am ha-arets*, are highly respectful and worthy of fulfilling their sacred duties in Jewish congregations. Therefore, it is the duty of each member of a congregation to select leaders of these last two types.

(2) Generally, a person who has a certain degree of culture is inclined to demonstrate it before others, but the true sage is he who refrains himself and has the patience to listen to what one who is wiser or more experienced than he may say. The Torah cites the example of Elazar and Itamar, the sons of Aaron, who dared not speak in the presence of their father who was wiser than they, and allowed Aaron to speak to Moses when the latter had gotten angry with them. (See Leviticus x:16–20.)

(3) He does not interrupt until his companion finishes saying all that he has to say in order not to confuse him, even if his companion is inferior to him. An interruption is considered an insult when it concerns a wiser or older person. Aaron did not interrupt Moses in the incident referred to above even though he knew beforehand that Moses was incorrect in his judgment. Another example of the same type can be found in the dialogue between God and the patriarch Abraham with regard to the destruction of the people of Sodom and Gomorrah. God allowed Abraham to speak until he finished and had no more to say. (See Genesis xviii:30–32.)

(4) People who are quick to respond, without prior thought, are apt to make mistakes. That is why they should not answer without having analyzed what they are going to say as much as possible, particularly if they are minors in the presence of adults or of those more learned

than they. We find a good example of this in Elihu, the youngest of the friends who visited Job. He was the last to speak although he possessed sufficient sagacity and wisdom to do so. (See Job XXXII:4–6.)

(5) In the Talmud (*Shabbat* 3), Rabbi Hiya recommended to Rav (Aba Ariha), "When you find yourself with the Master, and he is speaking about a certain tractate of the Talmud, don't ask him questions about another tractate; that is, when he is discoursing on a certain topic, don't talk to him about another." Another example: In the Torah, it says that the children of Israel asked Moses the Prophet about those who were impure and could not celebrate the Passover at the proper time. This occurred when Moses was speaking then about the holiday of Passover. To answer as is fit signifies also that just as the question should be asked clearly, with knowledge and intelligence, the answer should also be clear, learned, and intelligible. For example, the Torah relates that Jacob, the patriarch, did not wish to send his youngest son, Benjamin, to Egypt with his brothers. Reuven, the eldest son, answered (Genesis XLII:37), "Slay my two sons if I bring him not to thee." (The answer is quite foolish for what grandfather would kill his beloved grandchildren.) The fourth son, Yehudah, on the other hand, answered correctly, saying (Genesis XLIII:9) "I will be surety for him; of my hand shalt thou require him: if I bring him not to thee, and set him before thee, then I shall have sinned to thee forever." It is for this reason that Jacob took into consideration the words of Yehudah and not those of Reuven, which he considered inappropriate.

In my opinion, "to answer as is proper" (*kahalachah*), also means that the answer of the Jewish sage has to be "in accordance with the *Halachah*" (the legal decision based upon the teachings of the Torah and its commentaries). Likewise, I must add, that among the qualities of the sage is the fact that his questions and answers go directly to the grain and touch upon the relevant matter without circumlocutions or superfluous words.

(6) The author of *Avoth* of Rabbi Natan gives us the example of Rebecca to Eliezer when the latter asked her, "Whose daughter art thou? Tell me, I pray thee, is there room in thy father's house for us

to lodge in?" and she replied, "I am the daughter of Betuel." adding, "We have both straw and provender enough, and room to lodge in." (Genesis XXIV:23–25)

(7) The true wise man is not ashamed to say when he does not know the answer to the question asked of him, "I don't know." In contrast, those who do not possess this virtue answer whatever comes to their head, and do not care about the possibility of falling into error and causing others to err. The paragon of humility in this regard was Moses, who when asked how those who were in a state of impurity could celebrate the Passover, answered, "stand still, and I will hear what the Lord will command concerning you." (Numbers IX:8) In other words, he told them, "I don't know; I am going to ask."

(8) On the occasion in which the daughters of Zelophehad who claimed to have a right to the inheritance of their father, God gives us the example when he said to Moses, "The daughters of Zelophehad are right: thou shalt surely give them a possession of inheritance among their father's brethren" (Numbers XXVII:6) This teaches people that they should have the courage to admit the truth.

VERSE 5:10

5:10. Seven types of calamities come to the world (1) because of seven underlying sins (2). When some set aside the tithe (3) and others do not, famine comes due to drought; some suffer hunger while others have just enough to eat (4). If no one decides to set aside (to pay) the tithe, famine occurs due to popular uprisings (5) and the drought. And if they decide not to set aside the offering of *Challah* (the portion of dough consecrated to the *Kohanim* – priests), a famine of extermination occurs (6).

י שִׁבְעָה מִינֵי פֻּרְעָנִיּוֹת בָּאִין לָעוֹלָם עַל שִׁבְעָה גוּפֵי עֲבֵרָה. מִקְצָתָן מְעַשְּׂרִין וּמִקְצָתָן אֵינָן מְעַשְּׂרִין, רָעָב שֶׁל בַּצֹּרֶת בָּא, מִקְצָתָן רְעֵבִים וּמִקְצָתָן שְׂבֵעִים. גָּמְרוּ שֶׁלֹּא לְעַשֵּׂר, רָעָב שֶׁל מְהוּמָה וְשֶׁל בַּצֹּרֶת בָּא. וְשֶׁלֹּא לִטֹּל אֶת הַחַלָּה, רָעָב שֶׁל כְּלָיָה בָּא.

---

(1) According to traditional beliefs, whatever calamity befalls the world is due to the transgressions committed by human beings. Therefore, when such a misfortune occurs to the individual or collectively, everyone should examine his or her actions carefully with the aim of avoiding calamities, which are considered chastisements from heaven.

(2) Rav Tifereth Israel translates the words *gufe averoth* as sub multiples; i.e. partial transgressions lesser in quantity and character of complete sins.

(3) The Sabbatical year (*Shemita*) takes place every seventh year since the date of the Creation of the world. During this year, all work of the field such as plowing, planting, etc. was prohibited so that the land could rest according to the commandment of the Torah (Leviticus xxv:2). In the first and second year of the *shemita*, the Israelites were to separate what the land produced, the first tithe (10%) for the Levites (*maaser rishon*), and the second (*maaser sheni*) for themselves to be eaten in Jerusalem. They were to do the same

in the fourth and fifth year. But in the third year and sixth years of the *shemita*, they set aside the first tithe and the tithe for the poor (*maaser ani*) that was destined for the landless, the travelers, the orphans, and the widows.

The contribution of the *Maaser* was obligatory only in the land of Israel, not outside of it, but the prophets decreed that the Law of the *maaser ani* (the tithe for the poor) was also to be in effect in bordering countries, even in the Sabbatical year in which no tithe was obligatory in the Holy Land.

(4) When some separate any of the tithes previously mentioned and others do not, the punishment from heaven is a lack of rain and dew, and consequently, the poor suffer hunger due to the high cost of food, and only the wealthy have enough to live on. The penalty for making personal use of the tithe destined for the Levites, etc. was not celestial death unless it dealt with the *terumah* (the 2% due the *Kohanim*) and thus it is said here that hunger due to drought would be the outcome. The prophet Haggai (Ch. 1:9–11) foretold that a similar chastisement would ensue for the sin of leaving the House of God desolate.

(5) When no one separates the tithe, the punishment that befalls the land is the lack of rainfall as well as disturbances of the populace and banditry along the roads preventing people from traveling to other places in search of food and salvation from hunger.

(6) The Torah commands that one separate for the priest a part (*challah*) of the dough made of any of the following five cereal grains: wheat, barley, spelt, oats, and rye. The amount of dough required to be separated for each *omer* (approximately 1/10 of a bushel) was: 1/24 for family use, and 1/48 to be sold, as in the case of bakers. The *omer* consisted of the volume of 45 and 1/5 eggs, which means that the cereal ground and milled into flour, has this same content. According to the Torah, said precept applies only to the Israelites living in the land of Israel, but it was the custom to separate the *challah* even outside the land of Israel so that this commandment would not be forgotten. In this case, the *challah* is separated, but instead of giving it to the priest, it is burnt in the same oven in which the bread is baked. The punish-

139

ment for the one who unlawfully ate the *challah* (the portion set aside) was celestial (spiritual) death. But here, we are dealing with the sin of not having separated the *challah*, and not of having eaten it; therefore, the punishment is famine due to a complete lack of rainfall.

VERSE 5:11

5:11. Pestilence (1) occurs in the world for crimes whose punishment, as indicated in the Torah, was death, but which were not adjudicated in a court of law; also, for having commercial dealings concerning the agricultural products of the Sabbatical year (2). The sword (3) comes upon the land for justice that is delayed (4), or perverted (5), and also for the sins of those who interpret the Torah contrary to the *halachah* (6). Wild beasts (7) come to the world (people) for swearing in vain (or falsely), and for profanation of the Holy Name (8). Exile comes to the Jew for idolatry (9), immorality (10), incest, the shedding of blood (murder), and for not allowing the land to rest during the Sabbatical year (11).

יא דֶּבֶר בָּא לָעוֹלָם עַל מִיתוֹת הָאֲמוּרוֹת בַּתּוֹרָה שֶׁלֹּא נִמְסְרוּ לְבֵית דִּין, וְעַל פֵּרוֹת שְׁבִיעִית. חֶרֶב בָּאָה לָעוֹלָם עַל עִנּוּי הַדִּין, וְעַל עִוּוּת הַדִּין, וְעַל הַמּוֹרִים בַּתּוֹרָה שֶׁלֹּא כַהֲלָכָה. חַיָּה רָעָה בָּאָה לָעוֹלָם עַל שְׁבוּעַת שָׁוְא, וְעַל חִלּוּל הַשֵּׁם. גָּלוּת בָּאָה לָעוֹלָם עַל עוֹבְדֵי עֲבוֹדָה זָרָה, וְעַל גִּלּוּי עֲרָיוֹת, וְעַל שְׁפִיכוּת דָּמִים, וְעַל שְׁמִטַּת הָאָרֶץ.

---

(1) The pestilence referred to is a plague in which many die without having been previously ill. This comes to the world for transgressions committed which merit the penalty of death at God's hands and not those of man. This is true also in the case of those whose guilt could not be proven for lack of evidence, or because they fled. However, even those condemned to death by heaven, such as those who unlawfully

ate the sacred offerings, fodder, etc., were to be handed over to a human tribunal to verify their guilt or innocence.

(2) During the Sabbatical year called in Hebrew *shemita*, when one was not supposed to plow the earth or plant, the produce that grew spontaneously in the field was shared and belonged to everybody, including the animals, and not just to the owner of the field. It is for this reason that pestilence befell as punishment to those who sold these agricultural products.

(3) The "sword" symbolizes war, since, in ancient times, the sword was the principal weapon of war. These wars occurred when justice was unduly delayed.

(4) This refers to the judge who knowing clearly the decision that should be taken in a case in order to punish the guilty party or liberate the innocent one, delays justice, or puts off his decision leaving the parties in suspense and making them suffer in uncertainty.

(5) "Perversion of justice" implies finding the guilty party innocent and the innocent one guilty. It also signifies the purposeful pronouncement of an erroneous judgment.

(6) This refers in particular to rabbis and to those who interpret the law in accordance with what is convenient for them, allowing that which is prohibited and prohibiting that which is permissible. (Halachah signifies the legal and definitive decisions reached by the sages of the Law.)

(7) This refers to wild beasts who reach populated areas, as is said in Leviticus XXVI:22, "I will also send wild beasts among you, which shall rob you of your children, and destroy your cattle, and make you few in number; and your highways shall be desolate".

(8) "Profanation of the Holy Name" signifies committing in public an arrogant transgression of the precepts of the Torah, since this may lead others to follow the bad example. It is not the same as when a person

commits the same transgressions in private, which is not considered profanation of the Holy Name, though it is still a transgression.

(9) The punishment for the worshipping of idols is exile as it says in Leviticus XXVI:30–33, "And I will destroy your high places, and cut down your images… And I will scatter you among the heathen".

(10) God will withdraw His Divine Presence from where immorality abounds (Cf. Deuteronomy XXIII:15).

(11) To allow the land to rest signifies not to plow or to plant during the sabbatical year. These activities were prohibited every seventh year since the creation of the world. In Leviticus XXVI:33–34, it is written, "And I will scatter you among the heathen…Then shall the land enjoy her Sabbaths". The number of years that the Jews were exiled in Babylonia corresponds to the exact number of Sabbatical years that had not been observed when they were in land of Israel.

VERSE 5:12

יב בְּאַרְבָּעָה פְּרָקִים הַדֶּבֶר מִתְרַבֶּה: בָּרְבִיעִית, וּבַשְּׁבִיעִית, וּבְמוֹצָאֵי שְׁבִיעִית, וּבְמוֹצָאֵי הֶחָג שֶׁבְּכָל שָׁנָה וְשָׁנָה. בָּרְבִיעִית, מִפְּנֵי מַעְשַׂר עָנִי שֶׁבַּשְּׁלִישִׁית. בַּשְּׁבִיעִית, מִפְּנֵי מַעְשַׂר עָנִי שֶׁבַּשִּׁשִּׁית. בְּמוֹצָאֵי שְׁבִיעִית, מִפְּנֵי פֵרוֹת שְׁבִיעִית. בְּמוֹצָאֵי הֶחָג שֶׁבְּכָל שָׁנָה וְשָׁנָה, מִפְּנֵי גֶזֶל מַתְּנוֹת עֲנִיִּים.

5:12. The pestilence increases in four time periods: in the fourth and seventh years after the Sabbatical year, and in each year upon the conclusion of the festival of Succoth. It increases in the fourth year if the tithe had not been given to the poor (1) in the third year; it increases in the seventh year because of the tithe not having been given to the poor in the sixth year (2). After the seventh year, it increases because the law which ordains that the produce of the land be available to all had been violated. It increases every year after the festival of Succoth in which the poor had been deprived of the portion of the harvest due them at this season (3).

---

(1) The plagues mentioned in the previous Mishnah increase in four periods of the year for not giving the poor the allotment due them, and for trading in the produce of the Sabbatical year. This is considered theft according to the Talmud (*Bava Kama* 119). Here it says that God takes away before its time the soul of one who robs the poor. This is deduced from the verses of Proverbs XXII:22–23, "Do not rob the poor: nor oppress the afflicted in the gate; for the Lord will plead their cause and rob life of those who rob them."

(2) The tithe of the poor was set aside in the third and sixth years as previously explained.

(3) The festival of Succoth is also called in Hebrew "the Festival of Ingathering" [of the agricultural products of the year] (*Hag ha-asif*). The owners of the fields had to leave a portion of it for the poor so that they could glean the loose stems [see the Book of Ruth], and the sheaves forgotten in a corner of the field that had not been harvested. This is called in Hebrew *peah*. (See Leviticus XIX:9 and Deut. XXIV:19) All this belonged to the poor, and if the owner of the field did not comply with this commandment, God would punish him with a greater pestilence after the Festival of Succoth.

VERSE 5:13

5:13. People have four characteristics: there is the person who says, "What is mine is mine, and what is yours is yours"; such a person is average (1) (neither pious, nor wicked), although some believe that the people of Sodom (2) were like this. Another one says, "What is mine is yours, and what is yours is mine." One who says that is a fool (*am ha-aretz*) (3). He who says, "What is mine is yours, and what is yours, is yours." is a pious person (4). But one who says, "What is yours is mine, and what is mine is mine." is wicked (5).

יג. אַרְבַּע מִדּוֹת בָּאָדָם. הָאוֹמֵר שֶׁלִּי שֶׁלִּי וְשֶׁלְּךָ שֶׁלָּךְ, זוֹ מִדָּה בֵּינוֹנִית. וְיֵשׁ אוֹמְרִים, זוֹ מִדַּת סְדוֹם. שֶׁלִּי שֶׁלָּךְ וְשֶׁלְּךָ שֶׁלִּי, עַם הָאָרֶץ. שֶׁלִּי שֶׁלָּךְ וְשֶׁלְּךָ שֶׁלָּךְ, חָסִיד. שֶׁלִּי שֶׁלִּי וְשֶׁלְּךָ שֶׁלִּי, רָשָׁע.

---

(1) Some commentators consider this to be the character of the average person, and characteristic of those who give charity only out of fear of God, or to show people that they are generous, and not because they are really charitable by nature. Most people are like this, and are neither pious, nor wicked.

(2) The saying in the Talmud, "*ze nehene veze lo haser*" applies to the character of the people of Sodom. What they would not lack or would be deprived of if others might benefit from, they did not allow others to share. A person who gives nothing of his own may be indifferent to the welfare of others out of selfishness, much like the people of Sodom. Their land was fertile and they had an abundance of everything, but they would not permit immigrants or guests to stay in their city. They did not allow those who had nothing to derive benefit from their possessions. Their guiding principle was, "What is mine is mine, and what is yours is yours." (Cf. Ezekiel XVI:49.)

(3) This second category, those who say, "What is mine is yours and

what is yours is mine," is not praiseworthy, because they are willing to give of their own on condition of receiving from others. Sometimes an individual will behave in this way in order to receive much more than he gives, or because he covets the possessions of others. The *am ha-Aretz* belongs to this category. As was previously explained, in spite of having deficiencies in their character, they are not considered bad or as having intentionally profaned the Law. A good person, knowing the Torah, does good and gives of his own without setting conditions, or hoping to be compensated.

(4) The Torah does not require that a person give all he owns. The truly pious and knowledgeable of Torah know that they must reserve for themselves and their family what is necessary for their well-being. For this reason, the Talmud (*Ketuboth*) recommends that a generous individual not contribute more than one fifth of his assets so that he may not fall into need and become dependent upon others. To give beyond one's means would not be piety, but foolishness.

(5) This is a person who refuses to lend moral or material aid to others, but wants everyone to help him when he is in need. He is called 'evil' rather than selfish. He is in the class of people who do not do good even if it requires no sacrifice on their part, yet when they need something, they use whatever means possible in order to obtain it, not caring if others are harmed.

VERSE 5:14

5:14. There are four types of temperament. One who is easily angered and easily appeased (1). His loss is greater than his gain. One who is not easily provoked, but likewise not easily appeased (2). His gain is greater than his loss. One who is not easily angered, but easily appeased is truly pious (3). One who is easily angered and difficult to be appeased is wicked (4).

יד אַרְבַּע מִדוֹת בְּדֵעוֹת. נוֹחַ לִכְעוֹס וְנוֹחַ לִרְצוֹת, יָצָא שְׂכָרוֹ בְּהֶפְסֵדוֹ, קָשֶׁה לִכְעוֹס וְקָשֶׁה לִרְצוֹת, יָצָא הֶפְסֵדוֹ בִּשְׂכָרוֹ. קָשֶׁה לִכְעוֹס וְנוֹחַ לִרְצוֹת, חָסִיד. נוֹחַ לִכְעוֹס וְקָשֶׁה לִרְצוֹת, רָשָׁע.

---

(1) People who are easily provoked for the slightest and even unimportant reason, but who are also reconciled easily in a matter of moments, or their anger passes even without having received satisfaction belong to the first category. The loss of such people is greater than their gain for most people do not wish to have dealings with such individuals because of their unpleasant attitude.

(2) In the second category belong those people who get angry only for important reasons, overlooking those of minor importance. Since serious affronts occur less frequently, the text calls them "slow to anger" as well as "slow to be appeased". This does not mean that it takes them long to be provoked or to be reconciled. By virtue of the fact that they are not often angered for any little thing, their body and soul are not plagued by nervous agitation. For this reason, their gain is greater in comparison with their loss. For them there is a greater possibility of regeneration since they do not get angry for any little thing.

(3) A pious person does not get angry very easily and is forbearing with all people. But a person who never gets angry is difficult to find, for even Moses, whose greatest quality was humility, lost his temper on various occasions (See Exodus XVI:20, Exodus 32:19, and Numbers XXXI:14.).

For me, it would not be advisable for a person to never get angry. Sometimes it is necessary to get angry with someone one loves so that the latter improves, as when a father gets angry with his children, a teacher with his students, etc. All is permitted when the anger is meant to be constructive. Otherwise, it is necessary to control oneself by exerting a great effort of willpower so as not to let oneself be carried away by his anger.

(4) Those who fall into the fourth category have two great defects: that of being easily angered and appeased with difficulty. Such people are called "wicked" because they have nothing good to compensate for their faults as those in the first two categories have.

VERSE 5:15

5:15. There are four kinds of students: the one who learns quickly and forgets easily; his gain is canceled by his loss (1). Another who is slow to learn, but not easily forgets; his loss is annulled by his gain (2). The one who is quick to learn and does not easily forget; this is a good quality (3). The one who is a slow learner and who forgets quickly; he is unfortunate (4).

טו אַרְבַּע מִדּוֹת בַּתַּלְמִידִים. מָהִיר לִשְׁמוֹעַ וּמָהִיר לְאַבֵּד, יָצָא שְׂכָרוֹ בְּהֶפְסֵדוֹ. קָשֶׁה לִשְׁמוֹעַ וְקָשֶׁה לְאַבֵּד, יָצָא הֶפְסֵדוֹ בִּשְׂכָרוֹ. מָהִיר לִשְׁמוֹעַ וְקָשֶׁה לְאַבֵּד, זֶה חֵלֶק טוֹב. קָשֶׁה לִשְׁמוֹעַ וּמָהִיר לְאַבֵּד, זֶה חֵלֶק רָע.

---

(1) One of the remedies for not forgetting is to repeat the material several times paying close attention to what one wishes to learn.

(2) This one is in a better position than the first because he is in the habit of repeating the lesson several times so that it stays in his mind, and he will not forget it as easily as the first.

(3) His condition is preferable to the first two. If there is a scholar-

ship to be granted to a student, it is advisable to grant it to someone of his ability.

(4) This one should pray to God to open his mind so that he won't forget what he has learned.

VERSE 5:16

5:16. There are four categories of those who give charity (1): a person who wishes to give, but does not desire that others also give; such a person has an evil eye towards others. He who desires that others give, but not he, such a person is stingy (2). One who gives and desires that others also give; he is pious. One who does not give, and wishes that others would also not give; he is wicked.

טז אַרְבַּע מִדּוֹת בְּנוֹתְנֵי צְדָקָה. הָרוֹצֶה שֶׁיִּתֵּן וְלֹא יִתְּנוּ אֲחֵרִים, עֵינוֹ רָעָה בְּשֶׁל אֲחֵרִים. יִתְּנוּ אֲחֵרִים וְהוּא לֹא יִתֵּן, עֵינוֹ רָעָה בְּשֶׁלּוֹ. יִתֵּן וְיִתְּנוּ אֲחֵרִים, חָסִיד. לֹא יִתֵּן וְלֹא יִתְּנוּ אֲחֵרִים, רָשָׁע.

---

(1) According to the Talmud, charity enriches one who practices it. This belief is deduced from verse 10 of Malachi III, "Bring all the tithes into the storehouse, so that there may be food in My house, and put me to the test with that, say the Lord of Hosts, if I will not open for you the windows of heaven, and pour out for you blessings immeasurable." Therefore, he who desires that others not give has an evil eye towards others for he does not wish them to be enriched. It can also be said that the reason why the person wishes that others not give is out of egotism. He wishes to be the only one to be known for his generosity, and he does not take into account the deprivation he causes the poor. There also exist people who, although they give charity, are pained when a close relative or friend does so. In my capacity

as a rabbi, I have heard people say, "The contribution you intend to make is too much, give less." (See Ch. 11:14.)

(2) It seems to me that this kind of person, although he feels for the poor and thus wishes that they be helped, his degree of compassion for them is not great enough for him to put his hand in his pocket to give charity, for he is miserly with his possessions, and generous with the wealth of others. The words *eno raa beshelo* (he looks with covetous eyes upon what is his) mean that it bothers him not to have given, and if he gives, it weighs upon him.

Maimonides enumerates, in his philosophical work called *Shemonah Perakim* (The Eight Chapters), the eight levels of charity, the eighth being the highest That is, to give a person the necessary means for him to support himself so that he is not reduced to asking for alms. He also praises one who lends money to another in need [to start some sort of business, perhaps] and shares with him half of the profit without charging interest on the money lent. [In this sense, the giver becomes a partner rather than a lender and shares in the profit or loss that may derive from the money given.]

According to our sages, the most perfect form of charity is that which is practiced in secret. It is considered golden. Charity performed out of obligation is compared to silver, and charity compared to copper is that of a person who never practices it, but when he is dying, asks his relatives to use his wealth for charitable purposes. He thinks that perhaps by doing so, God will spare him from death, or he does it in order to leave a good name behind him once he is gone from this world.

VERSE 5:17

יז אַרְבַּע מִדּוֹת בְּהוֹלְכֵי בֵית הַמִּדְרָשׁ. הוֹלֵךְ וְאֵינוֹ עוֹשֶׂה, שְׂכַר הֲלִיכָה בְּיָדוֹ. עוֹשֶׂה וְאֵינוֹ הוֹלֵךְ, שְׂכַר מַעֲשֶׂה בְּיָדוֹ. הוֹלֵךְ וְעוֹשֶׂה, חָסִיד. לֹא הוֹלֵךְ וְלֹא עוֹשֶׂה, רָשָׁע.

5:17. There are four characteristics of those who attend (1) the house of religious study. One who attends, but does not put into practice what he learns (2) has the reward of having attended. The other who practices, but does not attend has the reward of his practice (3). The person who attends and puts into practice what he learns is a pious person (4). But he who neither attends nor practices conducts himself sinfully (5).

---

(1) The text of this Mishnah would be better worded if it said, "There are four categories in the act of attending or not attending the house of study." The second and fourth categories refer to persons who do not attend at all.

(2) One who attends, and does not put into practice what he learns refers to the person who is not apt to understand what is being taught and does not make the effort to assimilate the material. It does not refer to the person who attends the house of study just to be there, since such a person has no hope of being rewarded for his attendance.

(3) This refers to the person who studies alone and does not attend the Synagogue (House of Study) where those who are learned in the Torah are found; or to the person who thinks he does not need their company, and therefore does not attend, although he puts into practice what he learns on his own. Such a person earns the merit of an incomplete practice, for by attending the Synagogue he would have learned and practiced much more.

(4) The pious person, although he has sufficient knowledge, attends

the house of study, for it will always be beneficial to him, both for the study as well as for the observance of God's commandments.

(5) A person who has the chance to study and observe, and does not do either one is likely to fall into evil ways.

VERSE 5:18

5:18. Four are the characteristics of those who sit in the presence of sages: the sponge, the funnel the strainer, and the sieve. The sponge absorbs everything (1). The funnel allows things to enter into one ear and go out the other (2). The strainer allows the good wine to pass through, and retains the dregs (3). The sieve eliminates the powdery flour and retains the semolina (grits) (4).

יח אַרְבַּע מִדּוֹת בְּיוֹשְׁבִים לִפְנֵי חֲכָמִים. סְפוֹג, וּמַשְׁפֵּךְ, מְשַׁמֶּרֶת, וְנָפָה. סְפוֹג, שֶׁהוּא סוֹפֵג אֶת הַכֹּל. וּמַשְׁפֵּךְ, שֶׁמַּכְנִיס בְּזוֹ וּמוֹצִיא בְזוֹ. מְשַׁמֶּרֶת, שֶׁמּוֹצִיאָה אֶת הַיַּיִן וְקוֹלֶטֶת אֶת הַשְּׁמָרִים. וְנָפָה, שֶׁמּוֹצִיאָה אֶת הַקֶּמַח וְקוֹלֶטֶת אֶת הַסֹּלֶת.

---

(1) The sponge absorbs everything, the bad liquids as well as the good, the bitter and the sweet. The student compared to a sponge absorbs all the words of his teacher, and is not capable of separating the essential from what is secondary. He is also incapable of repeating what he learned until he is forced to do so, just like a sponge that has to be wrung out in order for it to emit its contents. However, when he does transmit what he has learned, his ideas are defective and illogical because he has them mixed up in his head.

(2) The student who is compared to a funnel easily absorbs all that he is taught, but does not retain it in his memory.

(3) The third category of student, the strainer, hears everything the teacher says, and retains in his memory only the trivia.

In my capacity as a rabbi and preacher, I have found that the majority of people belong to this third category, the strainer. They hear a discourse or a sermon, they remember what is said, the parable or the joke used in the talk, and they forget the essence of the lesson or the moral of the sermon.

(4) The student compared to a sieve, upon listening to a lesson, sifts the ideas put forth, and adopts as principles all that he heard that is good, discarding the unimportant things. On the other hand, Rav Tifereth Israel tells us that the sieve is the student who takes into consideration what is secondary and casts aside the essential. But upon examining the text that says "…retains the semolina", and by virtue of the fact that the semolina is the better part of the flour, the first opinion prevails.

The famous Rabbi Meir was wont to walk with his teacher, Elisha ben Avuya, even though the latter was considered a heretic. Rabbi Meir would hear all the words of his teacher, rejecting in his mind all that was bad, and retaining only the constructive ideas. The Talmud says in regard to this, "Rabbi Meir found a nut, he ate what was good in it, and threw away the shells."

VERSE 5:19

5:19. A love that is based upon material or vain interest will disappear once the interest is gone. On the other hand, a love that is unselfish; that is, not based upon interest, will never disappear. What is an example of a love based on a shallow interest, the love of Amnon for Tamar (1). What is an example of an unselfish interest, that of the love between David and Jonathan.

יט כָּל אַהֲבָה שֶׁהִיא תְלוּיָה בְדָבָר, בָּטֵל דָּבָר, בְּטֵלָה אַהֲבָה. וְשֶׁאֵינָהּ תְּלוּיָה בְדָבָר, אֵינָהּ בְּטֵלָה לְעוֹלָם. אֵיזוֹ הִיא אַהֲבָה שֶׁהִיא תְלוּיָה בְדָבָר, זוֹ אַהֲבַת אַמְנוֹן וְתָמָר. וְשֶׁאֵינָהּ תְּלוּיָה בְדָבָר, זוֹ אַהֲבַת דָּוִד וִיהוֹנָתָן.

---

(1) Amnon was strongly attracted to Tamar (See II Samuel Ch. XIII:1–17) for her physical beauty, but did not love her for herself with a true love. He wished to possess her to satisfy his carnal desire, or rather out of egoism. Therefore, after he violated her and thus, obtained what he desired, his love for her disappeared because what motivated his love disappeared. The same happens when husband and wife love each other only physically, and as time goes on, or by accident, he or she loses his or her personal attraction. Their love is bound to disappear. Likewise, when we love a person only for his or her money, influence, etc., the day that the riches or influence is lost, the affection will also be gone. On the other hand, a love free of all material interest, is like the love between David (before he became king) and King Saul's son, Jonathan, who loved David as his very own soul (See I Samuel XVIII: 11), knowing even that David might replace him as successor to the throne. Other examples are the love of a teacher for his student and vice versa, or the love of a woman for her beloved husband and vice versa, such a love will never disappear.

VERSE 5:20

5:20. Any controversy that concerns holy purposes (1) will finally lead to a lasting result, but that which does not have a holy aim will not result in anything worthwhile. What is an example of a controversy with sacred aims: the difference of opinion that existed between Hillel and Shammai? And what is an example of an unholy controversy: the rebellion of Korah and his followers against Moses.

כ כָּל מַחֲלֹקֶת שֶׁהִיא לְשֵׁם שָׁמַיִם, סוֹפָהּ לְהִתְקַיֵּם. וְשֶׁאֵינָהּ לְשֵׁם שָׁמַיִם, אֵין סוֹפָהּ לְהִתְקַיֵּם. אֵיזוֹ הִיא מַחֲלֹקֶת שֶׁהִיא לְשֵׁם שָׁמַיִם, זוֹ מַחֲלֹקֶת הִלֵּל וְשַׁמַּאי. וְשֶׁאֵינָהּ לְשֵׁם שָׁמַיִם, זוֹ מַחֲלֹקֶת קֹרַח וְכָל עֲדָתוֹ.

---

1) The controversies that have a lasting result for the participants and their followers are debates, or discussions that arise in order to establish truths, and do not have selfish motives or the personal ambition of the speakers to gain a reputation or glory at the expense of others, or in order to discredit them. Examples of these are those that took place in the religious academies (the *yeshivoth*). Their purposes were sacred and sincere and aimed to better serve God. Such controversies are lasting and do not create animosities or rancor. Also, they contribute to solidify the mental balance of those that engage in them. The academies of Hillel and Shammai argued constantly in order to uphold their opinions in matters of religion and the application of the laws of the Torah. They aimed to discover the true meaning of the words of God found in it. Consequently, according to the Talmud, a voice would sound from heaven saying, "All are equally the words of God."

On the other hand, the controversy of Korah, Dathan, Aviram, On and their whole group against Moses, Aaron and the others chosen by God arose out of destructive aims, based on envy, lust for power, etc. Such a controversy takes a person away from the paths of God and leads to sin. It is not lasting and causes the perdition of those who initiate it and those who adhere to it, as happened in the case of Korah and his followers (See Numbers XVI).

VERSE 5:21

5:21. Whoever leads many to do good will not occasion any sin thereby (1). And anyone who leads many to sin will have no help to do penance (for the evil that he did). Moses was virtuous and led many to be virtuous, therefore the merit of many is attributed to him, as is written	כא כָּל הַמְזַכֶּה אֶת הָרַבִּים, אֵין חֵטְא בָּא עַל יָדוֹ. וְכָל הַמַּחֲטִיא אֶת הָרַבִּים, אֵין מַסְפִּיקִין בְּיָדוֹ לַעֲשׂוֹת תְּשׁוּבָה. מֹשֶׁה זָכָה וְזִכָּה אֶת הָרַבִּים, זְכוּת הָרַבִּים תָּלוּי בּוֹ, שֶׁנֶּאֱמַר: צִדְקַת יְיָ עָשָׂה וּמִשְׁפָּטָיו עִם יִשְׂרָאֵל. יָרָבְעָם בֶּן נְבָט חָטָא וְהֶחֱטִיא אֶת הָרַבִּים, חֵטְא הָרַבִּים תָּלוּי בּוֹ, שֶׁנֶּאֱמַר: עַל חַטֹּאות יָרָבְעָם אֲשֶׁר חָטָא וַאֲשֶׁר הֶחֱטִיא אֶת יִשְׂרָאֵל.

in Deuteronomy XXXIII:21, "…and he came with the heads of the people, he executed the justice of the Lord, and his judgments with Israel." Jereboam, the son of Nebat, sinned and led many to sin. Therefore the sin of many is attributed to him, as is written in I Kings XV:30, "Because of the sins of Jereboam which he sinned, and made Israel sin."

---

(1) The person who leads many to do good, teaching them Judaism and morality by means of lessons, sermons, etc., as do rabbis of congregations, schoolteachers, leaders, presidents, etc. is helped by the Creator to not commit serious sins and thus not merit eternal punishment. Such a person leads others to have merits and good deeds. The merits of the many to whom he teaches what is right are attributed to him, and are reason for him to enter paradise. (See Talmud *Yoma* 86.) Moses could not perform the 613 commandments prescribed in

the Torah, since some of these commandments are applicable only in the Land of Israel and he never entered the Holy Land. Nevertheless, he taught these precepts to the Israelites who were able to enter and fulfill them; therefore, the merit of all of them is attributed to Moses as if he, himself, had performed them.

On the other hand, one who leads many to sin does not have the help of heaven to do penance, as when a lone individual has sinned and desires to repent in order to be cleansed of his transgressions. Such a person receives the assistance of heaven in order to do so. In reality, it is difficult for a person to do penance after having led others in the wrong path and these continue to practice evil because of him. Although such a person may desire to do penance, his arrogance prevents him from doing so, not counting the sins of his followers that are attributed to him as in the case of Jereboam, the son of Nebat, about whom it is written in 1 Kings xv:30, "…because of the sins of Jereboam which he sinned, and which he made Israel sin."

In my opinion, if a person who has sinned and made others sin, will try to correct himself and teach others leading them now in the right path to do good, God will certainly take this into account. According to the Talmud, "If indeed the gates of penitence are sometimes closed, the gate of tears arising from sincere repentence is never closed."

VERSE 5:22

5:22. All those who possess these three qualities: a generous eye, a humble spirit, and a modest soul, belong to the disciples of our father Abraham. And he who may have the following three qualities belong to the disciples of Bilam, the wicked: an envious eye, a haughty spirit, and lustful desires. What is the difference between the disciples of Abraham and those of Bilam? The disciples of Abraham enjoy the fruits of this world and inherit the World to Come, as is written, "That I may cause those who love Me (like Abraham, My friend – See Isaiah XLI:8) to inherit substance (the world to come) and I will fill their treasures (in this world)." (Proverbs VII:21) But the disciples of Bilam, the Wicked, will inherit Gehinam – Hell, and will fall into the pit of perdition, as is written, (Psalms LV:24) "But Thou, Oh God, shalt bring them down into the pit of destruction: bloody and deceitful men shall not live out half their days, but I will trust in Thee." (1).

כב כָּל מִי שֶׁיֵּשׁ בּוֹ שְׁלֹשָׁה דְבָרִים הַלָּלוּ, הוּא מִתַּלְמִידָיו שֶׁל אַבְרָהָם אָבִינוּ. וּשְׁלֹשָׁה דְבָרִים אֲחֵרִים, מִתַּלְמִידָיו שֶׁל בִּלְעָם הָרָשָׁע. עַיִן טוֹבָה, וְרוּחַ נְמוּכָה, וְנֶפֶשׁ שְׁפָלָה, מִתַּלְמִידָיו שֶׁל אַבְרָהָם אָבִינוּ. עַיִן רָעָה, וְרוּחַ גְּבוֹהָה, וְנֶפֶשׁ רְחָבָה, מִתַּלְמִידָיו שֶׁל בִּלְעָם הָרָשָׁע. מַה בֵּין תַּלְמִידָיו שֶׁל אַבְרָהָם אָבִינוּ לְתַלְמִידָיו שֶׁל בִּלְעָם הָרָשָׁע, תַּלְמִידָיו שֶׁל אַבְרָהָם אָבִינוּ, אוֹכְלִין בָּעוֹלָם הַזֶּה וְנוֹחֲלִין הָעוֹלָם הַבָּא, שֶׁנֶּאֱמַר: לְהַנְחִיל אֹהֲבַי יֵשׁ, וְאֹצְרֹתֵיהֶם אֲמַלֵּא. אֲבָל תַּלְמִידָיו שֶׁל בִּלְעָם הָרָשָׁע יוֹרְשִׁין גֵּיהִנֹּם וְיוֹרְדִין לִבְאֵר שַׁחַת, שֶׁנֶּאֱמַר: וְאַתָּה אֱלֹהִים תּוֹרִדֵם לִבְאֵר שַׁחַת, אַנְשֵׁי דָמִים וּמִרְמָה לֹא יֶחֱצוּ יְמֵיהֶם, וַאֲנִי אֶבְטַח בָּךְ.

---

(1) Abraham had an eye that was content with what God had pro-

vided him. That is why he did not wish to receive any gifts from the king of Sodom of the booty from the war, [in which he participated victoriously]. (See Genesis xiv:23), "I will take nothing; from a thread even to a shoe latchet, and that I will not take anything that is thine." Abraham also had a generous eye, for he offered the three guests a piece of bread, and ended up giving them a virtual banquet (See Genesis xviii:5–8), Abraham had a humble spirit, as is written in Genesis xviii:27, "Behold now, I have taken upon me to speak to the Lord, who am but dust and ashes." Abraham's will was modest for upon addressing Sarah, he said to her (Genesis xii:11), "Behold now, I know that thou art a fair woman to look upon." Because of his controlled desire, the patriarch did not realize how beautiful Sarah was until Pharaoh's princes praised her.

Bilam, on the other hand, had an envious eye, for it is written in Numbers xxii:18, "If Balak would give me his house full of silver and gold…" which signifies that he desired silver and gold. Bilam had a haughty spirit; he agreed to go to the king Balak only in the company of princes of rank higher than the first envoys. (See Numbers xxii:14–15), Bilam had lustful desires for otherwise he would not have counseled Balak, according to the Talmud; to have the daughters of his people prostitute themselves with the sons of Israel.

VERSE 5:23

5:23. Yehudah ben Tema (1) would say, be bold as a leopard (2), quick as an eagle (3), light and fast as a gazelle, and brave as a lion (4) to do the will of your Father who is in heaven. He would also say, the shameless are destined

כג יְהוּדָה בֶּן תֵּימָא אוֹמֵר: הֱוֵי עַז כַּנָּמֵר, וְקַל כַּנֶּשֶׁר, רָץ כַּצְּבִי, וְגִבּוֹר כָּאֲרִי, לַעֲשׂוֹת רְצוֹן אָבִיךְ שֶׁבַּשָּׁמָיִם. הוּא הָיָה אוֹמֵר: עַז פָּנִים לְגֵיהִנֹּם, וּבֹשֶׁת פָּנִים לְגַן עֵדֶן. יְהִי רָצוֹן מִלְּפָנֶיךָ, יְיָ אֱלֹהֵינוּ וֵאלֹהֵי אֲבוֹתֵינוּ, שֶׁיִּבָּנֶה בֵּית הַמִּקְדָּשׁ בִּמְהֵרָה בְיָמֵינוּ, וְתֵן חֶלְקֵנוּ בְּתוֹרָתֶךָ.

to go to hell, and the shamefaced to heaven (5). Be it Thy will, Lord our God and God of our fathers, that the Temple be rebuilt (6) speedily and in our days, and that our portion be in the study of Thy Torah (7).

---

(1) The name of this tannaite appears only once in the Mishnah.

(2) The Hebrew word *namer* that dictionaries translate as tiger, leopard or panther does not have an exact equivalent in any language. According to the Talmud, it is used here as an animal born of a cross between a lioness and a pig. Being a bastard, it has extraordinary boldness like the lion without possessing its strength.

(3) Yehudah ben Tema is referring to this animal when he says, "Be bold like the *namer* and don't be ashamed to ask your teacher, even though it be often, about what you have not understood, so that you learn to better serve your Creator.

(4) The eagle is fast and it climbs and dives swiftly. The disciple of the sages should be as quick to fulfill God's commandments, even if he should have to travel long distances. The same can be said with regard to being like the gazelle, run to fulfill the commandments.

(4) This does not refer solely to physical strength, but primarily to the power to overcome the evil instinct. The truly brave are those who know how to control their impulses, as was mentioned before, "Who is truly strong? he who knows how to restrain his evil impulses." It says in the first paragraph of the *Shulhan Aruh* (*Orah Hayim*) that a person should strive to be strong like a lion, and get up early to serve his Creator. The simile of the lion teaches us that man should dedicate himself to the commandments of the Torah with all his power, as if he were a lion.

The comparison "swifter than the eagle and stronger than the lion" was adapted from what King David said about King Saul and his son Jonathan (II Samuel, Ch. 1:23), "they were swifter than eagles, they were stronger than lions" alluding to the swiftness and strength of Saul and Jonathan. In my humble opinion, the tannaite Yehudah ben Tema is showing us by this comparison that we should practice physical culture in order to have a body with the characteristics of these animals with the aim of dedicating these powers to the will of God. As is known, a healthy soul and mind are generally found in a healthy body.

(5) Yehudah ben Tema recommends, as we said, that we be bold (*az, azpanim*) – brazenfaced, to do the will of God, but he warns us not to be arrogant with people, above all towards elders and those wiser in knowledge. This would be equivalent to being arrogant towards the commandments of the Torah, and consequently worthy of hell. On the other hand, modesty and respect are signs of a good soul, less likely to sin. The Talmud (*Yebamot* 79) tells us that three characteristics distinguish the true descent from our patriarch Abraham: being modest, compassionate, and a practitioner of acts of beneficence.

(6) It is more correct to say *shetivne* (that you should build) rather than *sheyibane bet Hamikdash* (that the temple be rebuilt). I say this basing myself on the words of Psalm CXXVII, "Unless the Lord builds the house, those who build it labor in vain."

(7) By virtue of the fact that the ancient custom was, after a religious service, to pray so that God should rebuild the Temple of Jerusalem and send the Messiah soon, this prayer, in being placed here, suggests

that the Pirkei Avoth ends here and that the paragraphs that follow were added later. In Izmir, Turkey, when someone had to recite the *Kaddish de-Rabanan* (read aloud by mourners) it was the custom to say this prayer first and then the traditional "Rabbi Hanina Ben Akashya".

VERSE 5:24

5:24. He, Yehudah ben Tema, also said, "the age of five (1) is proper for the study of the Hebrew Bible (2), ten for the study of the Mishnah (3), thirteen for the observance of the commandments (4), fifteen for the study of the Talmud (5), eighteen for contracting marriage (6), twenty for looking for a means of a livelihood (7), thirty for entering into full vigor (8), forty for understanding (9), fifty for judgment (10), sixty for reaching old age (11), seventy for old age (12), eighty for vigor if specially blessed (13), ninety to be bent with age (14), one hundred to be considered already dead and gone from this world (15).

כד הוּא הָיָה אוֹמֵר: בֶּן חָמֵשׁ שָׁנִים לַמִּקְרָא, בֶּן עֶשֶׂר לַמִּשְׁנָה, בֶּן שְׁלֹשׁ עֶשְׂרֵה לַמִּצְוֹת, בֶּן חֲמֵשׁ עֶשְׂרֵה לַגְּמָרָא, בֶּן שְׁמוֹנֶה עֶשְׂרֵה לַחֻפָּה, בֶּן עֶשְׂרִים לִרְדּוֹף, בֶּן שְׁלֹשִׁים לַכֹּחַ, בֶּן אַרְבָּעִים לַבִּינָה, בֶּן חֲמִשִּׁים לָעֵצָה, בֶּן שִׁשִּׁים לְזִקְנָה, בֶּן שִׁבְעִים לְשֵׂיבָה, בֶּן שְׁמוֹנִים לִגְבוּרָה, בֶּן תִּשְׁעִים לָשׁוּחַ, בֶּן מֵאָה כְּאִלּוּ מֵת וְעָבַר וּבָטֵל מִן הָעוֹלָם.

---

(1) In this Mishnah, a Jewish and also human life is classified according to what a person should normally do or be in each of the stages of life. Naturally, this cannot be applied everywhere and in all circumstances. For example, a child going to school in the Diaspora is first taught the language of the country and other indispensable matters.

(2) When the child reaches five, the Jewish father is obliged to teach him how to read and to explain to him the Bible in Hebrew. If the

father is not capable of doing so, he should hire a teacher for the child. In the time of the author of these lines, it was done, and therefore, it was rare to see a child who did not know how to read the prayers in Hebrew and did not have a basic knowledge of our religion. Nowadays, it is not rare to see children reach the age of Bar Mitzvah without any Jewish education, and young people who know neither the Hebrew alphabet, nor the history and the traditions of our people. This gives rise to alienation and indifference towards Judaism, assimilation, and other similar ills.

In the time of Yehoshua Ben Gamla, the founder of an organized Talmudic academy, the custom was established to accept a child of six and not less into primary school. From six on, it was possible to give abundant learning material to the child, just like the ox eats until his stomach is completely full.

(3) The Mishnah is the code of religious and civil law found principally in the first five books of the Bible, the Torah. It was compiled by the tannaite, Yehudah ha-Nasi around the second century of the Common Era. Therefore, one should not study the Mishnah until one has a thorough knowledge of the Bible. That is why a child is not prepared to study the Mishnah until he has completed five years of Bible study. The same is true of the study of the *Gemara*, which is but a detailed study of the legal decisions contained in the Mishnah. The child should begin to study the *Gemara* after five years of study of the Mishnah. [This sequence was and is, in many places, followed in Sephardic *yeshivoth*, but Ashkenazic *yeshivoth* begin the Mishnah and *Gemara* much sooner.]

(4) According to the Talmud, the word *ish* (man) is applied to a boy of thirteen. This is deduced from the reference to Jacob's son, Levy, mentioned in Genesis xxxiv:25 who was thirteen years old when he and his brother, Simeon, attacked the men of Shekhem. The Torah, taking into account the fact that a youth of thirteen begins to show signs of puberty, considers him a man *(ish)*, and holds him responsible for his actions. On the other hand, the Midrash (B.B. *Korah*) and the Talmud (*Shabbath* 9: 2) says that the Heavenly Tribunal does not punish young people under twenty. Proof of this is to be found in

Numbers xiv:29, which states, of the exiles from Egypt, "from twenty years old and upward, who have murmured against Me, shall by no means come into the (Holy) land."

It was on the basis of these words of Yehudah ben Tema, "At thirteen for the observance of the commandments," that the sages of Israel instituted the Bar Mitzvah ceremony for the youth who is considered an adult.

(5) The word Talmud originally referred to the *Gemara*, which we explained above, and later was applied to both the Mishnah and the *Gemara*, the Mishnah being the text, and the *Gemara*, the related commentary. The Talmud contains the thoughts, opinions, and teachings of the rabbis who lived from the year 300 Before the Common Era to 500 C.E. The Talmud contains the religious, civil, social and moral laws developed from of the Bible and the Oral Tradition passed down from generation to generation.

(6) This means that a youth from thirteen to eighteen who is in physical, moral, and material condition to contract matrimony, but who does not do so after eighteen is considered a sinner. On the other hand, the Torah (Deut. xx:5–7) gives us to understand that a man should first own a home and have a job, and only then marry.

(7) According to one version, a young man of twenty should observe the precepts of the Bible with greater ardor, since, as we said before, The Heavenly Tribunal does not punish those of less than twenty. Another version tells us that a young man of twenty should prepare himself for military service, and be heroic in pursuing the enemies of the nation, since in the time of Moses, those of twenty and above were mobilized for war. (See Numbers 1:3). A third version tells us that a young man of twenty should persevere and look for a means of a livelihood; that is, he should work hard to support his wife and children, since it is assumed that he married at eighteen.

(8) A man is considered to be at the height of his strength at the age of thirty. The Levites who had the responsibility of putting up and taking down the tabernacle in the desert, loading and unloading heavy

objects from the carts and carrying them on their shoulders, were called into this service at the age of thirty and on up. In my humble opinion, a lot depends, in this regard, on the use and the abuse one gives the human body, and not necessarily on age.

(9) The word *bina*, which we translate as "understanding", also means the ability to judge intelligently. A sage (*haham*) may have knowledge based upon what he has studied, but an intelligent one (*navon bina*) is one who understands and extracts teachings beyond his studies (*mevin davar mitoh davar*).

(10) The Levites retired from their labors at age fifty and served as advisors to those younger. In the majority of the circumstances that a person confronts in life, there are at least two possibilities: a man who reaches fifty has sufficient mental equilibrium to choose the most proper possibility, and is in a position to give better advice, for besides his maturity; he has in his favor the benefit of his years of experience.

(11) The word *zikna* is derived from "old" in Hebrew, but the Talmud translates this word as *ze shekana hohma* (the person who has acquired wisdom). Therefore, this does not mean here that one reaches old age at sixty, but rather it refers to the wisdom that one has accumulated by sixty. His or her words are like ripened grapes and aged wine that a person enjoys eating and drinking.

(12) The tannaite wishes to remind us of the commandment of the Torah to rise to honor an older person, Jewish or gentile, as a sign of respect for age (See Leviticus XIX:32). The word *seva* which we translate as old age indicates the age of seventy, as is written with reference to King David (1 Chronicles XXIX:28), "And he died in a good old age". He had lived seventy years.

(13) It means here that one has vigor in the soul, in spite of not having it in the body; thus, it is easier for such a person to observe God's commandments. For this reason, we see that the majority of those who attend the synagogue and come closer to everything referring to

religion are the old. It was King David who said (Psalm xc:10), "The days of our years are seventy; or if by means of special strength, eighty years", which means that people with a good constitution have a longevity greater than seventy years, above all when they lead a tranquil and less complicated life. Hence, King David, having had many tribulations in his life, lived only seventy years.

(14) The Hebrew word which we translate as "crooked" or "bent" (*lashuah*) can also be read as *lasuah* which means that the person of ninety can only make conversation (*siha*) regarding the Torah; in other words, he can employ the theory and not practice it, because he lacks the strength. As for the first version (*lashuah*), this word is also derived from *shuha*, which means "grave" in Hebrew; that is, at ninety, one is close to the grave.

(15) Upon reaching the age of one hundred, a person is closer to heaven than to earth, since he feels no desire, neither physical nor material, and it is as if his body no longer existed in this world, and he possessed only a soul. However, we see in our days that in certain places in the world, as for example, in the Caucus Mountains of Russia, some people are over a hundred years old and enjoy relatively good health. Nevertheless, these are exceptions to the rule. We are speaking here in general terms.

VERSE 5:25

5:25. Ben Bag Bag (1) would say, labor (2) (in the Torah) once and once again because all can be found in it (3). Put your mind to it (4), grow gray and grow old upon it (5), and don't move from it because you will not find any good better than the Torah (6).

כו בֶּן בַּג בַּג אוֹמֵר: הֲפָךְ בָּה וַהֲפָךְ בָּה, דְּכֹלָּא בָה. וּבָהּ תֶּחֱזֵי, וְסִיב וּבְלֵה בָה, וּמִנַּהּ לָא תָזוּעַ, שֶׁאֵין לְךָ מִדָּה טוֹבָה הֵימֶנָּה.

---

(1) There exist differences of opinion with regard to the identities of Ben Bag Bag and Ben He He. According to Rav Tifereth Israel, the first is rabbi Yohanan, the son of Bag Bag, mentioned in the Talmud (*Kiddushin* 10). The exegete, Icar Tosafot Yom Tov says it deals with two rabbis who died young, and for this reason the first name is not mentioned, as we find in the case of Ben Zoma and Ben Azay, mentioned previously. Nevertheless, the exegete Rishbam (Rashbam) believes that Ben Bag Bag and Ben He He were proselytes and students of the famous Hillel. As proof, he cites that Bag (Heb. *beth gimmel*) has the numerical value of five, the same as the letter *he* of the name of Ben He He.) As is known, the patriarch Abraham and his wife Sarah (whose names were originally Avram and Saray), were the first to recruit converts. God then changed their names to Abraham and Sarah; that is, he added the letter *he* to both their names. Therefore, when one enters into the Jewish religion, it is said that he or she is the son or daughter of Abraham and Sarah. In the case of Ben Bag Bag and Ben He He, they are called thus with the hidden meaning "sons of Abraham", in other words, converts who bear the letter *he* of Abraham (See Talmud *Hagiga, Tosafot*, 9:).

(2) Labor in the Torah; that is, go over the words of the Torah and all its precepts, since all the knowledge in the world is contained in it. The Talmud (*Eruvin* 54) tells us that just as a child receives complete support from its mother and its mother's milk, in like manner, one

who studies the Torah is fed spiritually and morally, etc. to perfection through it.

(3) As a person goes over the contents of the Torah, he will always find new insights that he had not perceived in previous readings, and answers to questions or doubts that he may have had. One who studies the Torah should not confide in his memory and say, "I have already read and studied it completely." It is not the same thing to read such a profound book as the Torah once as it is to have read it many times.

The Talmud relates that someone asked Rabbi Yehoshua, "Can a Jew teach his son Greek?" Yes, he can teach him at an hour that is neither day nor night, for the verse says, "Thou shalt meditate therein (on the Torah) day and night." (Joshua 1:8)

(4) By reading the Torah very attentively, you will discover in it the truth and you will be enlightened by its light, eliminating the darkness that there may be in your heart, and God will help you to fully expand your intelligence.

(5) Although you may have studied the Torah in your youth, continue studying it fervently until advanced age, for it will contribute to maintaining your spirit lucid until the end. What difference is there between an *am ha-aretz* (one who is ignorant in matters of Torah) and a student of a sage? The *am ha-aretz* suffers mental disturbances as he ages, while the student of a sage is lucid even in advanced old age. It says in Psalm XCII:15, "They still bring forth fruit in old age; they are fat and flourishing to declare that the Lord is upright…"

(6) The Torah is the best acquisition one can obtain. One who studies and practices it enjoys its fruits in this world and its capital is kept for him in the World to Come. It is the best investment one can make. King David in Psalm CXIX:72 said, "The Torah of thy mouth is better to me than thousands of gold and silver." It is for this reason that God said to the people of Israel (Proverbs IV:2), "For I give you good doctrine, forsake not my Torah."

VERSE 5:26

5:26. Ben He He would say, according to the effort (in the study of the Torah), so is the reward. (1).

כו בֶּן הֵא הֵא אוֹמֵר: לְפוּם צַעֲרָא אַגְרָא.

רַבִּי חֲנַנְיָא בֶּן עֲקַשְׁיָא אוֹמֵר: רָצָה הַקָּדוֹשׁ בָּרוּךְ הוּא לְזַכּוֹת אֶת יִשְׂרָאֵל, לְפִיכָךְ הִרְבָּה לָהֶם תּוֹרָה וּמִצְוֹת, שֶׁנֶּאֱמַר: יְיָ חָפֵץ לְמַעַן צִדְקוֹ, יַגְדִּיל תּוֹרָה וְיַאְדִּיר.

Rabbi Hanania, son of Akashia used to say, the Holy One, blessed be He, wishing to render Israel the more worthy enlarged for them the Torah and its commandments. For so we may read the words of the prophet Isaiah (XLII:21), "The Lord was pleased for His righteousness' sake to magnify Torah and to make it glorious." (2)

---

(1) In my humble opinion, the words of Ben He He refer not only to the study of Torah and the observance of its commandments, but also to all efforts a person makes to acquire knowledge, riches or moral perfection.

Note that the words of Ben Bag Bag and of Ben He He are in Aramaic. The majority of the tannaites whose names appear in the Babylonian Talmud knew Aramaic and perhaps used it in the home and in the street to better communicate with the people even after the return of the exiles from Babylonia where this language was used exclusively, except for prayers, which were said in Hebrew. In my humble opinion, they wrote these words here in Aramaic, and Yehudah ha-Nasi left them in the original so that people would understand them better. An example of this can be found in the *Ha lahma anya* (This is the bread of affliction, etc.) that we find in the Haggadah of Passover.

This is an invitation to the poor who would walk around houses so that they might be invited to eat and participate in the Seder. The paragraph was said in Aramaic so that the poor would understand in their own language, in this case, Aramaic, that they were being invited to eat. If the invitation were made In Hebrew, they might not have understood it. Proof of what was just said is that the other parts of the Haggadah are written in Hebrew,

(2) Rabbi Hanania. See the translation and commentary at the end of Chapter 1.

Chapter VI פרק ו׳

VERSE 6:1

"כָּל יִשְׂרָאֵל יֵשׁ לָהֶם חֵלֶק לָעוֹלָם הַבָּא, שֶׁנֶּאֱמַר: וְעַמֵּךְ כֻּלָּם צַדִּיקִים, לְעוֹלָם יִירְשׁוּ אָרֶץ, נֵצֶר מַטָּעַי מַעֲשֵׂה יָדַי לְהִתְפָּאֵר.
שָׁנוּ חֲכָמִים בִּלְשׁוֹן הַמִּשְׁנָה, בָּרוּךְ שֶׁבָּחַר בָּהֶם וּבְמִשְׁנָתָם.
א רַבִּי מֵאִיר אוֹמֵר: כָּל הָעוֹסֵק בַּתּוֹרָה לִשְׁמָהּ, זוֹכֶה לִדְבָרִים הַרְבֵּה, וְלֹא עוֹד אֶלָּא שֶׁכָּל הָעוֹלָם כֻּלּוֹ כְּדַאי הוּא לוֹ. נִקְרָא רֵעַ, אָהוּב, אוֹהֵב אֶת הַמָּקוֹם, אוֹהֵב אֶת הַבְּרִיּוֹת, מְשַׂמֵּחַ אֶת הַמָּקוֹם, מְשַׂמֵּחַ אֶת הַבְּרִיּוֹת, וּמַלְבַּשְׁתּוֹ עֲנָוָה וְיִרְאָה, וּמַכְשַׁרְתּוֹ לִהְיוֹת צַדִּיק, חָסִיד, יָשָׁר, וְנֶאֱמָן, וּמְרַחַקְתּוֹ מִן הַחֵטְא, וּמְקָרַבְתּוֹ לִידֵי זְכוּת, וְנֶהֱנִין מִמֶּנּוּ עֵצָה וְתוּשִׁיָּה בִּינָה וּגְבוּרָה, שֶׁנֶּאֱמַר: לִי עֵצָה וְתוּשִׁיָּה, אֲנִי בִינָה, לִי גְבוּרָה. וְנוֹתֶנֶת לוֹ מַלְכוּת וּמֶמְשָׁלָה וְחִקּוּר דִּין, וּמְגַלִּין לוֹ רָזֵי תוֹרָה, וְנַעֲשֶׂה כְּמַעְיָן הַמִּתְגַּבֵּר וּכְנָהָר שֶׁאֵינוֹ פוֹסֵק, וְהֹוֶה צָנוּעַ וְאֶרֶךְ רוּחַ, וּמוֹחֵל עַל עֶלְבּוֹנוֹ, וּמְגַדַּלְתּוֹ וּמְרוֹמַמְתּוֹ עַל כָּל הַמַּעֲשִׂים.

6:1 "All Israel has a share in the World to Come…" (1) The sages taught (the following *baraitoth* – "lessons") (2) in the style of the Mishnah. Blessed be He (God) who chose them (3) and their Mishnah (teaching).

Rabbi Meir used to say, one who occupies oneself in the study of the Torah for the love of it (4) deserves many rewards. Not only that, but the whole world is indebted to him (5). He is called friend (6), beloved (7), that he loves God, that he loves his fellow human creatures (8); he pleases God and humanity. The Torah dresses him with (9) with qualities of humility and reverence; it makes him just, pious, righteous and faithful. It distances him from sin (10), and draws him towards virtue, and people benefit from his (good) advice, his wisdom, his judgment, and his moral strength as is written in Proverbs VIII:14, "Counsel is mine, and sound wisdom; I am understanding; I have strength." (11). It confers upon him royalty (12), authority and clarity in judgment. The secrets of the Torah are revealed unto him (13) and he becomes like a spring that does not lose its strength, and like a river whose waters are never-ending (14). He becomes chaste (pure and honest) and patient; he pardons those who insult him, and the Torah broadens him and raises him above all that has been created (under the heavens).

---

(1) See the commentary that precedes Chapter 1.

(2) The sixth chapter of the Pirkei Avoth is called *Perek Kinian ha-Torah* (The chapter of acquisition of the Law) or the *baraita* of Rabbi Meir, and is composed of several *baraitoth* (Aramaic – supplementary study). These are the teachings that do not enter into the canon of the Mishnah compiled by Rabbi Yehudah ha-Nasi. The Mishnah, as we have said, is the code of civil and religious laws gathered together in six volumes in the Second Century C.E. by Yehudah ha-Nasi. The *baraita* was written in the same style as the Mishnah and deals with the same theme, only it was not included in the official text of the Mishnah. As it is the custom to read the Pirkei Avoth in the six weeks between Passover and Shavuoth (for it was on this day, the 5th of the Hebrew month of Sivan, fifty days after Passover, that the Torah was given on Mount Sinai) that the sixth chapter was added so as not to leave the Sabbath before Shavuoth without a reading similar to the Pirkei Avoth. It deals with the praise of the Torah and of those who study it.

(3) God selected the sages of the Law for their human qualities and virtues. He also selected their studies and teachings, since they did not do them in order to glorify themselves or for their own benefit, but in order to divulge Divine Truth.

One should not think that the sages wrote this chapter praising the Torah and those who study it out of self-interest or because the Torah was their profession. It is from the Torah itself, and not from the sages of the Law, that all the virtues enumerated arise.

Another version of the Mishnah tells us that the words, "Blessed be he who chose them" refer to the compiler who selected the teachers of the Law and their teachings.

(4) For the intrinsic value of the Torah, and not out of fear that God might punish one who does not study it, and not for self-aggrandizement or with the aim of receiving some reward. On the other hand, the Talmud teaches us that although one does not study the Torah simply for the love of it, in the end, he will come to love it. (*Mitoh shelo lishmah ba lishmah*).

(5) The Torah, being the principal objective of the Creation of the world, it can be said that only for the merit of those who study it was the world created.

(6) Happy is one who joins with another who studies the Torah for he is considered the best of friends.

(7) He is beloved by all due to the qualities he acquired through the study of Torah.

(8) He loves all human beings without exception for God created them all.

(9) The virtues that a person possesses are here represented by the clothes he wears, for just as one notices his clothing, in like manner are his moral qualities noted, such as humility, the fear of God, respect for superiors, etc.

(10) The precepts of the Torah cause a person to stay away from sin, and to practice good deeds.

(11) King Solomon made the Torah speak, as if it said, "Counsel is mine and sound wisdom, etc. and one who studies me acquires all this."

(12) The Torah causes one to see the splendor of a king in one who studies it.

(13) One who studies the Torah deeply sees the secrets hidden in its

words and precepts, just as a prophet perceives things that are mysteries to others.

(14) In my humble opinion, the comparison of those who study the Law to a spring or a river means that such persons do not limit their knowledge of the Torah to what they learned from their teacher. They produce new teachings based on the Torah; they constantly progress in their studies, like a spring that does not lose its force in spewing forth water continuously, or the river whose waters are inexhaustible. (Cf. II, 11).

VERSE 6:2

6:2. Rabbi Yehoshua ben Levi used to say, day in and day out a *"bat kol"*, a heavenly voice (1) resounds from Mount Horeb and proclaims, "Woe to the people who do not revere the Torah!" This is said because all who do not engage in the study of the Torah merit reproach (2), as is written in Proverbs XI:22, "Like a jewel of gold in a swine's snout, so is a fair woman without discretion." It also says in Exodus XXXII:16, "And the Tablets were the work of God, and the writing was the writing of God, engraved upon the Tablets." This is not to be read as *"harut"* – engraved, but *"herut"* – liberty (3), for there is not to be found a free man, who does not occupy himself with the study of the Torah, and

ב אָמַר רַבִּי יְהוֹשֻׁעַ בֶּן לֵוִי: בְּכָל יוֹם וָיוֹם בַּת קוֹל יוֹצֵאת מֵהַר חוֹרֵב וּמַכְרֶזֶת וְאוֹמֶרֶת: אוֹי לָהֶם לַבְּרִיּוֹת מֵעֶלְבּוֹנָהּ שֶׁל תּוֹרָה. שֶׁכָּל מִי שֶׁאֵינוֹ עוֹסֵק בַּתּוֹרָה נִקְרָא נָזוּף, שֶׁנֶּאֱמַר: נֶזֶם זָהָב בְּאַף חֲזִיר, אִשָּׁה יָפָה וְסָרַת טָעַם. וְאוֹמֵר: וְהַלֻּחֹת מַעֲשֵׂה אֱלֹהִים הֵמָּה, וְהַמִּכְתָּב מִכְתַּב אֱלֹהִים הוּא חָרוּת עַל הַלֻּחֹת. אַל תִּקְרָא חָרוּת אֶלָּא חֵרוּת, שֶׁאֵין לְךָ בֶּן חוֹרִין אֶלָּא מִי שֶׁעוֹסֵק בְּתַלְמוּד תּוֹרָה. וְכָל מִי שֶׁעוֹסֵק בְּתַלְמוּד תּוֹרָה הֲרֵי זֶה מִתְעַלֶּה, שֶׁנֶּאֱמַר: וּמִמַּתָּנָה נַחֲלִיאֵל, וּמִנַּחֲלִיאֵל בָּמוֹת.

all who do so are exalted as is written in Numbers XXI:19, "and from Mattana (where the Torah was given) to Nahaliel (God's heritage): and from Nahaliel to Bamot (high places)".

---

(1) *Bat Kol*, which can be translated as "echo", means literally, "daughter of the voice" for it is a reproduction of the original sound. The Talmud calls it "a voice from heaven". In tractate *Yoma* 9: it says that even though communication between Israel and God ended with the death of the last prophet, His voice can be heard by means of the *bat kol*. In a controversy between the academies of Shammai and Hillel, a *bat kol* decided that the latter was correct (*Yoma Talmud Berahot* 1). On the other hand, when during a controversy a *bat kol* was heard saying that the opinion of Rabbi Elazar should prevail over that of Rabbi Yehoshua, the latter did not take it into consideration. He said, quoting Deut. XXX:11, "It (the Torah) is not in heaven," and also, in Exodus XXIII:2, the implication is that the opinion of the majority should prevail, and we are the majority." Nevertheless, many rabbis consider the *bat kol* as a voice that comes from the Divine Presence. Therefore, this voice, which descends from Mount Horeb, (Mt. Sinai) is a heavenly voice, for it was there that the Torah was given to Israel, and when people do not study it, the voice protests saying, "Woe to the people…"

(2) The word *nazuf* was taken from the first two Hebrew letters of the word *nazem* (a hoop earring) and from the last letter of the word *be'af* meaning snout. Together, they form the word *nazef* (reproach), as it appears in the verse of Proverbs cited above. The verse signifies that just as a golden hoop in the snout of a pig does not add to its beauty, a beautiful woman lacking in good qualities has no grace. A man who has no aptitude for the study of Torah, or who is knowledgeable therein, but does not observe its commandments is thus compared to a pig with a golden hoop in its snout. This can also be said of a person who has all the means, such as books, teachers, etc., and still does not study. Such people are reproachable, but their indifference does not affect the value and the sanctity of the Torah. The golden

hoop is also compared to human intelligence and knowledge when it is used for evil purposes. Those who do so are compared to pigs that wallow in mud and garbage. Intelligence and knowledge are likewise compared to a beautiful woman, whose husband gives her jewels and fine clothes, but she being slovenly does not make good use of them, and therefore, her husband scolds her. God similarly reproaches those who do not make good use of their knowledge. The Torah is compared to a beautiful woman, and one who does not give her proper respect becomes a boor.

(3) This play on words *harut* (engraved) transformed into *herut* (liberty) was not done to correct the text of the Torah, but to reveal the following thought. One who has in his heart the commandments engraved on the Tablets of the Law is considered free, for his soul is not slave to human vices and passions. This is true liberty. There are people who are physically free, but slave to their evil inclinations. The verse quoted from Numbers XXI:19 can be interpreted in this way: God has given man the gift (*matana*) of the Torah, and if he knows how to make good use of it, he inherits God's reward, by means of which he rises to the heights (*bamot*).

VERSE 6:3

6:3. One who learns from his companion (1) just one chapter or a single *halachah* (law of the Torah), or a verse, or a word, or even a single letter (2) should treat him with honor. We see this in the case of King David who learned from Ahitophel (3) nothing more than two things (4), and nevertheless called him his teacher, his guide and his familiar friend as is written in Psalm LV:14 "...but it was thou, a man my equal, my companion, and my familiar friend." Now then, if King David learned from Ahitophel only two things and called him his teacher, etc., how much more should one honor a companion from whom he learned a chapter, a law, a verse, a word, or even a single letter? And 'honor' applies only to the Torah, as it says in Proverbs III:35, "The wise shall inherit honor." (5), and in Proverbs XXVIII:10, "...but the innocent shall inherit good."(6) The 'good' referred to is nothing else but the Torah, as is written in Proverbs IV:2 "For I give you good doctrine; forsake not my Torah."

ג הַלּוֹמֵד מֵחֲבֵרוֹ פֶּרֶק אֶחָד, אוֹ הֲלָכָה אַחַת, אוֹ פָּסוּק אֶחָד, אוֹ דִבּוּר אֶחָד, אוֹ אֲפִילוּ אוֹת אַחַת, צָרִיךְ לִנְהָג בּוֹ כָּבוֹד, שֶׁכֵּן מָצִינוּ בְּדָוִד מֶלֶךְ יִשְׂרָאֵל, שֶׁלֹּא לָמַד מֵאֲחִיתֹפֶל אֶלָּא שְׁנֵי דְבָרִים בִּלְבָד, קְרָאוֹ רַבּוֹ אַלּוּפוֹ וּמְיֻדָּעוֹ, שֶׁנֶּאֱמַר: וְאַתָּה אֱנוֹשׁ כְּעֶרְכִּי אַלּוּפִי וּמְיֻדָּעִי. וַהֲלֹא דְבָרִים קַל וָחֹמֶר, וּמַה דָּוִד מֶלֶךְ יִשְׂרָאֵל שֶׁלֹּא לָמַד מֵאֲחִיתֹפֶל אֶלָּא שְׁנֵי דְבָרִים בִּלְבָד קְרָאוֹ רַבּוֹ אַלּוּפוֹ וּמְיֻדָּעוֹ, הַלּוֹמֵד מֵחֲבֵרוֹ פֶּרֶק אֶחָד, אוֹ הֲלָכָה אַחַת, אוֹ פָּסוּק אֶחָד, אוֹ דִבּוּר אֶחָד, אוֹ אֲפִילוּ אוֹת אַחַת, עַל אַחַת כַּמָּה וְכַמָּה שֶׁצָּרִיךְ לִנְהָג בּוֹ כָּבוֹד. וְאֵין כָּבוֹד אֶלָּא תוֹרָה, שֶׁנֶּאֱמַר: כָּבוֹד חֲכָמִים יִנְחָלוּ, וּתְמִימִים יִנְחֲלוּ טוֹב. וְאֵין טוֹב אֶלָּא תוֹרָה, שֶׁנֶּאֱמַר: כִּי לֶקַח טוֹב נָתַתִּי לָכֶם, תּוֹרָתִי אַל תַּעֲזֹבוּ.

(1) The text refers to one who learns from his companion a chapter, etc. of Torah, Talmud or other similar holy works. In my humble opinion, it should also be applied to students who gain any positive knowledge or moral concepts. They should honor the person who teaches them whether he or she is younger or older than they.

(2) Sometimes a single letter can change the meaning of a word, a sentence, or a law. When there is doubt, the person who teaches the correct letter deserves respect.

(3) Ahitophel was an advisor to King David, and his advice was of such quality that it was considered as if one were consulting the word of God (II Samuel, XVI:23). He was greatly appreciated by King David, but he later became the king's enemy, `perhaps because he was the grandfather of Bath-Sheba whose husband, Uriah, the Hittite, was killed by order of King David. Ahitophel joined Absalom in his rebellion against his father, King David, advising him to pursue the king in his defeat, but Absalom did not heed his advice, and took the counsel of Hushai, sent by David to pretend to be Absalom's freiend. This displeased Ahitophel who withdraw to his home and killed himself (II Samuel XVII:1–23).

(4) The first thing that David learned from Ahitophel was not to study the Torah alone, for as is written in Jeremiah L:36, "a sword upon her mighty men; and they shall be dismayed." According to the Talmud (*Berahot* 63), this means figuratively, "A sword upon those disciples of sages that study the Torah alone, because they will be dumbfounded by the doubts they may have in their study.

The second thing that Ahitophel taught David was not to enter the house of study with his head held high. It is a sign of pride. The Talmud also relates that Ahitophel saw David going alone and slowly to the house of study, and said to him, "Is it not perhaps written, 'In the multitude of his people lies the glory of the king, and in the scarcity of people, the ruin of a prince.' Let us walk together, as it says in Psalm LV: 15, "We took sweet counsel together, and walked to the House of God in company."

Meanwhile, there are those who believe that David did not learn two things from Ahitophel, but that they only conversed, and David derived benefit from the conversation. This is deduced from the words *shenei devarim* (two words) which can be transformed into one, *shenidbarim* (that they spoke to one another).

(5) No one merits an honor as much as one who is dedicated to the study of Torah. Thus, one who honors such a person is honoring the Torah itself.

(6) By virtue of the fact that "the good" means the Torah, the sages deserve the honors due it.

VERSE 6:4

6:4. The pathway to the study of Torah is this, a morsel of bread with salt to eat, water to drink with measure, sleep on the ground, live a life of toil (1), but work diligently in the study of Torah. And if you do so, you will be happy and you will have a good life, as the psalmist said, "Happy shalt thou be (in this world), and it shall be well with thee (in the World to Come)." (Psalm CXXVIII: 2)

ד כַּךְ הִיא דַרְכָּהּ שֶׁל תּוֹרָה, פַּת בְּמֶלַח תֹּאכֵל, וּמַיִם בִּמְשׂוּרָה תִּשְׁתֶּה, וְעַל הָאָרֶץ תִּישָׁן, וְחַיֵּי צַעַר תִּחְיֶה, וּבַתּוֹרָה אַתָּה עָמֵל. אִם אַתָּה עֹשֶׂה כֵן, אַשְׁרֶיךָ וְטוֹב לָךְ, אַשְׁרֶיךָ בָּעוֹלָם הַזֶּה, וְטוֹב לָךְ לָעוֹלָם הַבָּא.

---

(1) In my opinion, this does not mean that a person who possesses material comforts should deprive himself of the good that God has given him, and that he should eat only bread and salt, etc. Abstinence from the benefits this world has to offer is alien to the spirit of Judaism. God created the world so that His creatures should enjoy the fruits of what is in it, as is written in Isaiah XLV:18, "He did not create it a wasteland; He formed it to be inhabited." According to the opinion

of Rabbi Elazar Hakapar, the sin of the *nazir* (Nazirite – see Numbers VI) was that he deprived himself of the pleasures of a normal human being, and for this reason he was obliged to bring a sin offering [to the Temple] when the time stipulated in his vow expired. What is being said here refers to a person who even when he finds himself in extreme poverty, not having anything else to eat but bread and salt, etc., is still obliged to study Torah. This also refers to a person who, in spite of living a life of deprivation, on beginning his studies, he should persist and not abandon the Torah, for in the end he will be rewarded for his sacrifices.

VERSE 6:5

ה אַל תְּבַקֵּשׁ גְּדֻלָּה לְעַצְמְךָ, וְאַל תַּחְמוֹד כָּבוֹד, יוֹתֵר מִלִּמּוּדְךָ עֲשֵׂה, וְאַל תִּתְאַוֶּה לְשֻׁלְחָנָם שֶׁל מְלָכִים, שֶׁשֻּׁלְחָנְךָ גָּדוֹל מִשֻּׁלְחָנָם, וְכִתְרְךָ גָּדוֹל מִכִּתְרָם, וְנֶאֱמָן הוּא בַּעַל מְלַאכְתְּךָ שֶׁיְּשַׁלֵּם לְךָ שְׂכַר פְּעֻלָּתֶךָ.

6:5. Do not seek greatness (1) for yourself and do not chase after honors (2). Put into practice more than what you have learned (3), and do not wish for the table of kings, because your table is superior to theirs (4), and your crown (5) higher than theirs, and worthy of faith is your Master (God) to repay the reward of your (good) deeds.

---

(1) Although you reach a higher level in your studies, do not exalt yourself and show that you are superior to others. It can also be said that one should not look for the spiritual or material reward for his efforts for having achieved a higher level of superiority. (Cf. 1, 10).

(2) Do not study so that you should be called Mr. Rabbi, Your Eminence, Your Excellency, Honorable so and so, but study [Torah] for its intrinsic value.

(3) A person who studies, but does not put into practice his learning

has little value. One who practices what he has learned is worthy of admiration. But one who observes more than what he has been taught should be praised even more. (Cf. I:17 and III:12).

(4) Do not wish for the table of kings who, without any work or effort, have the best of everything. The king acquires his crown not because of any special ability, but out of royal descent. But you acquired your table, your greatness, and your crown through your own merit. This is my humble opinion in this regard.

(5) This refers to the crown of Torah that is more valuable than the crown of royalty (See Ch. IV:17). The table of the studious one is crowned and sanctified by the words and glory of the Torah. This refers not only to the table, but to any circumstance; one who studies the Holy Law carries the crown of Torah upon him.

verse 6:6

6:6. The Torah is greater than the priesthood and royalty, for royalty demands (is acquired through) thirty requirements (1), and the priesthood through twenty-four (2), while the Torah is attained through forty-eight. These are: studying with a master, listening carefully (not through meditation), oral practice (repeating aloud), understanding of the heart, discernment of the heart (3),

ו גְּדוֹלָה תוֹרָה יוֹתֵר מִן הַכְּהֻנָּה וּמִן הַמַּלְכוּת, שֶׁהַמַּלְכוּת נִקְנֵית בִּשְׁלֹשִׁים מַעֲלוֹת, וְהַכְּהֻנָּה נִקְנֵית בְּעֶשְׂרִים וְאַרְבָּעָה, וְהַתּוֹרָה נִקְנֵית בְּאַרְבָּעִים וּשְׁמוֹנָה דְבָרִים. וְאֵלּוּ הֵן: בְּתַלְמוּד, בִּשְׁמִיעַת הָאֹזֶן, בַּעֲרִיכַת שְׂפָתַיִם, בְּבִינַת הַלֵּב, בְּשִׂכְלוּת הַלֵּב, בְּאֵימָה, בְּיִרְאָה, בַּעֲנָוָה, בְּשִׂמְחָה, בְּטָהֳרָה, בְּשִׁמּוּשׁ חֲכָמִים, בְּדִקְדּוּק חֲבֵרִים, בְּפִלְפּוּל הַתַּלְמִידִים, בְּיִשּׁוּב, בְּמִקְרָא, בְּמִשְׁנָה, בְּמִעוּט סְחוֹרָה, בְּמִעוּט דֶּרֶךְ אֶרֶץ, בְּמִעוּט תַּעֲנוּג, בְּמִעוּט שֵׁנָה, בְּמִעוּט שִׂיחָה, בְּמִעוּט שְׂחוֹק, בְּאֶרֶךְ אַפַּיִם, בְּלֵב טוֹב, בֶּאֱמוּנַת חֲכָמִים, בְּקַבָּלַת הַיִּסּוּרִין, הַמַּכִּיר אֶת

fear of God, reverence (for the teacher) (4), attending to the sages (5), the interchange of ideas with fellow students (6), detailed analysis of what is studied with students (7), serenity, Bible study (8), study of the Mishnah, moderation in business (9), moderation in sexual relations (10), moderation in pleasures, moderate sleep, moderation in conversation, moderation in laughter (11); with forbearance (12), with a good heart, with confidence (in the words of the sages) (13), with acceptance of suffering (14), with consciousness of one's place (15), with acceptance on one's lot with contentment (16), with care in one's choice of words (17), with not seeking merits for oneself (18), with making oneself esteemed by others (19), with love of God, and with love of humanity (29), with love of charity (21), with love of things being right, with love of the just reprimand that others make of you (22), fleeing honors, not taking pride in one's knowledge, not enjoying passing judgment (23, with prudence, with sharing the yoke with one's companion (24), judging him or her favorably (25), guiding him or her to truth and peace (26), with preparing carefully the lesson one is to teach (27), with proper questions and answers (28), with listening and expand-

מְקוֹמוֹ, וְהַשָּׂמֵחַ בְּחֶלְקוֹ, וְהָעוֹשֶׂה סְיָג לִדְבָרָיו, וְאֵינוֹ מַחֲזִיק טוֹבָה לְעַצְמוֹ, אָהוּב, אוֹהֵב אֶת הַמָּקוֹם, אוֹהֵב אֶת הַבְּרִיּוֹת, אוֹהֵב אֶת הַצְּדָקוֹת, אוֹהֵב אֶת הַמֵּישָׁרִים, אוֹהֵב אֶת הַתּוֹכָחוֹת, וּמִתְרַחֵק מִן הַכָּבוֹד, וְלֹא מֵגִיס לִבּוֹ בְּתַלְמוּדוֹ, וְאֵינוֹ שָׂמֵחַ בְּהוֹרָאָה, נוֹשֵׂא בְעֹל עִם חֲבֵרוֹ, וּמַכְרִיעוֹ לְכַף זְכוּת, וּמַעֲמִידוֹ עַל הָאֱמֶת, וּמַעֲמִידוֹ עַל הַשָּׁלוֹם, וּמִתְיַשֵּׁב לִבּוֹ בְּתַלְמוּדוֹ, שׁוֹאֵל וּמֵשִׁיב, שׁוֹמֵעַ וּמוֹסִיף, הַלּוֹמֵד עַל מְנָת לְלַמֵּד, וְהַלּוֹמֵד עַל מְנָת לַעֲשׂוֹת, הַמַּחְכִּים אֶת רַבּוֹ, וְהַמְכַוֵּן אֶת שְׁמוּעָתוֹ, וְהָאוֹמֵר דָּבָר בְּשֵׁם אוֹמְרוֹ, הָא לָמַדְתָּ: כָּל הָאוֹמֵר דָּבָר בְּשֵׁם אוֹמְרוֹ מֵבִיא גְאֻלָּה לָעוֹלָם, שֶׁנֶּאֱמַר: וַתֹּאמֶר אֶסְתֵּר לַמֶּלֶךְ בְּשֵׁם מָרְדֳּכָי.

ing on what one is taught (29), by learning in order to teach (30), by learning in order to put into practice (31), by helping one's teacher to become more learned (32), paying attention to the pronouncement of one's teacher (33); by quoting the name of the person from whom one learned what one says (34) for all who cite a passage with the name of the author brings redemption to the world, as is written (35), "And Esther reported it to the king in Mordecai's name" (Esther 11:22)

---

(1) These thirty requisites are as follows: 1. The king does not act as judge. 2. He is not to be brought to trial to be judged. This refers to the ancient kings of the tribes of Israel. The tribunals did not have the power to apply any chastisement upon them. Nevertheless, the kings of the tribe of Judah obeyed the orders of the tribunal and could be judged. 3. He should not serve as a witness. 4. No one should testify against him. 5. He is not subject to the laws of levirate marriage (See Deuteronomy xxv:7–10) 6. His wife is likewise not subject to the levirate ceremony. 7. He does not have to marry his brother's widow. 8. His widow is not required to marry by means of the levirate [to marry the king's brother upon the king's death] 9. No one is allowed to marry the king's widow. 10. He is not to accompany a dead relative [to the grave] on leaving the palace. 11. In the meal following the funeral (*Seudat Havraah*), the other relatives sit on the ground, but he should sit in a higher place. 12. He can proclaim an optional war (not an obligatory one). 13. He can disregard private property in order to make a road for himself. 14. The king's road has no limits. 15. The booty taken in a war should be placed before him. 16. He has the first privilege of taking part of the booty. 17. He should not take more than eighteen wives. 18. He should not have more horses than he needs for his chariot. 19. He should not possess more gold and silver than he needs for his palace. 20. He must write a Torah scroll for his personal use alone. 21. He should go out to war with a Torah scroll. 22. He should enter his house with this same Torah scroll. 23. He should have this Torah scroll with him when he attends a trial. 24. The scroll should be with him at mealtime and at the hour of repose. 25. No

one can ride upon his horse. 26. No one can sit upon his throne. 27. No one can use his scepter. No one should look upon him when he is having his hair cut. 29. No one should see him naked. 30. No one should see him when he is bathing. (See Deut. XVII:14–20 and the tractate *Sanhedrin* 18.)

In addition, only a prophet could designate the king; the king had to be of Jewish origin, and not from a foreign land, nor be a foreigner. He should not be a slave or a bastard. (See Deut. XVII:15.)

(2) The twenty-four requirements for the priesthood are as follows: 1. Saintliness, 2. Purity, 3. Linen vestments, 4. cutting the hair and nails every thirty days (the High Priest had to do so every seven days), 5. Not to become defiled because of the death of one of his relatives, 6. Not to remove the hair of his head as a sign of mourning, 7. Not to shave his beard with a razor, 8. Not to make incisions in his flesh, 9. Not to marry a prostitute, 10. nor a profane woman (a woman from a marriage prohibited by the Torah), 11. nor a woman divorced from her husband. 12. He should have no blemishes. 13. He should not be blind, 14. nor lame, 15. nor have a flat nose, 16. nor be disproportionate of limbs, 17. nor have a broken foot, 18. nor a broken hand, 19. nor overly thick eyebrows, 20. nor have cataracts in his eyes, 21. nor have a spot in his eye, 22. nor have scaly skin, 23. nor have herpes, 24. nor have crushed or collapsed testicles. Nevertheless, priests with defects could partake of the holy offerings, and handle holy objects, but they could not go beyond the veil of the Sanctuary nor approach the altar. These twenty-four conditions are parallel to another twenty-four conditions that applied to the High priest. (See Leviticus XXI–XXII, Numbers XVIII:8–20 and Talmud, *Sanhedrin* 2.)

(3) Just as King Solomon asked God when he said to Him, "Give therefore, Thy servant, an understanding heart to judge Thy people, that I may discern between good and evil…" (1 Kings III:9)

(4) Some translators interpret *ema* as fear of the teacher, and *yira* as reverence for God.

(5) One who studies and attends to the sages in their daily tasks has more opportunity to learn from them important things that present

themselves on certain occasions in life. One witnesses their behavior and their reasoning and, thus, acquires more experience. That is why the Talmud (*Berahot* 7) says, "It is even more important to serve sages than to study the Law." (Cf. 1, 6)

(6) The interchange of opinions with colleagues on what has been studied gives rise to questions and answers that clarify details that had not appeared in the lesson. This kind of discussion often sheds light on obscure points.

(7) Teachers who engage in the interchange of opinions with their students also learn from them, as Rabbi Yehudah ha-Nasi says in the Talmud (*Makot* 10, 1), "I have learned from my teachers, but I have learned even more from my students."

(8) I have seen many people who, never having read the Bible, enter into discussions about the Jewish religion. The least that such people ought to do is to study Torah and the Holy Scriptures with a good teacher, and then enter into details regarding the commentaries explained in the Mishnah and the Gemara; that is, the Talmud. The lack of knowledge of the Bible and the Mishnah disqualifies even the disciples of the sages of the Law.

(9) According to the interpretation of the Talmud with regard to verses 12 and 13 of Deuteronomy xxx, the Torah "is not in heaven", meaning that it is not found in people whose vanity rises up to the skies; nor is it beyond the sea." meaning that it is not found in those who dedicate themselves all the time to business matters (Cf. II:6 and IV:12).

(10) Overindulgence in sex weakens the mind according to the general consensus of all the doctors in the world. (See Tiferet Israel.)

(11) Cf. III:17

(12) One who is forbearing and is not easily angered over any slight matter does not easily lose control of himself, and his memory remains sharp, which is indispensable for study.

(13) Even when one does not fully understand the words of the sages,

or has not investigated whether or not what they say is true, one should trust their words, but not in the words of anyone else who is not learned in the Law. One should verify beforehand if their thoughts are correct. Only a fool believes all he is told.

(14) When misfortunes beyond one's control befall a person, he should accept them with love, and not rebel against God, nor against the Torah saying, "How is it possible that I, being good, being so religious, and so diligent in the study of Torah, should have such things happen to me?" On the contrary, in spite of all, one should remain steadfast in his faith.

(15) One who has a proper and true concept of his value as a person knows that his place is in the House of Study [the Synagogue or a yeshivah] in order to better learn the paths of God.

(16) The ambition to acquire material wealth in this world does not allow a person to dedicate himself to the study of Torah. In addition, this brings him sadness and anxiety on not being able to obtain what he desires, causing him to be morose and melancholy, etc. On the contrary, one should rejoice in his lot just for being a student of the Torah, in spite of material deprivations.

(17) One who thinks before he speaks is less likely to be wrong or to profane holy things with his speech.

(18) One should not attribute to himself praise and merit for the good he has done, or for all that he has studied, for this is his duty and it was for this that God created him. And when others praise him, he should try to flee from vanity and pride. (Cf. II:9).

In the Book of Proverbs (Chapter XXVII:2) one reads, "Let another man praise thee, and not thy own mouth."

(19) Cause yourself to be esteemed by all for your righteous conduct, and not through hypocrisy and deceit. (Cf. III:13)

(20) To love God means here to love His Torah and do His will. To love humanity means to love human beings because they were cre-

ated in the image of God, and because the Torah commands us to do so (Cf. VI:1).

(21) In Hebrew, the word *tzedakah* means "justice" and is also translated as "charity" because when we give charity we are acting justly towards the poor. To stand up for justice is one of the prime duties of a Jew, just as Moses defended the daughters of Jethro at the well against the injustices of the shepherds (Exodus II:16–17). The Torah (Deut. XVI:20) command us, "Justice, only justice shalt thou pursue…"

(22) When someone reprimands us in a positive moral sense, and he is correct in what he says, we should not only accept his words, but also love him; even though this may be difficult for us to do. In the Book of Proverbs (Chapter IX:8) we read, "rebuke a wise man and he will love thee."

(23) Do not rejoice; that is, be not proud for becoming one who makes decisions; on the contrary, reflect that perhaps you do not merit this responsibility or that you may make a mistake in judging. This will lead you to have greater care in fulfilling the duties of your high office.

(24) To bear the yoke with one's fellow student is to be bonded to him, physically, and materially, to share suffering, to give good advice, to teach the Torah, and to be of help to him whenever he needs you. Also, you should rejoice in the well-being of your companion.

(25) This also signifies that you should encourage your companion to judge others favorably and not malevolently (Cf. I:6).

(26) If your companion is following a wrong path, try by all means, to guide him along the path of truth. If you notice that he has had some differences with someone, guide him so that peace shall reign between them. (Woe to him or her who enjoys provoking quarrels, or who does not contribute towards the peace of his fellow man!)

(27) A person who is going to teach others, a preacher who is going to give a sermon, or a teacher who is going to give a class to students

has to be well prepared beforehand. Otherwise he may have to improvise or have doubts about questions that may arise. Others explain *umityashev Betalmudo* as being calm and deliberate upon acquiring the teachings of a master.

(28) Teaching that is done in the form of questions and answers becomes much more interesting than lengthy lectures by one person. One should not be wordy in formulating a question or in answering one because often, in doing so, one often deviates from the theme of the discussion. Likewise, one should take care not to make a play on words for this may cause his listeners to become confused. Therefore, it is of paramount importance that the questions relate to the theme under discussion and that the answers be directed exclusively to the questions asked.

(29) A teacher who hears an incomplete question, or who sees that his answer was not sufficient for the required explanation, should have the question amplified as well as his answer so that the matter may be more clearly understood.

(30) Although a teacher may be sufficiently prepared to teach his subject, and not need further study, still and all, he should strive to acquire more knowledge so as to be able to contribute more to his students.

(31) One who learns but does not practice is not as worthy as one who studies and puts into practice what he has learned. Our sages said, "What matters most is the practice and not the study." (Cf. IV:6)

(32) Intelligent students force a teacher to try to study more in order to be better able to answer their questions. That is why it was said above that teachers learn more from their students than from their own teachers.

(33) The admonition to cite the source of a thought can be interpreted in two ways as follows: although the words of a teacher may seem contradictory, the student will try to reconcile them. It can also be said that the student is so careful to pay attention to what is being

taught that on transmitting the learning he does not add or subtract a word of what he has heard.

(34) This means that one should not take credit for what some one else has said. He should name the source from which he has taken this knowledge, or as the case may be, the teacher or the person from whom he learned it, or the book in which he read it.

(35) In the Book of Esther (Chapter II:22), we read that when Mordecai was seated at the gate of the palace, he heard two of the king's eunuchs, Bigtan and Teresh, plan to kill the king. He passed this knowledge on to Queen Esther, and she then informed the king in Mordecai's name. Because of this, King Ahasuerus eventually decided to honor Mordecai, and told Haman, his Prime Minister, to carry out the honors. Thus began the fall of Haman, the enemy of the Jews whom he wished to annihilate. As a result, it was due to Esther's report to the king in the name of Mordecai about the plan of the eunuchs that salvation came to the Jews. From this, the Talmud deduces that a person who cites the source of the good he has learned, and does not take credit for it for himself, acts justly, attracting the Divine Presence so that the deed may be recorded among the acts in favor of the oppressed. (See Megilat Esther, pp. 10 and 17).

VERSE 6:7

6:7. The Torah is great because it give life (1) to those who observe it in this world as well as in the World to Come, as it says in Proverbs IV:22 "For they [His words] are life to those who find them, and health to all their flesh," and in Proverbs III:8, "It shall be health to thy navel, and marrow to thy bones." Also in Proverbs III:18, we read, "She (the Torah) is a tree of life (2) to those who lay hold on her (3), and happy are those who hold her fast." And it says in Proverbs I:9, "Because they [the instructions of thy father and the Torah of thy mother] shall be a graceful garland for thy head, and chains [necklaces] about thy neck." and in Proverbs IV:9, "She (wisdom) (4) shall give to thy head an ornament of grace, a crown of glory," Proverbs IX:11 reads, "For by Me shall thy days be multiplied, and the years of thy life shall be increased". In Proverbs III:16, it says, "Length of days is in her right hand; and in her left hand are riches and honor." In Proverbs III:2, we read, "For length of days, and long life, and peace shall they [His commandments] add to thee."

ז גְּדוֹלָה תוֹרָה, שֶׁהִיא נוֹתֶנֶת חַיִּים לְעוֹשֶׂיהָ בָּעוֹלָם הַזֶּה וּבָעוֹלָם הַבָּא, שֶׁנֶּאֱמַר: כִּי חַיִּים הֵם לְמוֹצְאֵיהֶם, וּלְכָל בְּשָׂרוֹ מַרְפֵּא. וְאוֹמֵר: רִפְאוּת תְּהִי לְשָׁרֶּךָ וְשִׁקּוּי לְעַצְמוֹתֶיךָ. וְאוֹמֵר: עֵץ חַיִּים הִיא לַמַּחֲזִיקִים בָּהּ, וְתֹמְכֶיהָ מְאֻשָּׁר. וְאוֹמֵר: כִּי לִוְיַת חֵן הֵם לְרֹאשֶׁךָ וַעֲנָקִים לְגַרְגְּרֹתֶיךָ. וְאוֹמֵר: תִּתֵּן לְרֹאשְׁךָ לִוְיַת חֵן, עֲטֶרֶת תִּפְאֶרֶת תְּמַגְּנֶךָּ. וְאוֹמֵר: כִּי בִי יִרְבּוּ יָמֶיךָ וְיוֹסִיפוּ לְךָ שְׁנוֹת חַיִּים. וְאוֹמֵר: אֹרֶךְ יָמִים בִּימִינָהּ, בִּשְׂמֹאלָהּ עֹשֶׁר וְכָבוֹד. וְאוֹמֵר: כִּי אֹרֶךְ יָמִים וּשְׁנוֹת חַיִּים וְשָׁלוֹם יוֹסִיפוּ לָךְ.

---

(1) Note that the Torah says, "The Torah gives life to those who observe it." and it does not say, "to those who study it." Nevertheless,

one should bear in mind that study is in itself also important, for if one does not have knowledge of the Torah, he will not be able to put it into practice properly.

In addition to the Torah, there are other studies that bring a person riches, honor, power, etc., but not life in this world and good fortune in the next. This is achieved only through the study and observance of Torah. Neither riches, nor power, nor honor are of any value if one does not lead a pure and healthy life. This is only possible through the teachings of the Torah, which are like marrow for the bones and the best way to acquire a healthy mind and soul.

(2) The Torah is like the Tree of (eternal) Life that was in the Garden of Eden (See Genesis 11:9). Adam would have lived forever if he had eaten the fruit of this tree. In like manner, the Torah grants eternal life to those who study and practice it. The just, even after death, are considered to be alive in this world and also in the World to Come the splendor of which emanates from the light of the eternal life.

(3) The Torah is a tree of life for those who study it as well as those who support them. This is deduced from the Hebrew words *Mahazikim ba*, which mean "for those who lay hold of it or cause it to be held [words said when the Torah is lifted].

(4) In this paragraph Torah and wisdom are used as synonyms.

VERSE 6:8

6:8. Rabbi Simeon ben Judah said in the name of Rabbi Simeon bar Yohai, "beauty, strength, riches, honor, wisdom, old age, a hoary head (1), and children (2) sit well for the righteous (3), and also for the world (4) as it says in Proverbs XVI:31, "The hoary head is a crown of glory; it is found in the way of the righteous." (5) It also says in Proverbs XVII:6, "Children's children are the crown of old men, and the glory of the children are their fathers." (6). In Proverbs XX:29, we read, "The glory of young men is their strength (7), and the beauty of old men is the gray head." It is also said (Isaiah: XXIV:23), "Then the moon shall be confounded and the sun ashamed, when the Lord of Hosts shall reign in Mount Zion, and in Jerusalem, and before His elders will be His glory." (8)

ח רַבִּי שִׁמְעוֹן בֶּן יְהוּדָה מִשּׁוּם רַבִּי שִׁמְעוֹן בֶּן יוֹחַאי אוֹמֵר: הַנּוֹי וְהַכֹּחַ וְהָעֹשֶׁר וְהַכָּבוֹד וְהַחָכְמָה וְהַזִּקְנָה וְהַשֵּׂיבָה וְהַבָּנִים, נָאֶה לַצַּדִּיקִים וְנָאֶה לָעוֹלָם, שֶׁנֶּאֱמַר: עֲטֶרֶת תִּפְאֶרֶת שֵׂיבָה, בְּדֶרֶךְ צְדָקָה תִּמָּצֵא. וְאוֹמֵר: תִּפְאֶרֶת בַּחוּרִים כֹּחָם וַהֲדַר זְקֵנִים שֵׂיבָה. וְאוֹמֵר: עֲטֶרֶת זְקֵנִים בְּנֵי בָנִים, וְתִפְאֶרֶת בָּנִים אֲבוֹתָם. וְאוֹמֵר: וְחָפְרָה הַלְּבָנָה וּבוֹשָׁה הַחַמָּה, כִּי מָלַךְ יְיָ צְבָאוֹת בְּהַר צִיּוֹן וּבִירוּשָׁלַיִם, וְנֶגֶד זְקֵנָיו כָּבוֹד.

---

(1) When people are just and good, they become beautiful, even if they are not, and they make a better impression. There are people whose goodness of soul is reflected in their face. The just employ their good looks for the good, their strength for the defense of the oppressed, their wealth to help the poor and needy, honor, in order to give good advice that leads to honor and to be honored, wisdom, for the good of the community, old age, to help others benefit from their experience, the hoary head, to make the younger generation see how the path of evil leads to perdition. The just, who even though they suf-

fer at times in this world, attain the good fortune of the World to Come, for they have their conscience clear, even in old age, while the perverse who apparently flourish, lead a bitter life in the end, and are destroyed by their evil deeds. They had used their beauty for licentiousness, their strength, to oppress the weak, etc. in contrast to what is done by the righteous.

(2) This refers to good children who learn from the example and virtues of their parents and grandparents, adopting them for their own.

(3) It is proper for the just to have all these good things for they will use them for good, as we have said, but it is not right for the wicked to have them for they will make bad use of them.

(4) This refers to the generation in which such people exist.

(5) When an older person led an impeccable life in his youth, his gray hairs serve as an adornment to be more respected.

(6) When one sees well brought up children who fear God, people will think that it is due to their parents and grandparents that they possess these virtues. Thus, they constitute a crown of glory for their elders. Likewise, when children have good parents, these are the glory of the children and the best recommendation for them everywhere.

(7) Which is put to use for good.

(8) These allegorical words of the prophet Isaiah are interpreted here as follows: When the light of the moon, a symbol of beauty as previously mentioned, disappears in the future, and strength, symbolized by the sun, are dimmed by the light of the Lord of Hosts that will shine on Mount Zion, respect for the aged, even then, will not be neglected. That is, when the kingdom of God will reign on all the earth, there will no longer be beauty, or strength, or riches, or wisdom that matter before the honor due the aged who were righteous. Another interpretation, informs us that in spite of the fact that the elders and the sages of the Torah will lose the strength of their senses and their

VERSE 6:9

6:9. Rabbi Simeon ben Menasya said, these seven qualities (1) that the sages enumerated for the righteous were personified in Rabbi Yehudah ha-Nasi (2) and his children.

ט רַבִּי שִׁמְעוֹן בֶּן מְנַסְיָא אוֹמֵר: אֵלּוּ שֶׁבַע מִדּוֹת שֶׁמָּנוּ חֲכָמִים לַצַּדִּיקִים, כֻּלָּם נִתְקַיְּמוּ בְּרַבִּי וּבְבָנָיו.

---

(1) The previous Mishnah lists eight qualities rather than seven. Some books omit "wisdom", and in Talmud *Yerushalmi*, old age is not mentioned. Nevertheless, almost all other books always list eight qualities and not seven.

(2) Rabbi Yehudah ha-Nasi, (the Prince) who compiled the Mishnah, is also known as *Rabi haKadosh* (our saintly teacher); he was outstanding for the purity of his soul. He used his immense material wealth to do the will of God, and not for his own benefit. Therefore, he and his sons, who followed his example, deserved to have all these qualities mentioned above. Their example is evidence of the reward that the righteous merit for the good use they make of the benefits bestowed upon them [by God].

VERSE 6:10

6:10. Rabbi Yose ben Kisma (1) said, "Once when I was walking along the road, I met a man who greeted me, and I returned his greeting (2). He asked me, "Rabbi, where are you from?" (3) I answered, "I am from a city where there are great sages and scribes." He said to me, "Rabbi, if you consent to live with us in our town, I will give you a million dinars of gold, precious stones, and pearls." (4) I replied, "Even if you were to give me all the gold, precious stones, and pearls in the world, I would not live in any place unless there is Torah in it.(5) for it is written in the Book of Psalms, (CXIX:72) by the hand of King David, 'The Torah of Thy mouth (learning) is better to me than thousands of gold and silver.' And not only that, but in the hour in which man leaves this world, neither gold, nor precious stones, nor pearls accompany him, but only the Torah and

י אָמַר רַבִּי יוֹסֵי בֶּן קִסְמָא: פַּעַם אַחַת הָיִיתִי מְהַלֵּךְ בַּדֶּרֶךְ, וּפָגַע בִּי אָדָם אֶחָד, וְנָתַן לִי שָׁלוֹם, וְהֶחֱזַרְתִּי לוֹ שָׁלוֹם, אָמַר לִי, רַבִּי, מֵאֵיזֶה מָקוֹם אַתָּה, אָמַרְתִּי לוֹ, מֵעִיר גְּדוֹלָה שֶׁל חֲכָמִים וְשֶׁל סוֹפְרִים אָנִי, אָמַר לִי, רַבִּי, רְצוֹנְךָ שֶׁתָּדוּר עִמָּנוּ בִּמְקוֹמֵנוּ, וַאֲנִי אֶתֵּן לְךָ אֶלֶף אֲלָפִים דִּינְרֵי זָהָב וַאֲבָנִים טוֹבוֹת וּמַרְגָּלִיּוֹת, אָמַרְתִּי לוֹ, אִם אַתָּה נוֹתֵן לִי כָּל כֶּסֶף וְזָהָב וַאֲבָנִים טוֹבוֹת וּמַרְגָּלִיּוֹת שֶׁבָּעוֹלָם, אֵינִי דָר אֶלָּא בִּמְקוֹם תּוֹרָה, וְכֵן כָּתוּב בְּסֵפֶר תְּהִלִּים עַל יְדֵי דָוִד מֶלֶךְ יִשְׂרָאֵל: טוֹב לִי תוֹרַת פִּיךָ מֵאַלְפֵי זָהָב וָכָסֶף. וְלֹא עוֹד, אֶלָּא שֶׁבִּשְׁעַת פְּטִירָתוֹ שֶׁל אָדָם, אֵין מְלַוִּין לוֹ לְאָדָם לֹא כֶסֶף וְלֹא זָהָב וְלֹא אֲבָנִים טוֹבוֹת וּמַרְגָּלִיּוֹת, אֶלָּא תּוֹרָה וּמַעֲשִׂים טוֹבִים בִּלְבָד, שֶׁנֶּאֱמַר: בְּהִתְהַלֶּכְךָ תַּנְחֶה אֹתָךְ, בְּשָׁכְבְּךָ תִּשְׁמֹר עָלֶיךָ, וַהֲקִיצוֹתָ הִיא תְשִׂיחֶךָ. בְּהִתְהַלֶּכְךָ תַּנְחֶה אֹתָךְ, בָּעוֹלָם הַזֶּה. בְּשָׁכְבְּךָ תִּשְׁמֹר עָלֶיךָ, בַּקֶּבֶר. וַהֲקִיצוֹתָ הִיא תְשִׂיחֶךָ, לָעוֹלָם הַבָּא. וְאוֹמֵר: לִי הַכֶּסֶף וְלִי הַזָּהָב, נְאֻם יְיָ צְבָאוֹת.

good deeds, as it is written, (Proverbs VI: 22) 'When thou walkest, it shall guide thee (in this world), when thou liest down (in the grave), it shall protect thee (6), and when thou awakest (in the next world), it shall talk with thee.' It is also written in Psalm (CXIX:72) by King David, "The Torah of Thy mouth is better to me than thousands of gold and silver (7)." And in the same sense, Haggai II:8 reads, "The silver is mine and the gold is mine, says the Lord of Hosts." (8)

---

(1) Rabbi Yose ben Kisma lived in the Second Century of the Common Era. He wishes to tell us in this passage that in spite of the fact that the righteous are worthy of riches, honor, etc., they should not abandon the Torah for anything in this world. (Cf. IV:18)

(2) Relating that they greeted each other is to show the respect in which rabbis were formerly held, and the modesty they had in entering into conversation with anyone, even one who was courteous and well brought up. Rabbi Yose refused the offer only so as not to exchange the Torah for the material goods of this world, for no authentic rabbi is materialistic. The man knew him to be a rabbi because of his clothing and not for the beard and sideburns that he wore. In olden times, all men allowed their beards and sideburns to grow, whereas a rabbi's vestments were different from those of others.

(3) In my opinion, the reason why the rabbi was asked where he came from was because the man wondered at how the people of his community left him to wander about looking for a way to make a living, and did not pay him enough to remain in his city. Rabbi Yose explained in his reply that he was from a city full of sages and scribes, and thus, he could not support himself comfortably.

(4) The man's offer seems rather exaggerated. I think that what the man wished to say to the rabbi was that he would give him a sufficient amount to amply support himself so that his city might have a competent rabbi. I believe the reason why the man's proposition is

mentioned here is to teach wealthy Jews to be more generous towards rabbis when the congregation cannot adequately support them.

(5) No matter how learned a rabbi may be, he needs to interchange opinions with his colleagues. That is why Rabbi Yose ben Kisma preferred to remain in his city and not to reside in a place where there was no study of Torah, and also for the reasons cited below.

(6) When a righteous person dies, it is as if he lay down to sleep. This is said of King David (1 Kings 11:10), "So David slept with his fathers, and was buried in the city of David." The righteous also feel protected from the fear of death, as David said in Psalm XXIII, "Yeah, though I walk through the valley of the shadow of death, I will fear no evil, for Thou (God) art with me."

(7) David, who was king and hence, possessed much gold and silver, loved the teachings of the sages of the Torah, more than his wealth.

(8) This verse is also an answer to the man who had made the offer. Rabbi Yose ben Kisma wished to state that by virtue of the fact that silver and gold belong to God; He distributes His riches to whom he pleases. If God judged that Rabbi Yose should have much gold and silver, He would give it to him no matter where he lived.

VERSE 6:11

יא חֲמִשָּׁה קִנְיָנִים קָנָה הַקָּדוֹשׁ בָּרוּךְ הוּא בְּעוֹלָמוֹ, וְאֵלּוּ הֵן: תּוֹרָה קִנְיָן אֶחָד, שָׁמַיִם וָאָרֶץ קִנְיָן אֶחָד, אַבְרָהָם קִנְיָן אֶחָד, יִשְׂרָאֵל קִנְיָן אֶחָד, בֵּית הַמִּקְדָּשׁ קִנְיָן אֶחָד. תּוֹרָה מִנַּיִן, דִּכְתִיב: יְיָ קָנָנִי רֵאשִׁית דַּרְכּוֹ, קֶדֶם מִפְעָלָיו מֵאָז. שָׁמַיִם וָאָרֶץ מִנַּיִן, דִּכְתִיב: כֹּה אָמַר יְיָ, הַשָּׁמַיִם כִּסְאִי וְהָאָרֶץ הֲדֹם רַגְלָי, אֵי זֶה בַיִת אֲשֶׁר תִּבְנוּ לִי וְאֵי זֶה מָקוֹם מְנוּחָתִי. וְאוֹמֵר: מָה רַבּוּ מַעֲשֶׂיךָ יְיָ, כֻּלָּם בְּחָכְמָה עָשִׂיתָ, מָלְאָה הָאָרֶץ קִנְיָנֶךָ. אַבְרָהָם מִנַּיִן, דִּכְתִיב: וַיְבָרְכֵהוּ וַיֹּאמַר, בָּרוּךְ אַבְרָם לְאֵל עֶלְיוֹן, קוֹנֵה שָׁמַיִם וָאָרֶץ. יִשְׂרָאֵל מִנַּיִן, דִּכְתִיב: עַד יַעֲבֹר עַמְּךָ יְיָ, עַד יַעֲבֹר עַם זוּ קָנִיתָ. וְאוֹמֵר: לִקְדוֹשִׁים אֲשֶׁר בָּאָרֶץ הֵמָּה, וְאַדִּירֵי כָּל חֶפְצִי בָם. בֵּית הַמִּקְדָּשׁ מִנַּיִן, דִּכְתִיב: מָכוֹן לְשִׁבְתְּךָ פָּעַלְתָּ יְיָ, מִקְּדָשׁ אֲדֹנָי כּוֹנְנוּ יָדֶיךָ. וְאוֹמֵר: וַיְבִיאֵם אֶל גְּבוּל קָדְשׁוֹ, הַר זֶה קָנְתָה יְמִינוֹ.

6:11. Five possessions (1) did the Holy One, Blessed be He, specify as His own in this world. They are the Torah, heaven and earth, the patriarch Abraham (2), the people of Israel, and the Holy Temple. How do we know that the Torah is His? Because it says in Proverbs VIII:22 "The Lord created me (the Torah) as the beginning of His way, the first of His works of old: I was set up from everlasting, from the beginning, before ever the earth was." With regard to the heavens and the earth, it says in Isaiah LXVI:1, "Thus says the Lord, the heaven is my throne, and the earth is my footstool, where is the house that you would build for Me? And where is the place of My rest?" And it is said (Psalm CIV:24), "O Lord, how manifold are Thy works! In wisdom hast Thou made them all; the earth is full of Thy creatures." (3). How do we know about Abraham? Because it is written (Genesis XIV:19), "And He blessed him, and said, Blessed be Avram of the most high God, possessor of heaven and earth." With regard to Israel, how do we know this? Because it is written (Exodus xv:16), "Till Thy people pass over, O Lord, till the people pass over, whom Thou hast acquired." And in Psalm LXXVIII:54, "And He brought them to His holy border, to the mountain, which His right hand had purchased."

---

(1) The universe and all it contains are possession of the Creator, but these five things are more prized by Him than others, for they are as if He acquired them for His own. Each one of these things is joined to the other; that is, if one did not exist, there would be no reason for the other to exist. This is affirmed by the prophet Jeremiah (XXXI:35), "If these ordinances depart from before Me, says the Lord, then the seed of Israel also shall cease from being a nation before Me forever." Elsewhere, Jeremiah affirms (XXXIII:25), "Thus says the Lord, if I have not appointed My covenant with day and night, the ordinances of heaven and earth…"

In the Talmud and in the Midrash, only three things are mentioned as being possessions of the Creator: the Torah, Israel, and the Temple.

(2) This does not diminish the merit of the other patriarchs, prophets, etc. The aim here is to point out that the patriarch Abraham was the first to recognize the existence of the one true God, to propagate monotheism, and to recruit followers. It is not clear in the verse cited to prove that Abraham is one of the possessions of God, whether the *kinyan* (possession) refers to Abraham, but rather to heaven and earth. This led the scholar, the Gaon of Vilna, to count four possessions instead of five. It seems to me, the *derasha* (interpretation) is that the Talmud and the Midrash sometimes have similar characteristics, as in this case. The fact that word *kone* (possessor) is found in the same verse in which Abraham is mentioned, implies that the possessions of God include heaven and earth as well as the person of Abraham.

(3) The reason for adding more verses is in order to fill in the words

missing from the previous verses, as in this case, *kinianeha – kinian* (possessions).

VERSE 6:12

6:12. All that the Holy One, Blessed be He, created in this world, He created for His glory (1), as is said in Isaiah XLIII:7, "…every one that is called by My name; for I have created him for My glory. I have formed him; yeah, I have made him." And it is also said in Exodus XV:18, The Lord shall reign for ever and ever." (2).

יב כָּל מַה שֶׁבָּרָא הַקָּדוֹשׁ בָּרוּךְ הוּא בְּעוֹלָמוֹ, לֹא בְרָאוֹ אֶלָּא לִכְבוֹדוֹ, שֶׁנֶּאֱמַר: כֹּל הַנִּקְרָא בִשְׁמִי וְלִכְבוֹדִי בְּרָאתִיו יְצַרְתִּיו אַף עֲשִׂיתִיו. וְאוֹמֵר: יְיָ יִמְלֹךְ לְעֹלָם וָעֶד.

---

(1) Each of the things that God created in this world has a purpose, and is, in itself, testimony to the existence of God and glorifies Him.

(2) The verse was put here to tell us that God would reign over all humanity so that all will worship Him in the same way, and not differently by each group. This will happen in the end of days when all hearts shall be purified, and God will make them see the great mystery of Creation. That is the reason why each living being was created, from the tiniest insect, plant, etc. to the wisest among mortals, the purpose of which is unknown. Then all as one will glorify the Holy Name of the one God, Ruler of the Universe, and will say, "The Lord shall reign for ever and ever." (Amen)

רַבִּי חֲנַנְיָא בֶּן עֲקַשְׁיָא אוֹמֵר: רָצָה הַקָּדוֹשׁ בָּרוּךְ הוּא לְזַכּוֹת אֶת יִשְׂרָאֵל, לְפִיכָךְ הִרְבָּה לָהֶם תּוֹרָה וּמִצְוֹת, שֶׁנֶּאֱמַר: יְיָ חָפֵץ לְמַעַן צִדְקוֹ, יַגְדִּיל תּוֹרָה וְיַאְדִּיר.

Rabbi Hanania ben Akasha (1) used to say, the Holy One, Blessed be He, wishing to render Israel the more worthy, enlarged for them the Torah and its commandments. For as we may read in the words of the prophet Isaiah (XLII:21), "The Lord was well pleased for His righteousness sake (2) to magnify Torah (3) and to make it glorious."

---

(1) This paragraph, which is not part of the Pirkei Avoth, is found in the Talmud at the end of Tractate *Macoth*. Since its content is related to God, Torah, and Israel, it was placed here as well as at the end of each of the five chapters of Pirkei Avoth. It was also done this way due to the custom of always reciting this paragraph before *Kaddish DeRabanan (*the Rabbis' Kaddish).

(2) *Leman Tzidko:* these words, which literally mean, "for the love of His justice", were interpreted as if one said *Leman leha tzidko* (in order to make Israel just and worthy).

(3) Torah signifies in this verse, the logical precepts that just and humane people would observe even if they were not recommended. This includes not committing murder, or stealing, or eating insects, and others. As for *mitzvoth* which include *hukim* (ordinances), these are precepts that would not be observed if they were not recommended for we do not understand the reason for them. Examples of these are: *shatnes* (not wearing, clothing made of both wool and linen), not cooking a kid in its mother's milk, and others.

The prohibition of not cooking the kid (which includes also the lamb, calf, etc.) was repeated three times in the Torah. According to the Talmud (*Pesahim 26, Holin 115*), the first is to prohibit the eating of meat with milk or its derivatives, the second, to prohibit benefiting from this mixture, and the third to prohibit the cooking of these foods together.

This precept belongs to the category of laws denominated *hukim*, which as we said, are precepts the reason for which were not revealed to us.

The commandments relating to foods do not depend solely on hygienic reasons. This is obvious. Many of those who do not observe these commandments, and who eat meat with cheese, or eat pork, shellfish, and other animal products considered impure [not kosher] by the Torah, are often healthy and enjoy good health. The true reason for these prohibitions is mainly of a spiritual nature. Their purpose is to keep the soul healthy and pure, and to protect it from contamination or impure inclinations that harm it. That is why animals and foods permitted or prohibited by the Torah are classified as pure or impure. This teaches us that the reason for prohibiting them is not only for hygienic considerations. Proof of this is that the Torah (Leviticus XI:43–47) tells us clearly, "You shall not make yourselves abominable with any creeping thing that creeps, neither shall you make yourselves unclean with them, that you should be defiled by them…you shall therefore be holy, for I am holy…."

∼

I lift my heart full of appreciation to God for allowing me to reach the end of this work, beseeching Him that peace and universal brotherhood reign in all human beings as children of one Father, the Lord, and as members of one single family.

AMEN!